C000128806

Daily Stock Market Trends

DAILY STOCK MARKET TRENDS

Compiled by
David Schwartz

Burleigh Publishing Company

Compiled and edited by David Schwartz
Published by Burleigh Publishing Company Limited,
Burleigh Hall, Burleigh, Stroud, Gloucestershire GL5 2PF

ISBN 09523961 7 3

A CIP record for this book is available from the British Library

Printed in England by
Redwood Books, Trowbridge, Wiltshire

Notice

Whilst every effort has been made to ensure that information in this book is correct, no liability can be accepted for any loss incurred in any way whatsoever by any person relying solely on the information contained herein.

Contents

DISCLAIMER

This book is a review of past stock market trends. It is based upon an historical analysis of every closing price on the various share price indices available at the time this book was prepared.

Every reference we make to possible future price movements is a statistical projection derived from past trends. No one knows if any of these relationships will continue in the future. Our observations are not intended to be recommendations to buy or sell any particular stock or the market as a whole.

Remember that the price of any stock market investment can go down as well as up. You can easily lose some or all of your investment. This is especially true when investing in various derivatives which are very volatile.

Be sure to discuss the risk of any investment you are considering with a qualified advisor before making any investment decision.

INTRODUCTION

Consciously or unconsciously, most investors make an effort to forecast the future. Rightly so. Future prospects play an important role in establishing future stock market valuations. Investment programmes that ignore future prospects can easily end in tears.

But looking ahead is hard to do. Few private investors have the skills or the time to make accurate forecasts about the future. The business news media as well as many independent commentators and fee-charging advisory services attempt to fill this void.

The quality of their offerings varies. Some are quite good. Others are poor. But, in one important respect, most forecasters share a common trait. Their time horizon typically is weeks or months ahead. Little attention is focused upon the very short term – like the next 24 hours.

It is an important omission. After all, how many times were you on the verge of making a trade but were unsure whether to proceed at that very moment, or to wait a few days in the hope of executing your transaction at a better price? Did you ever sell part of your portfolio, believing a rally was running out of steam, only to find that shares continued to rise for several more days after you sold?

The simple truth is that very short-term forecasting is a frustrating and difficult undertaking. Even worse, many private investors have nowhere to turn for help. Today's news reports do a fine job of describing yesterday's stock market behaviour. But as most investors have learned the hard way, a thorough knowledge of yesterday's trend often provides little help in forecasting where shares will be heading tomorrow.

Daily Stock Market Trends addresses this critical problem. It provides the precise odds of a price rise in the UK stock market for each day of the year, in a concise tabular manner. The goal is to help you to make the very best investment decision at the moment of truth – the day you plan to buy or sell.

There are no subjective opinions in *Daily Stock Market Trends*, just solid historical facts. They are based on an analysis of every single daily closing price from July 1935 when daily price changes were first systematically recorded in the UK, to the present. Price changes to 1965 are based upon the FT-Ordinary Shares Index, the only reputable daily index in existence during that period. Daily trends from 1965 to the present are based on the FTSE All Shares index, a larger and more broadly-based index.

My thanks to Primark Datastream for providing much of the historical data used in this analysis.

David Schwartz
January 2000

How To Use This Book

It is widely believed that short-term share price fluctuations are random and unpredictable. According to Efficient Market Theory, today's price reflects everything that is known – all past information, newly-breaking news and future hopes. In the absence of fresh news, short-term price swings are nothing more than random gyrations.

EMT is a fine theory but the facts are different. History reveals that there are huge differences in the odds of a daily price rise, depending upon day of the year, whether prices rose or fell yesterday or how far prices spurted above or below the underlying trend.

These non-random price fluctuations occur on a daily basis with astonishing regularity. Some have been apparent for many decades. The presence of a systematic tendency to rise or fall does not guarantee an advance or decline on any single trading day, of course. The stock market is too complex an institution to obey blindly any single historical pattern. Still, awareness of these historical trends can help investors to increase the odds of correctly anticipating which way shares will shift on any specific trading day.

Daily Stock Market Trends analyses some of these trends and their effect on the UK stock market for each trading day of the year. The following pages will show you how to use the data to maximise your short-term trading profits.

Section A – Overall Profit Odds

The top line on each daily price page provides investors with the precise odds of a price rise for that day. The calculations are based on a statistical analysis of all price changes that have occurred on this day from 1935 to the present.

Knowing the overall record on any trading day is a good place to start before you decide whether to buy or sell on that day. A table for January 27 is shown on page xiii for illustrative purposes. Note that the odds of a price rise on January 27 are 47%.

Section B – Size of Shift

Directly below the overall trend is an analysis of all previous price shifts that have occurred on January 27. These shifts are divided into three groups, small changes no greater than 0.25% from the previous closing price and larger rises or falls in excess of 0.25%. A shift of 0.25% or one-quarter of a per cent is the equivalent of 15 points on an FTSE-100 in the area of 6000.

The size of the typical price swing can provide investors with a useful perspective about what might lie ahead. For example, our chart reveals that 43% of all price changes on January 27 are small, one quarter of a per cent or less. In contrast, fluctuation patterns are much more extreme on October 22, to pick another day at random. Small swings occur just 19% of the time. In other words, the odds of a big price change are much greater on October 22 than January 27.

Information like this does not tell us which way prices will shift in any single year. But it provides a useful context within which to gauge the odds of a big move on each trading day.

Section C – Yesterday's Influence

We then provide profit odds for each trading day based upon the previous trading day's behaviour. In most years, the previous trading day is the preceding calendar day but it could also be several calendar days earlier if a weekend or holiday intervenes.

History repeatedly demonstrates that a price swing on any specific day provides useful insights about the likely trend on the following day. Our example shows that UK shares rise 79% of the time on January 27 following a large price increase in excess of 0.25% on the preceding day. There are no guarantees for any single year of course. Prices might still fall, despite the stock market's propensity to rise on the back of this historical signal. Still, 79% profit odds is a strong signal. The figure tells us that shares rise more than three out of four times on January 27 following a solid price rise the previous day.

A

JANUARY 27 ODDS OF A PRICE RISE: 47%

A

Odds of different size price shift

B

	1935 to present
Large rise *(above +0.25%)*	32%
Small swing *(+0.25% to -0.25%)*	43%
Large fall (*below -0.25%)*	26%

B

Odds of rise based on yesterday

C

	1935 to present
Large rise yesterday *(above +0.25%)*	79%
Small swing yesterday *(+0.25% to -0.25%)*	25%
Large fall yesterday (*below -0.25%)*	*25%

C

DIAGNOSTICS

Odds of price rise based on direction of 5-day and 20-day trend yesterday

D

	5-day trend	20-day trend
Yesterday rose more than +0.1%	59%	60%
Little change *(+0.1% to -0.1%)*	50%	40%
Yesterday fell more than -0.1%	29%	*14%

D

Odds of rise based upon distance between trend and yesterday s closing price

E

	5-day trend	20-day trend
Yesterday more than +0.5% above trend	69%	62%
Yesterday near trend *(+0.5% to -0.5%)*	40%	33%
Yesterday more than -0.5% below trend	27%	*22%

E

Looking ahead: odds of rise in future

F

	Next 3 days	Next 5 days
Today rose over +0.25%	80%	100%
Today small swing *(+0.25% to -0.25%)*	60%	60%
Today fell below -0.25%	50%	58%

F

On the other hand, history also signals that the odds of a rise are just one in four on January 27 if the previous day's price swing was small (up or down by less than 0.25%) or if yesterday dropped by a large amount.

The asterisk (*) adjacent to one of the three percentages in this sequence warns that specific computation is based upon fewer than 10 observations. It is our way of flagging that the percentage may be less reliable because of the small number of observations. In this example, there were eight occasions in history when prices fell on the previous trading day more than 0.25%. Shares rose on January 27 in just two of those eight years, a 25% success rate.

Profit odds of 25% are worth thinking about if you are planning to make a purchase on January 27. The stock market will rise in some years of course but over the long-run, history warns that an investment on January 27 is typically a money-loser following a large drop on the preceding trading day.

Section D – Direction of Five-day and 20-day Trends

Moving on to mid-page, experienced investors will gain a great deal of insight into daily profit prospects from this diagnostic section. It is based upon the five-day and 20-day trend averages.

The five-day average is calculated by summing the closing price on each of the last five trading days and dividing by five. The 20-day average is calculated by summing the last 20 closing prices and dividing by 20. Experience shows that the five-day and 20-day averages are important diagnostic tools. Investors should make it a point to record each day's closing price in a systematic fashion so that all necessary data are always available.

The first diagnostic in the series measures the direction of the five-day and 20-day trends and the degree of change. The degree of change is another way of describing the speed with which the trend rises or falls. Think of it as the angle of ascent or descent of a trend line. The more sharply a trend rises or falls from one day to the next, the larger will be the degree of change.

History teaches that a trend's direction and rate of change often provides a useful perspective about where the stock market will be heading on the following trading day.

Here is how to calculate the direction and degree of change from one day to the next. Assume that the FTSE-100 closes as follows on five consecutive days: 5900, 5950, 6000, 6050 and 6100. The five-day average at the end of this period is the sum of all five closing prices, divided by five. In this case, the five-day average is exactly 6000.

Further assume that shares rise to 6150 on the sixth day in the sequence. The new five-day average is based upon the five most recent closing prices from day two to day six. It is the sum of 5950, 6000, 6050, 6100 and 6150, divided by five, or 6050.

To calculate direction and degree of change, merely divide the five-day average on day six by the five-day average on day five or 6050 by 6000. This produces a change of +0.83%. In other words, the five-day average increased by almost 1% between day five and day six.

As far as January 27 is concerned, history teaches that the odds of a price rise are 59% if the five-day average rises at the end of the 26th by more than a tenth of a per cent above the average on the preceding day (the 25th).

These profit odds are not arbitrarily selected. They are based on an intensive analysis of every single closing price, from 1935 to the present. The analysis finds that a rise on the five-day average at the end of trading on January 26 by more than +0.10% above the previous night's average is associated with a price rise 59% of the time on January 27.

Going back to our hypothetical example, the five-day average increased +0.83%. If an increase of this magnitude occurred on January 26, we would conclude that the profit odds on January 27 are 59%.

At the other extreme, history also teaches that five-day average declines in excess of -0.10% are followed by price rises on January 27 just 29% of the time. Putting it an other way, a downward sloping five-day trend that slipped more than -0.10% on the preceding day is associated with a drop on January 27 in 71% of all years. Prices might rise in any single year, of course, but history warns that the odds are poor.

This discussion about the five-day average also applies to the 20-day average, shown in the adjacent column. Note the asterisk next to the figure of 14% at the bottom of the 20-day series. It warns that the calculation is based upon fewer than 10 occasions. In other words, the percentage may be an unreliable representation of the underlying trend because of the small number of observations.

SECTION E – DISTANCE BETWEEN YESTERDAY AND FIVE-DAY OR 20-DAY AVERAGE

History also teaches that the distance or gap between the five-day or 20-day average and yesterday's closing price is a useful forecasting tool. Closing prices that are well above or well below either average are often associated with atypical profit odds on the following trading day.

Let us return to our hypothetical example of the FTSE-100 closing on five successive days at 5950, 6000, 6050, 6100 and 6150. As before, the five-day average is the sum of all five closing prices, divided by five, or 6050.

But now, we measure the distance or gap between the final closing price and the five-day average, stated as a percent. The calculation is 6150 (the final closing price of the series) divided by 6050 (the five-day average) or +1.65%

Over the long run, the profit odds on January 27 are best when yesterday's closing price is greater than +0.5% above its five-day average. In our hypothetical example, the gap or distance between the closing price and the five-day trend is +1.65%, well above one-half of a percent. If this gap occurred at the end of trading on January 26, it would tell us that the odds of a price rise on January 27 are 69%.

The profit odds slip to just 40% if yesterday's closing price is closer to its five-day average, no greater than 0.5% above or below the average. The profit odds slip even further to 27% if yesterday's closing price is more than -0.5% below its five-day average

The same procedure is used to calculate the gap or distance between the 20-day average and yesterday's closing price. Those profit odds are showing in the right hand column.

SECTION F – LOOKING AHEAD THREE TO FIVE DAYS

The final set of diagnostics at the bottom of the page makes use of today's share price shift to forecast the odds of a future price rise. Two forecasts are provided: for the next three trading days and the next five trading days. Keep in mind that these profit forecasts show the odds of a rise at the very end of each period. They ignore all ebbs or flows that may occur in mid-period.

Our table shows that prices have risen 80% of the time in the next three trading days and 100% of the time in the next five trading days following a large price increase on January 27th in excess of +0.25%. There are no guarantees for any future year of course. Still history suggests that a clear-cut profit opportunity exists if prices rise by a solid amount on January 27.

On the other hand, history also teaches that the profit odds for the next few days slip if prices rise on January 27 by less than 0.25% or if they drop by any amount.

JANUARY

PROFIT ODDS SUMMARY FOR THE MONTH

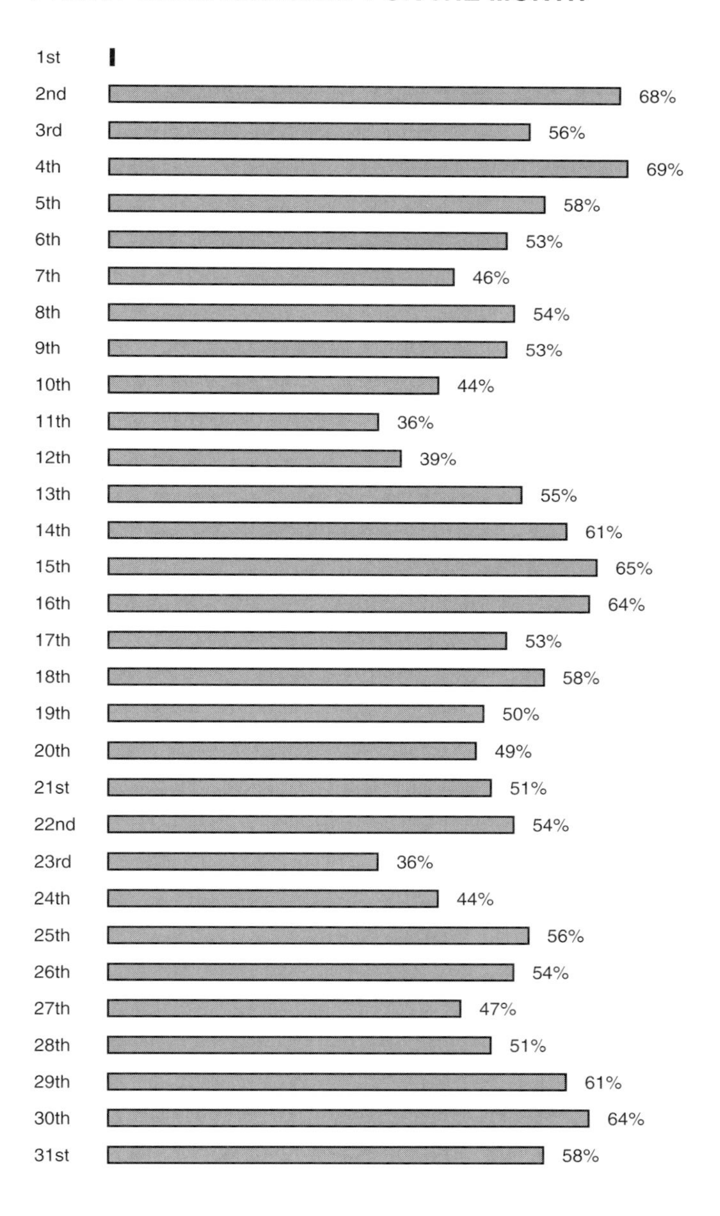

JANUARY 2 ODDS OF A PRICE RISE: 68%

Odds of different size price shift

	1935 to present
Large rise *(above +0.25%)*	47%
Small swing *(+0.25% to -0.25%)*	26%
Large fall *(below -0.25%)*	26%

Odds of rise based on yesterday

	1935 to present
Large rise yesterday *(above +0.25%)*	88%
Small swing yesterday *(+0.25% to -0.25%)*	56%
Large fall yesterday *(below -0.25%)*	*40%

DIAGNOSTICS

Odds of price rise based on direction of 5-day and 20-day trend yesterday

	5-day trend	20-day trend
Yesterday rose more than +0.1%	82%	75%
Little change *(+0.1% to -0.1%)*	*14%	57%
Yesterday fell more than -0.1%	*67%	*75%

Odds of rise based upon distance between trend and yesterday s closing price

	5-day trend	20-day trend
Yesterday more than +0.5% above trend	80%	73%
Yesterday near trend *(+0.5% to -0.5%)*	56%	*50%
Yesterday more than -0.5% below trend	*50%	*63%

Looking ahead: odds of rise in future

	Next 3 days	Next 5 days
Today rose over +0.25%	61%	50%
Today small swing *(+0.25% to -0.25%)*	70%	80%
Today fell below -0.25%	70%	70%

* *Per cent based on fewer than 10 observations*

JANUARY 3 ODDS OF A PRICE RISE: 56%

Odds of different size price shift

	1935 to present
Large rise *(above +0.25%)*	47%
Small swing *(+0.25% to -0.25%)*	37%
Large fall (*below -0.25%)*	16%

Odds of rise based on yesterday

	1935 to present
Large rise yesterday *(above +0.25%)*	67%
Small swing yesterday *(+0.25% to -0.25%)*	53%
Large fall yesterday (*below -0.25%)*	40%

DIAGNOSTICS

Odds of price rise based on direction of 5-day and 20-day trend yesterday

	5-day trend	20-day trend
Yesterday rose more than +0.1%	61%	63%
Little change *(+0.1% to -0.1%)*	*56%	52%
Yesterday fell more than -0.1%	*33%	*50%

Odds of rise based upon distance between trend and yesterday s closing price

	5-day trend	20-day trend
Yesterday more than +0.5% above trend	74%	58%
Yesterday near trend *(+0.5% to -0.5%)*	35%	*75%
Yesterday more than -0.5% below trend	*57%	*38%

Looking ahead: odds of rise in future

	Next 3 days	Next 5 days
Today rose over +0.25%	55%	35%
Today small swing *(+0.25% to -0.25%)*	69%	63%
Today fell below -0.25%	*86%	*71%

JANUARY 4 ODDS OF A PRICE RISE: 69%

Odds of different size price shift

	1935 to present
Large rise *(above +0.25%)*	44%
Small swing *(+0.25% to -0.25%)*	40%
Large fall *(below -0.25%)*	16%

Odds of rise based on yesterday

	1935 to present
Large rise yesterday *(above +0.25%)*	69%
Small swing yesterday *(+0.25% to -0.25%)*	65%
Large fall yesterday *(below -0.25%)*	*78%

DIAGNOSTICS

Odds of price rise based on direction of 5-day and 20-day trend yesterday

	5-day trend	20-day trend
Yesterday rose more than +0.1%	56%	63%
Little change *(+0.1% to -0.1%)*	86%	68%
Yesterday fell more than -0.1%	*83%	*100%

Odds of rise based upon distance between trend and yesterday s closing price

	5-day trend	20-day trend
Yesterday more than +0.5% above trend	59%	63%
Yesterday near trend *(+0.5% to -0.5%)*	70%	*100%
Yesterday more than -0.5% below trend	*100%	*83%

Looking ahead: odds of rise in future

	Next 3 days	Next 5 days
Today rose over +0.25%	80%	45%
Today small swing *(+0.25% to -0.25%)*	61%	56%
Today fell below -0.25%	*57%	*43%

* *Per cent based on fewer than 10 observations*

JANUARY 5 ODDS OF A PRICE RISE: 58%

Odds of different size price shift

	1935 to present
Large rise *(above +0.25%)*	42%
Small swing *(+0.25% to -0.25%)*	31%
Large fall (*below -0.25%)*	27%

Odds of rise based on yesterday

	1935 to present
Large rise yesterday *(above +0.25%)*	72%
Small swing yesterday *(+0.25% to -0.25%)*	61%
Large fall yesterday (*below -0.25%)*	*22%

DIAGNOSTICS

Odds of price rise based on direction of 5-day and 20-day trend yesterday

	5-day trend	20-day trend
Yesterday rose more than +0.1%	53%	62%
Little change *(+0.1% to -0.1%)*	*78%	50%
Yesterday fell more than -0.1%	*50%	*67%

Odds of rise based upon distance between trend and yesterday s closing price

	5-day trend	20-day trend
Yesterday more than +0.5% above trend	50%	59%
Yesterday near trend *(+0.5% to -0.5%)*	65%	*40%
Yesterday more than -0.5% below trend	*50%	*67%

Looking ahead: odds of rise in future

	Next 3 days	Next 5 days
Today rose over +0.25%	63%	53%
Today small swing *(+0.25% to -0.25%)*	64%	50%
Today fell below -0.25%	42%	17%

JANUARY 6 ODDS OF A PRICE RISE: 53%

Odds of different size price shift

	1935 to present
Large rise *(above +0.25%)*	34%
Small swing *(+0.25% to -0.25%)*	38%
Large fall *(below -0.25%)*	28%

Odds of rise based on yesterday

	1935 to present
Large rise yesterday *(above +0.25%)*	67%
Small swing yesterday *(+0.25% to -0.25%)*	46%
Large fall yesterday *(below -0.25%)*	30%

DIAGNOSTICS

Odds of price rise based on direction of 5-day and 20-day trend yesterday

	5-day trend	20-day trend
Yesterday rose more than +0.1%	52%	56%
Little change *(+0.1% to -0.1%)*	58%	59%
Yesterday fell more than -0.1%	*50%	*0%

Odds of rise based upon distance between trend and yesterday s closing price

	5-day trend	20-day trend
Yesterday more than +0.5% above trend	64%	59%
Yesterday near trend *(+0.5% to -0.5%)*	44%	*14%
Yesterday more than -0.5% below trend	*43%	*67%

Looking ahead: odds of rise in future

	Next 3 days	Next 5 days
Today rose over +0.25%	38%	50%
Today small swing *(+0.25% to -0.25%)*	50%	56%
Today fell below -0.25%	38%	38%

* *Per cent based on fewer than 10 observations*

JANUARY 7 ODDS OF A PRICE RISE: 46%

Odds of different size price shift

	1935 to present
Large rise *(above +0.25%)*	39%
Small swing *(+0.25% to -0.25%)*	26%
Large fall (*below -0.25%)*	35%

Odds of rise based on yesterday

	1935 to present
Large rise yesterday *(above +0.25%)*	59%
Small swing yesterday *(+0.25% to -0.25%)*	44%
Large fall yesterday (*below -0.25%)*	27%

DIAGNOSTICS

Odds of price rise based on direction of 5-day and 20-day trend yesterday

	5-day trend	20-day trend
Yesterday rose more than +0.1%	36%	42%
Little change *(+0.1% to -0.1%)*	58%	43%
Yesterday fell more than -0.1%	*56%	*67%

Odds of rise based upon distance between trend and yesterday s closing price

	5-day trend	20-day trend
Yesterday more than +0.5% above trend	41%	43%
Yesterday near trend *(+0.5% to -0.5%)*	43%	*50%
Yesterday more than -0.5% below trend	*63%	*60%

Looking ahead: odds of rise in future

	Next 3 days	Next 5 days
Today rose over +0.25%	61%	56%
Today small swing *(+0.25% to -0.25%)*	58%	50%
Today fell below -0.25%	31%	44%

JANUARY 8 ODDS OF A PRICE RISE: 54%

Odds of different size price shift

	1935 to present
Large rise *(above +0.25%)*	39%
Small swing *(+0.25% to -0.25%)*	33%
Large fall (*below -0.25%)*	28%

Odds of rise based on yesterday

	1935 to present
Large rise yesterday *(above +0.25%)*	63%
Small swing yesterday *(+0.25% to -0.25%)*	62%
Large fall yesterday (*below -0.25%)*	41%

DIAGNOSTICS

Odds of price rise based on direction of 5-day and 20-day trend yesterday

	5-day trend	20-day trend
Yesterday rose more than +0.1%	62%	59%
Little change *(+0.1% to -0.1%)*	*67%	53%
Yesterday fell more than -0.1%	27%	*40%

Odds of rise based upon distance between trend and yesterday s closing price

	5-day trend	20-day trend
Yesterday more than +0.5% above trend	64%	63%
Yesterday near trend *(+0.5% to -0.5%)*	61%	*44%
Yesterday more than -0.5% below trend	*22%	*20%

Looking ahead: odds of rise in future

	Next 3 days	Next 5 days
Today rose over +0.25%	56%	56%
Today small swing *(+0.25% to -0.25%)*	40%	47%
Today fell below -0.25%	54%	54%

* *Per cent based on fewer than 10 observations*

JANUARY 9 ODDS OF A PRICE RISE: 53%

Odds of different size price shift

	1935 to present
Large rise *(above +0.25%)*	31%
Small swing *(+0.25% to -0.25%)*	36%
Large fall (*below -0.25%)*	33%

Odds of rise based on yesterday

	1935 to present
Large rise yesterday *(above +0.25%)*	61%
Small swing yesterday *(+0.25% to -0.25%)*	47%
Large fall yesterday (*below -0.25%)*	50%

DIAGNOSTICS

Odds of price rise based on direction of 5-day and 20-day trend yesterday

	5-day trend	20-day trend
Yesterday rose more than +0.1%	63%	57%
Little change *(+0.1% to -0.1%)*	30%	48%
Yesterday fell more than -0.1%	55%	*67%

Odds of rise based upon distance between trend and yesterday s closing price

	5-day trend	20-day trend
Yesterday more than +0.5% above trend	73%	53%
Yesterday near trend *(+0.5% to -0.5%)*	44%	*29%
Yesterday more than -0.5% below trend	42%	*83%

Looking ahead: odds of rise in future

	Next 3 days	Next 5 days
Today rose over +0.25%	79%	79%
Today small swing *(+0.25% to -0.25%)*	44%	63%
Today fell below -0.25%	33%	60%

JANUARY 10 ODDS OF A PRICE RISE: 44%

Odds of different size price shift

	1935 to present
Large rise *(above +0.25%)*	27%
Small swing *(+0.25% to -0.25%)*	40%
Large fall *(below -0.25%)*	33%

Odds of rise based on yesterday

	1935 to present
Large rise yesterday *(above +0.25%)*	57%
Small swing yesterday *(+0.25% to -0.25%)*	44%
Large fall yesterday *(below -0.25%)*	33%

DIAGNOSTICS

Odds of price rise based on direction of 5-day and 20-day trend yesterday

	5-day trend	20-day trend
Yesterday rose more than +0.1%	46%	48%
Little change *(+0.1% to -0.1%)*	45%	43%
Yesterday fell more than -0.1%	40%	*0%

Odds of rise based upon distance between trend and yesterday s closing price

	5-day trend	20-day trend
Yesterday more than +0.5% above trend	50%	42%
Yesterday near trend *(+0.5% to -0.5%)*	48%	*80%
Yesterday more than -0.5% below trend	30%	*29%

Looking ahead: odds of rise in future

	Next 3 days	Next 5 days
Today rose over +0.25%	67%	92%
Today small swing *(+0.25% to -0.25%)*	61%	61%
Today fell below -0.25%	40%	47%

* *Per cent based on fewer than 10 observations*

JANUARY 11 ODDS OF A PRICE RISE: 36%

Odds of different size price shift

	1935 to present
Large rise *(above +0.25%)*	18%
Small swing *(+0.25% to -0.25%)*	42%
Large fall (*below -0.25%)*	40%

Odds of rise based on yesterday

	1935 to present
Large rise yesterday *(above +0.25%)*	33%
Small swing yesterday *(+0.25% to -0.25%)*	39%
Large fall yesterday (*below -0.25%)*	33%

DIAGNOSTICS

Odds of price rise based on direction of 5-day and 20-day trend yesterday

	5-day trend	20-day trend
Yesterday rose more than +0.1%	33%	32%
Little change *(+0.1% to -0.1%)*	*63%	41%
Yesterday fell more than -0.1%	23%	*33%

Odds of rise based upon distance between trend and yesterday s closing price

	5-day trend	20-day trend
Yesterday more than +0.5% above trend	40%	41%
Yesterday near trend *(+0.5% to -0.5%)*	28%	*25%
Yesterday more than -0.5% below trend	42%	*20%

Looking ahead: odds of rise in future

	Next 3 days	Next 5 days
Today rose over +0.25%	*75%	*75%
Today small swing *(+0.25% to -0.25%)*	63%	58%
Today fell below -0.25%	44%	61%

JANUARY 12 ODDS OF A PRICE RISE: 39%

Odds of different size price shift

	1935 to present
Large rise *(above +0.25%)*	22%
Small swing *(+0.25% to -0.25%)*	30%
Large fall (*below -0.25%)*	48%

Odds of rise based on yesterday

	1935 to present
Large rise yesterday *(above +0.25%)*	80%
Small swing yesterday *(+0.25% to -0.25%)*	39%
Large fall yesterday (*below -0.25%)*	17%

DIAGNOSTICS

Odds of price rise based on direction of 5-day and 20-day trend yesterday

	5-day trend	20-day trend
Yesterday rose more than +0.1%	53%	42%
Little change *(+0.1% to -0.1%)*	38%	35%
Yesterday fell more than -0.1%	21%	*33%

Odds of rise based upon distance between trend and yesterday s closing price

	5-day trend	20-day trend
Yesterday more than +0.5% above trend	*56%	45%
Yesterday near trend *(+0.5% to -0.5%)*	42%	33%
Yesterday more than -0.5% below trend	23%	*20%

Looking ahead: odds of rise in future

	Next 3 days	Next 5 days
Today rose over +0.25%	80%	70%
Today small swing *(+0.25% to -0.25%)*	64%	57%
Today fell below -0.25%	73%	50%

* *Per cent based on fewer than 10 observations*

JANUARY 13 ODDS OF A PRICE RISE: 55%

Odds of different size price shift

	1935 to present
Large rise *(above +0.25%)*	45%
Small swing *(+0.25% to -0.25%)*	32%
Large fall (*below -0.25%)*	23%

Odds of rise based on yesterday

	1935 to present
Large rise yesterday *(above +0.25%)*	80%
Small swing yesterday *(+0.25% to -0.25%)*	18%
Large fall yesterday (*below -0.25%)*	57%

DIAGNOSTICS

Odds of price rise based on direction of 5-day and 20-day trend yesterday

	5-day trend	20-day trend
Yesterday rose more than +0.1%	67%	81%
Little change *(+0.1% to -0.1%)*	67%	21%
Yesterday fell more than -0.1%	35%	*50%

Odds of rise based upon distance between trend and yesterday s closing price

	5-day trend	20-day trend
Yesterday more than +0.5% above trend	83%	69%
Yesterday near trend *(+0.5% to -0.5%)*	56%	40%
Yesterday more than -0.5% below trend	37%	*25%

Looking ahead: odds of rise in future

	Next 3 days	Next 5 days
Today rose over +0.25%	90%	71%
Today small swing *(+0.25% to -0.25%)*	80%	53%
Today fell below -0.25%	55%	55%

JANUARY 14 ODDS OF A PRICE RISE: 61%

Odds of different size price shift

	1935 to present
Large rise *(above +0.25%)*	46%
Small swing *(+0.25% to -0.25%)*	28%
Large fall (*below -0.25%)*	26%

Odds of rise based on yesterday

	1935 to present
Large rise yesterday *(above +0.25%)*	75%
Small swing yesterday *(+0.25% to -0.25%)*	69%
Large fall yesterday (*below -0.25%)*	20%

DIAGNOSTICS

Odds of price rise based on direction of 5-day and 20-day trend yesterday

	5-day trend	20-day trend
Yesterday rose more than +0.1%	61%	80%
Little change *(+0.1% to -0.1%)*	82%	44%
Yesterday fell more than -0.1%	47%	*0%

Odds of rise based upon distance between trend and yesterday s closing price

	5-day trend	20-day trend
Yesterday more than +0.5% above trend	77%	71%
Yesterday near trend *(+0.5% to -0.5%)*	58%	*56%
Yesterday more than -0.5% below trend	50%	*33%

Looking ahead: odds of rise in future

	Next 3 days	Next 5 days
Today rose over +0.25%	67%	62%
Today small swing *(+0.25% to -0.25%)*	77%	69%
Today fell below -0.25%	75%	58%

* *Per cent based on fewer than 10 observations*

JANUARY 15 ODDS OF A PRICE RISE: 65%

Odds of different size price shift

	1935 to present
Large rise *(above +0.25%)*	54%
Small swing *(+0.25% to -0.25%)*	22%
Large fall (*below -0.25%)*	24%

Odds of rise based on yesterday

	1935 to present
Large rise yesterday *(above +0.25%)*	72%
Small swing yesterday *(+0.25% to -0.25%)*	71%
Large fall yesterday (*below -0.25%)*	50%

DIAGNOSTICS

Odds of price rise based on direction of 5-day and 20-day trend yesterday

	5-day trend	20-day trend
Yesterday rose more than +0.1%	75%	78%
Little change *(+0.1% to -0.1%)*	*56%	53%
Yesterday fell more than -0.1%	62%	*50%

Odds of rise based upon distance between trend and yesterday s closing price

	5-day trend	20-day trend
Yesterday more than +0.5% above trend	67%	65%
Yesterday near trend *(+0.5% to -0.5%)*	76%	*63%
Yesterday more than -0.5% below trend	46%	67%

Looking ahead: odds of rise in future

	Next 3 days	Next 5 days
Today rose over +0.25%	48%	44%
Today small swing *(+0.25% to -0.25%)*	60%	80%
Today fell below -0.25%	64%	36%

JANUARY 16 ODDS OF A PRICE RISE: 64%

Odds of different size price shift

	1935 to present
Large rise *(above +0.25%)*	47%
Small swing *(+0.25% to -0.25%)*	31%
Large fall *(below -0.25%)*	22%

Odds of rise based on yesterday

	1935 to present
Large rise yesterday *(above +0.25%)*	77%
Small swing yesterday *(+0.25% to -0.25%)*	70%
Large fall yesterday *(below -0.25%)*	38%

DIAGNOSTICS

Odds of price rise based on direction of 5-day and 20-day trend yesterday

	5-day trend	20-day trend
Yesterday rose more than +0.1%	88%	77%
Little change *(+0.1% to -0.1%)*	50%	53%
Yesterday fell more than -0.1%	50%	*50%

Odds of rise based upon distance between trend and yesterday s closing price

	5-day trend	20-day trend
Yesterday more than +0.5% above trend	82%	78%
Yesterday near trend *(+0.5% to -0.5%)*	67%	*75%
Yesterday more than -0.5% below trend	38%	36%

Looking ahead: odds of rise in future

	Next 3 days	Next 5 days
Today rose over +0.25%	62%	48%
Today small swing *(+0.25% to -0.25%)*	36%	43%
Today fell below -0.25%	40%	30%

* *Per cent based on fewer than 10 observations*

JANUARY 17 ODDS OF A PRICE RISE: 53%

Odds of different size price shift

	1935 to present
Large rise *(above +0.25%)*	33%
Small swing *(+0.25% to -0.25%)*	38%
Large fall (*below -0.25%)*	29%

Odds of rise based on yesterday

	1935 to present
Large rise yesterday *(above +0.25%)*	65%
Small swing yesterday *(+0.25% to -0.25%)*	50%
Large fall yesterday (*below -0.25%)*	36%

DIAGNOSTICS

Odds of price rise based on direction of 5-day and 20-day trend yesterday

	5-day trend	20-day trend
Yesterday rose more than +0.1%	63%	69%
Little change *(+0.1% to -0.1%)*	46%	21%
Yesterday fell more than -0.1%	46%	*60%

Odds of rise based upon distance between trend and yesterday s closing price

	5-day trend	20-day trend
Yesterday more than +0.5% above trend	47%	61%
Yesterday near trend *(+0.5% to -0.5%)*	68%	*25%
Yesterday more than -0.5% below trend	*33%	40%

Looking ahead: odds of rise in future

	Next 3 days	Next 5 days
Today rose over +0.25%	60%	53%
Today small swing *(+0.25% to -0.25%)*	53%	53%
Today fell below -0.25%	46%	54%

JANUARY 18 ODDS OF A PRICE RISE: 58%

Odds of different size price shift

	1935 to present
Large rise *(above +0.25%)*	42%
Small swing *(+0.25% to -0.25%)*	33%
Large fall *(below -0.25%)*	24%

Odds of rise based on yesterday

	1935 to present
Large rise yesterday *(above +0.25%)*	67%
Small swing yesterday *(+0.25% to -0.25%)*	57%
Large fall yesterday *(below -0.25%)*	46%

DIAGNOSTICS

Odds of price rise based on direction of 5-day and 20-day trend yesterday

	5-day trend	20-day trend
Yesterday rose more than +0.1%	73%	75%
Little change *(+0.1% to -0.1%)*	56%	47%
Yesterday fell more than -0.1%	43%	*0%

Odds of rise based upon distance between trend and yesterday s closing price

	5-day trend	20-day trend
Yesterday more than +0.5% above trend	67%	71%
Yesterday near trend *(+0.5% to -0.5%)*	54%	*38%
Yesterday more than -0.5% below trend	*50%	*33%

Looking ahead: odds of rise in future

	Next 3 days	Next 5 days
Today rose over +0.25%	47%	58%
Today small swing *(+0.25% to -0.25%)*	60%	67%
Today fell below -0.25%	36%	27%

* *Per cent based on fewer than 10 observations*

JANUARY 19 ODDS OF A PRICE RISE: 50%

Odds of different size price shift

	1935 to present
Large rise *(above +0.25%)*	26%
Small swing *(+0.25% to -0.25%)*	41%
Large fall (*below -0.25%)*	33%

Odds of rise based on yesterday

	1935 to present
Large rise yesterday *(above +0.25%)*	61%
Small swing yesterday *(+0.25% to -0.25%)*	41%
Large fall yesterday (*below -0.25%)*	45%

DIAGNOSTICS

Odds of price rise based on direction of 5-day and 20-day trend yesterday

	5-day trend	20-day trend
Yesterday rose more than +0.1%	61%	50%
Little change *(+0.1% to -0.1%)*	45%	61%
Yesterday fell more than -0.1%	33%	*0%

Odds of rise based upon distance between trend and yesterday s closing price

	5-day trend	20-day trend
Yesterday more than +0.5% above trend	55%	57%
Yesterday near trend *(+0.5% to -0.5%)*	47%	*50%
Yesterday more than -0.5% below trend	*43%	30%

Looking ahead: odds of rise in future

	Next 3 days	Next 5 days
Today rose over +0.25%	58%	50%
Today small swing *(+0.25% to -0.25%)*	63%	68%
Today fell below -0.25%	40%	47%

JANUARY 20 ODDS OF A PRICE RISE: 49%

Odds of different size price shift

	1935 to present
Large rise *(above +0.25%)*	28%
Small swing *(+0.25% to -0.25%)*	36%
Large fall *(below -0.25%)*	36%

Odds of rise based on yesterday

	1935 to present
Large rise yesterday *(above +0.25%)*	57%
Small swing yesterday *(+0.25% to -0.25%)*	55%
Large fall yesterday *(below -0.25%)*	31%

DIAGNOSTICS

Odds of price rise based on direction of 5-day and 20-day trend yesterday

	5-day trend	20-day trend
Yesterday rose more than +0.1%	56%	48%
Little change *(+0.1% to -0.1%)*	42%	57%
Yesterday fell more than -0.1%	40%	*25%

Odds of rise based upon distance between trend and yesterday s closing price

	5-day trend	20-day trend
Yesterday more than +0.5% above trend	67%	58%
Yesterday near trend *(+0.5% to -0.5%)*	38%	*20%
Yesterday more than -0.5% below trend	*38%	36%

Looking ahead: odds of rise in future

	Next 3 days	Next 5 days
Today rose over +0.25%	38%	62%
Today small swing *(+0.25% to -0.25%)*	76%	59%
Today fell below -0.25%	59%	59%

* *Per cent based on fewer than 10 observations*

JANUARY 21 ODDS OF A PRICE RISE: 51%

Odds of different size price shift

	1935 to present
Large rise *(above +0.25%)*	36%
Small swing *(+0.25% to -0.25%)*	31%
Large fall (*below -0.25%)*	33%

Odds of rise based on yesterday

	1935 to present
Large rise yesterday *(above +0.25%)*	67%
Small swing yesterday *(+0.25% to -0.25%)*	44%
Large fall yesterday (*below -0.25%)*	43%

DIAGNOSTICS

Odds of price rise based on direction of 5-day and 20-day trend yesterday

	5-day trend	20-day trend
Yesterday rose more than +0.1%	48%	52%
Little change *(+0.1% to -0.1%)*	*67%	57%
Yesterday fell more than -0.1%	45%	*25%

Odds of rise based upon distance between trend and yesterday s closing price

	5-day trend	20-day trend
Yesterday more than +0.5% above trend	63%	57%
Yesterday near trend *(+0.5% to -0.5%)*	35%	*60%
Yesterday more than -0.5% below trend	*56%	30%

Looking ahead: odds of rise in future

	Next 3 days	Next 5 days
Today rose over +0.25%	69%	69%
Today small swing *(+0.25% to -0.25%)*	50%	64%
Today fell below -0.25%	47%	40%

JANUARY 22 ODDS OF A PRICE RISE: 54%

Odds of different size price shift

	1935 to present
Large rise *(above +0.25%)*	37%
Small swing *(+0.25% to -0.25%)*	30%
Large fall (*below -0.25%)*	33%

Odds of rise based on yesterday

	1935 to present
Large rise yesterday *(above +0.25%)*	64%
Small swing yesterday *(+0.25% to -0.25%)*	50%
Large fall yesterday (*below -0.25%)*	50%

DIAGNOSTICS

Odds of price rise based on direction of 5-day and 20-day trend yesterday

	5-day trend	20-day trend
Yesterday rose more than +0.1%	50%	48%
Little change *(+0.1% to -0.1%)*	71%	69%
Yesterday fell more than -0.1%	42%	*40%

Odds of rise based upon distance between trend and yesterday s closing price

	5-day trend	20-day trend
Yesterday more than +0.5% above trend	73%	48%
Yesterday near trend *(+0.5% to -0.5%)*	42%	*63%
Yesterday more than -0.5% below trend	56%	62%

Looking ahead: odds of rise in future

	Next 3 days	Next 5 days
Today rose over +0.25%	59%	71%
Today small swing *(+0.25% to -0.25%)*	57%	64%
Today fell below -0.25%	47%	53%

* *Per cent based on fewer than 10 observations*

JANUARY 23 ODDS OF A PRICE RISE: 36%

Odds of different size price shift

	1935 to present
Large rise *(above +0.25%)*	22%
Small swing *(+0.25% to -0.25%)*	36%
Large fall (*below -0.25%)*	42%

Odds of rise based on yesterday

	1935 to present
Large rise yesterday *(above +0.25%)*	54%
Small swing yesterday *(+0.25% to -0.25%)*	47%
Large fall yesterday (*below -0.25%)*	12%

DIAGNOSTICS

Odds of price rise based on direction of 5-day and 20-day trend yesterday

	5-day trend	20-day trend
Yesterday rose more than +0.1%	47%	52%
Little change *(+0.1% to -0.1%)*	*33%	15%
Yesterday fell more than -0.1%	24%	*14%

Odds of rise based upon distance between trend and yesterday s closing price

	5-day trend	20-day trend
Yesterday more than +0.5% above trend	45%	52%
Yesterday near trend *(+0.5% to -0.5%)*	45%	*29%
Yesterday more than -0.5% below trend	14%	13%

Looking ahead: odds of rise in future

	Next 3 days	Next 5 days
Today rose over +0.25%	90%	90%
Today small swing *(+0.25% to -0.25%)*	50%	56%
Today fell below -0.25%	47%	53%

JANUARY 24 ODDS OF A PRICE RISE: 44%

Odds of different size price shift

	1935 to present
Large rise *(above +0.25%)*	36%
Small swing *(+0.25% to -0.25%)*	27%
Large fall *(below -0.25%)*	38%

Odds of rise based on yesterday

	1935 to present
Large rise yesterday *(above +0.25%)*	58%
Small swing yesterday *(+0.25% to -0.25%)*	31%
Large fall yesterday *(below -0.25%)*	47%

DIAGNOSTICS

Odds of price rise based on direction of 5-day and 20-day trend yesterday

	5-day trend	20-day trend
Yesterday rose more than +0.1%	39%	50%
Little change *(+0.1% to -0.1%)*	60%	23%
Yesterday fell more than -0.1%	41%	*63%

Odds of rise based upon distance between trend and yesterday s closing price

	5-day trend	20-day trend
Yesterday more than +0.5% above trend	38%	50%
Yesterday near trend *(+0.5% to -0.5%)*	44%	*17%
Yesterday more than -0.5% below trend	50%	47%

Looking ahead: odds of rise in future

	Next 3 days	Next 5 days
Today rose over +0.25%	88%	88%
Today small swing *(+0.25% to -0.25%)*	50%	50%
Today fell below -0.25%	41%	71%

* *Per cent based on fewer than 10 observations*

JANUARY 25 ODDS OF A PRICE RISE: 56%

Odds of different size price shift

	1935 to present
Large rise *(above +0.25%)*	36%
Small swing *(+0.25% to -0.25%)*	31%
Large fall (*below -0.25%)*	33%

Odds of rise based on yesterday

	1935 to present
Large rise yesterday *(above +0.25%)*	65%
Small swing yesterday *(+0.25% to -0.25%)*	80%
Large fall yesterday (*below -0.25%)*	27%

DIAGNOSTICS

Odds of price rise based on direction of 5-day and 20-day trend yesterday

	5-day trend	20-day trend
Yesterday rose more than +0.1%	47%	52%
Little change *(+0.1% to -0.1%)*	67%	56%
Yesterday fell more than -0.1%	57%	*63%

Odds of rise based upon distance between trend and yesterday s closing price

	5-day trend	20-day trend
Yesterday more than +0.5% above trend	*44%	52%
Yesterday near trend *(+0.5% to -0.5%)*	60%	60%
Yesterday more than -0.5% below trend	56%	57%

Looking ahead: odds of rise in future

	Next 3 days	Next 5 days
Today rose over +0.25%	69%	50%
Today small swing *(+0.25% to -0.25%)*	57%	57%
Today fell below -0.25%	73%	87%

JANUARY 26 ODDS OF A PRICE RISE: 54%

Odds of different size price shift

	1935 to present
Large rise *(above +0.25%)*	43%
Small swing *(+0.25% to -0.25%)*	41%
Large fall (*below -0.25%)*	15%

Odds of rise based on yesterday

	1935 to present
Large rise yesterday *(above +0.25%)*	67%
Small swing yesterday *(+0.25% to -0.25%)*	53%
Large fall yesterday (*below -0.25%)*	44%

DIAGNOSTICS

Odds of price rise based on direction of 5-day and 20-day trend yesterday

	5-day trend	20-day trend
Yesterday rose more than +0.1%	46%	52%
Little change *(+0.1% to -0.1%)*	59%	58%
Yesterday fell more than -0.1%	56%	*50%

Odds of rise based upon distance between trend and yesterday s closing price

	5-day trend	20-day trend
Yesterday more than +0.5% above trend	64%	52%
Yesterday near trend *(+0.5% to -0.5%)*	52%	55%
Yesterday more than -0.5% below trend	50%	57%

Looking ahead: odds of rise in future

	Next 3 days	Next 5 days
Today rose over +0.25%	75%	85%
Today small swing *(+0.25% to -0.25%)*	53%	58%
Today fell below -0.25%	*57%	*57%

* *Per cent based on fewer than 10 observations*

JANUARY 27 ODDS OF A PRICE RISE: 47%

Odds of different size price shift

	1935 to present
Large rise *(above +0.25%)*	32%
Small swing *(+0.25% to -0.25%)*	43%
Large fall (*below -0.25%)*	26%

Odds of rise based on yesterday

	1935 to present
Large rise yesterday *(above +0.25%)*	79%
Small swing yesterday *(+0.25% to -0.25%)*	25%
Large fall yesterday (*below -0.25%)*	*25%

DIAGNOSTICS

Odds of price rise based on direction of 5-day and 20-day trend yesterday

	5-day trend	20-day trend
Yesterday rose more than +0.1%	59%	60%
Little change *(+0.1% to -0.1%)*	50%	40%
Yesterday fell more than -0.1%	29%	*14%

Odds of rise based upon distance between trend and yesterday s closing price

	5-day trend	20-day trend
Yesterday more than +0.5% above trend	69%	62%
Yesterday near trend *(+0.5% to -0.5%)*	40%	33%
Yesterday more than -0.5% below trend	27%	*22%

Looking ahead: odds of rise in future

	Next 3 days	Next 5 days
Today rose over +0.25%	80%	100%
Today small swing *(+0.25% to -0.25%)*	60%	60%
Today fell below -0.25%	50%	58%

JANUARY 28 ODDS OF A PRICE RISE: 51%

Odds of different size price shift

	1935 to present
Large rise *(above +0.25%)*	36%
Small swing *(+0.25% to -0.25%)*	42%
Large fall *(below -0.25%)*	22%

Odds of rise based on yesterday

	1935 to present
Large rise yesterday *(above +0.25%)*	64%
Small swing yesterday *(+0.25% to -0.25%)*	50%
Large fall yesterday *(below -0.25%)*	36%

DIAGNOSTICS

Odds of price rise based on direction of 5-day and 20-day trend yesterday

	5-day trend	20-day trend
Yesterday rose more than +0.1%	52%	61%
Little change *(+0.1% to -0.1%)*	*44%	33%
Yesterday fell more than -0.1%	53%	*57%

Odds of rise based upon distance between trend and yesterday s closing price

	5-day trend	20-day trend
Yesterday more than +0.5% above trend	56%	52%
Yesterday near trend *(+0.5% to -0.5%)*	61%	70%
Yesterday more than -0.5% below trend	27%	30%

Looking ahead: odds of rise in future

	Next 3 days	Next 5 days
Today rose over +0.25%	81%	63%
Today small swing *(+0.25% to -0.25%)*	58%	63%
Today fell below -0.25%	90%	80%

* *Per cent based on fewer than 10 observations*

JANUARY 29 ODDS OF A PRICE RISE: 61%

Odds of different size price shift

	1935 to present
Large rise *(above +0.25%)*	37%
Small swing *(+0.25% to -0.25%)*	41%
Large fall (*below -0.25%)*	22%

Odds of rise based on yesterday

	1935 to present
Large rise yesterday *(above +0.25%)*	65%
Small swing yesterday *(+0.25% to -0.25%)*	59%
Large fall yesterday (*below -0.25%)*	58%

DIAGNOSTICS

Odds of price rise based on direction of 5-day and 20-day trend yesterday

	5-day trend	20-day trend
Yesterday rose more than +0.1%	60%	68%
Little change *(+0.1% to -0.1%)*	*56%	50%
Yesterday fell more than -0.1%	65%	60%

Odds of rise based upon distance between trend and yesterday s closing price

	5-day trend	20-day trend
Yesterday more than +0.5% above trend	59%	64%
Yesterday near trend *(+0.5% to -0.5%)*	65%	*14%
Yesterday more than -0.5% below trend	58%	79%

Looking ahead: odds of rise in future

	Next 3 days	Next 5 days
Today rose over +0.25%	65%	53%
Today small swing *(+0.25% to -0.25%)*	68%	58%
Today fell below -0.25%	60%	70%

JANUARY 30 ODDS OF A PRICE RISE: 64%

Odds of different size price shift

	1935 to present
Large rise *(above +0.25%)*	44%
Small swing *(+0.25% to -0.25%)*	38%
Large fall *(below -0.25%)*	18%

Odds of rise based on yesterday

	1935 to present
Large rise yesterday *(above +0.25%)*	75%
Small swing yesterday *(+0.25% to -0.25%)*	67%
Large fall yesterday *(below -0.25%)*	45%

DIAGNOSTICS

Odds of price rise based on direction of 5-day and 20-day trend yesterday

	5-day trend	20-day trend
Yesterday rose more than +0.1%	65%	74%
Little change *(+0.1% to -0.1%)*	*71%	67%
Yesterday fell more than -0.1%	61%	45%

Odds of rise based upon distance between trend and yesterday s closing price

	5-day trend	20-day trend
Yesterday more than +0.5% above trend	64%	80%
Yesterday near trend *(+0.5% to -0.5%)*	61%	*43%
Yesterday more than -0.5% below trend	*75%	56%

Looking ahead: odds of rise in future

	Next 3 days	Next 5 days
Today rose over +0.25%	70%	70%
Today small swing *(+0.25% to -0.25%)*	59%	53%
Today fell below -0.25%	*38%	*38%

* *Per cent based on fewer than 10 observations*

JANUARY 31 ODDS OF A PRICE RISE: 58%

Odds of different size price shift

	1935 to present
Large rise *(above +0.25%)*	47%
Small swing *(+0.25% to -0.25%)*	22%
Large fall (*below -0.25%)*	31%

Odds of rise based on yesterday

	1935 to present
Large rise yesterday *(above +0.25%)*	79%
Small swing yesterday *(+0.25% to -0.25%)*	50%
Large fall yesterday (*below -0.25%)*	*17%

DIAGNOSTICS

Odds of price rise based on direction of 5-day and 20-day trend yesterday

	5-day trend	20-day trend
Yesterday rose more than +0.1%	47%	67%
Little change *(+0.1% to -0.1%)*	64%	47%
Yesterday fell more than -0.1%	64%	*56%

Odds of rise based upon distance between trend and yesterday s closing price

	5-day trend	20-day trend
Yesterday more than +0.5% above trend	59%	70%
Yesterday near trend *(+0.5% to -0.5%)*	60%	*17%
Yesterday more than -0.5% below trend	*33%	56%

Looking ahead: odds of rise in future

	Next 3 days	Next 5 days
Today rose over +0.25%	71%	52%
Today small swing *(+0.25% to -0.25%)*	50%	50%
Today fell below -0.25%	50%	64%

FEBRUARY

PROFIT ODDS SUMMARY FOR THE MONTH

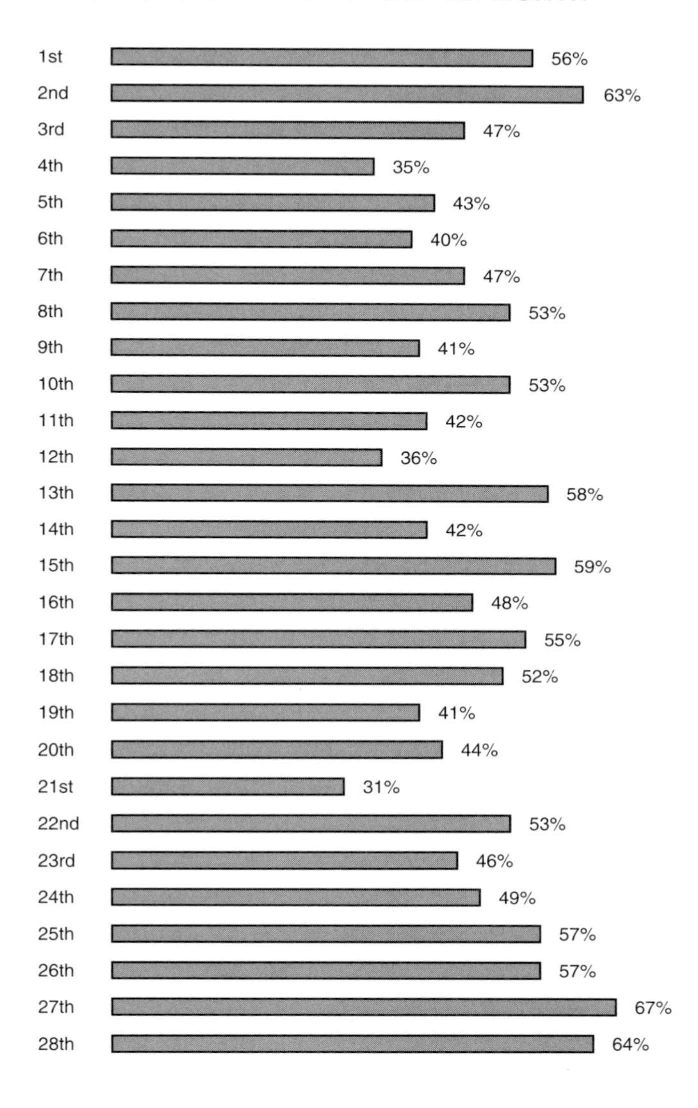

FEBRUARY 1 ODDS OF A PRICE RISE: 56%

Odds of different size price shift

	1935 to present
Large rise *(above +0.25%)*	40%
Small swing *(+0.25% to -0.25%)*	36%
Large fall (*below -0.25%)*	24%

Odds of rise based on yesterday

	1935 to present
Large rise yesterday *(above +0.25%)*	60%
Small swing yesterday *(+0.25% to -0.25%)*	50%
Large fall yesterday (*below -0.25%)*	54%

DIAGNOSTICS

Odds of price rise based on direction of 5-day and 20-day trend yesterday

	5-day trend	20-day trend
Yesterday rose more than +0.1%	59%	50%
Little change *(+0.1% to -0.1%)*	47%	43%
Yesterday fell more than -0.1%	*67%	82%

Odds of rise based upon distance between trend and yesterday s closing price

	5-day trend	20-day trend
Yesterday more than +0.5% above trend	63%	50%
Yesterday near trend *(+0.5% to -0.5%)*	48%	*44%
Yesterday more than -0.5% below trend	*60%	75%

Looking ahead: odds of rise in future

	Next 3 days	Next 5 days
Today rose over +0.25%	56%	50%
Today small swing *(+0.25% to -0.25%)*	50%	31%
Today fell below -0.25%	55%	64%

* *Per cent based on fewer than 10 observations*

FEBRUARY 2 ODDS OF A PRICE RISE: 63%

Odds of different size price shift

	1935 to present
Large rise *(above +0.25%)*	39%
Small swing *(+0.25% to -0.25%)*	46%
Large fall (*below -0.25%)*	15%

Odds of rise based on yesterday

	1935 to present
Large rise yesterday *(above +0.25%)*	67%
Small swing yesterday *(+0.25% to -0.25%)*	60%
Large fall yesterday (*below -0.25%)*	60%

DIAGNOSTICS

Odds of price rise based on direction of 5-day and 20-day trend yesterday

	5-day trend	20-day trend
Yesterday rose more than +0.1%	68%	67%
Little change *(+0.1% to -0.1%)*	58%	53%
Yesterday fell more than -0.1%	*56%	*75%

Odds of rise based upon distance between trend and yesterday s closing price

	5-day trend	20-day trend
Yesterday more than +0.5% above trend	59%	65%
Yesterday near trend *(+0.5% to -0.5%)*	67%	*50%
Yesterday more than -0.5% below trend	*63%	67%

Looking ahead: odds of rise in future

	Next 3 days	Next 5 days
Today rose over +0.25%	39%	39%
Today small swing *(+0.25% to -0.25%)*	52%	48%
Today fell below -0.25%	*43%	*29%

FEBRUARY 3 ODDS OF A PRICE RISE: 47%

Odds of different size price shift

	1935 to present
Large rise *(above +0.25%)*	36%
Small swing *(+0.25% to -0.25%)*	36%
Large fall *(below -0.25%)*	28%

Odds of rise based on yesterday

	1935 to present
Large rise yesterday *(above +0.25%)*	53%
Small swing yesterday *(+0.25% to -0.25%)*	44%
Large fall yesterday *(below -0.25%)*	40%

DIAGNOSTICS

Odds of price rise based on direction of 5-day and 20-day trend yesterday

	5-day trend	20-day trend
Yesterday rose more than +0.1%	46%	48%
Little change *(+0.1% to -0.1%)*	54%	47%
Yesterday fell more than -0.1%	40%	*43%

Odds of rise based upon distance between trend and yesterday s closing price

	5-day trend	20-day trend
Yesterday more than +0.5% above trend	45%	50%
Yesterday near trend *(+0.5% to -0.5%)*	55%	60%
Yesterday more than -0.5% below trend	*20%	*22%

Looking ahead: odds of rise in future

	Next 3 days	Next 5 days
Today rose over +0.25%	65%	47%
Today small swing *(+0.25% to -0.25%)*	41%	47%
Today fell below -0.25%	31%	38%

* *Per cent based on fewer than 10 observations*

FEBRUARY 4 ODDS OF A PRICE RISE: 35%

Odds of different size price shift

	1935 to present
Large rise *(above +0.25%)*	26%
Small swing *(+0.25% to -0.25%)*	33%
Large fall (*below -0.25%)*	41%

Odds of rise based on yesterday

	1935 to present
Large rise yesterday *(above +0.25%)*	38%
Small swing yesterday *(+0.25% to -0.25%)*	33%
Large fall yesterday (*below -0.25%)*	33%

DIAGNOSTICS

Odds of price rise based on direction of 5-day and 20-day trend yesterday

	5-day trend	20-day trend
Yesterday rose more than +0.1%	46%	32%
Little change *(+0.1% to -0.1%)*	9%	37%
Yesterday fell more than -0.1%	*33%	*40%

Odds of rise based upon distance between trend and yesterday s closing price

	5-day trend	20-day trend
Yesterday more than +0.5% above trend	41%	36%
Yesterday near trend *(+0.5% to -0.5%)*	30%	*33%
Yesterday more than -0.5% below trend	*33%	*33%

Looking ahead: odds of rise in future

	Next 3 days	Next 5 days
Today rose over +0.25%	58%	67%
Today small swing *(+0.25% to -0.25%)*	40%	40%
Today fell below -0.25%	32%	42%

FEBRUARY 5 ODDS OF A PRICE RISE: 43%

Odds of different size price shift

	1935 to present
Large rise *(above +0.25%)*	26%
Small swing *(+0.25% to -0.25%)*	37%
Large fall (*below -0.25%)*	37%

Odds of rise based on yesterday

	1935 to present
Large rise yesterday *(above +0.25%)*	50%
Small swing yesterday *(+0.25% to -0.25%)*	44%
Large fall yesterday (*below -0.25%)*	36%

DIAGNOSTICS

Odds of price rise based on direction of 5-day and 20-day trend yesterday

	5-day trend	20-day trend
Yesterday rose more than +0.1%	46%	48%
Little change *(+0.1% to -0.1%)*	*38%	29%
Yesterday fell more than -0.1%	42%	*63%

Odds of rise based upon distance between trend and yesterday s closing price

	5-day trend	20-day trend
Yesterday more than +0.5% above trend	53%	44%
Yesterday near trend *(+0.5% to -0.5%)*	35%	*38%
Yesterday more than -0.5% below trend	40%	46%

Looking ahead: odds of rise in future

	Next 3 days	Next 5 days
Today rose over +0.25%	58%	50%
Today small swing *(+0.25% to -0.25%)*	47%	41%
Today fell below -0.25%	41%	35%

* *Per cent based on fewer than 10 observations*

FEBRUARY 6 ODDS OF A PRICE RISE: 40%

Odds of different size price shift

	1935 to present
Large rise *(above +0.25%)*	27%
Small swing *(+0.25% to -0.25%)*	40%
Large fall (*below -0.25%)*	33%

Odds of rise based on yesterday

	1935 to present
Large rise yesterday *(above +0.25%)*	57%
Small swing yesterday *(+0.25% to -0.25%)*	33%
Large fall yesterday (*below -0.25%)*	31%

DIAGNOSTICS

Odds of price rise based on direction of 5-day and 20-day trend yesterday

	5-day trend	20-day trend
Yesterday rose more than +0.1%	52%	53%
Little change *(+0.1% to -0.1%)*	*33%	32%
Yesterday fell more than -0.1%	23%	*33%

Odds of rise based upon distance between trend and yesterday s closing price

	5-day trend	20-day trend
Yesterday more than +0.5% above trend	67%	58%
Yesterday near trend *(+0.5% to -0.5%)*	30%	*11%
Yesterday more than -0.5% below trend	30%	25%

Looking ahead: odds of rise in future

	Next 3 days	Next 5 days
Today rose over +0.25%	92%	75%
Today small swing *(+0.25% to -0.25%)*	50%	67%
Today fell below -0.25%	47%	33%

FEBRUARY 7 ODDS OF A PRICE RISE: 47%

Odds of different size price shift

	1935 to present
Large rise *(above +0.25%)*	33%
Small swing *(+0.25% to -0.25%)*	36%
Large fall (*below -0.25%)*	31%

Odds of rise based on yesterday

	1935 to present
Large rise yesterday *(above +0.25%)*	*78%
Small swing yesterday *(+0.25% to -0.25%)*	47%
Large fall yesterday (*below -0.25%)*	29%

DIAGNOSTICS

Odds of price rise based on direction of 5-day and 20-day trend yesterday

	5-day trend	20-day trend
Yesterday rose more than +0.1%	53%	56%
Little change *(+0.1% to -0.1%)*	27%	47%
Yesterday fell more than -0.1%	64%	30%

Odds of rise based upon distance between trend and yesterday s closing price

	5-day trend	20-day trend
Yesterday more than +0.5% above trend	53%	52%
Yesterday near trend *(+0.5% to -0.5%)*	50%	40%
Yesterday more than -0.5% below trend	33%	43%

Looking ahead: odds of rise in future

	Next 3 days	Next 5 days
Today rose over +0.25%	53%	73%
Today small swing *(+0.25% to -0.25%)*	69%	56%
Today fell below -0.25%	14%	14%

* *Per cent based on fewer than 10 observations*

FEBRUARY 8 ODDS OF A PRICE RISE: 53%

Odds of different size price shift

	1935 to present
Large rise *(above +0.25%)*	31%
Small swing *(+0.25% to -0.25%)*	42%
Large fall (*below -0.25%)*	27%

Odds of rise based on yesterday

	1935 to present
Large rise yesterday *(above +0.25%)*	69%
Small swing yesterday *(+0.25% to -0.25%)*	56%
Large fall yesterday (*below -0.25%)*	31%

DIAGNOSTICS

Odds of price rise based on direction of 5-day and 20-day trend yesterday

	5-day trend	20-day trend
Yesterday rose more than +0.1%	65%	76%
Little change *(+0.1% to -0.1%)*	33%	45%
Yesterday fell more than -0.1%	56%	*25%

Odds of rise based upon distance between trend and yesterday s closing price

	5-day trend	20-day trend
Yesterday more than +0.5% above trend	80%	74%
Yesterday near trend *(+0.5% to -0.5%)*	55%	38%
Yesterday more than -0.5% below trend	33%	38%

Looking ahead: odds of rise in future

	Next 3 days	Next 5 days
Today rose over +0.25%	36%	36%
Today small swing *(+0.25% to -0.25%)*	53%	47%
Today fell below -0.25%	58%	58%

FEBRUARY 9 ODDS OF A PRICE RISE: 41%

Odds of different size price shift

	1935 to present
Large rise *(above +0.25%)*	22%
Small swing *(+0.25% to -0.25%)*	43%
Large fall (*below -0.25%)*	35%

Odds of rise based on yesterday

	1935 to present
Large rise yesterday *(above +0.25%)*	60%
Small swing yesterday *(+0.25% to -0.25%)*	38%
Large fall yesterday (*below -0.25%)*	27%

DIAGNOSTICS

Odds of price rise based on direction of 5-day and 20-day trend yesterday

	5-day trend	20-day trend
Yesterday rose more than +0.1%	50%	45%
Little change *(+0.1% to -0.1%)*	27%	40%
Yesterday fell more than -0.1%	42%	36%

Odds of rise based upon distance between trend and yesterday s closing price

	5-day trend	20-day trend
Yesterday more than +0.5% above trend	60%	48%
Yesterday near trend *(+0.5% to -0.5%)*	40%	30%
Yesterday more than -0.5% below trend	31%	40%

Looking ahead: odds of rise in future

	Next 3 days	Next 5 days
Today rose over +0.25%	50%	60%
Today small swing *(+0.25% to -0.25%)*	55%	55%
Today fell below -0.25%	44%	38%

* *Per cent based on fewer than 10 observations*

FEBRUARY 10 ODDS OF A PRICE RISE: 53%

Odds of different size price shift

	1935 to present
Large rise *(above +0.25%)*	34%
Small swing *(+0.25% to -0.25%)*	32%
Large fall (*below -0.25%)*	34%

Odds of rise based on yesterday

	1935 to present
Large rise yesterday *(above +0.25%)*	77%
Small swing yesterda y*(+0.25% to -0.25%)*	50%
Large fall yesterday (*below -0.25%)*	39%

DIAGNOSTICS

Odds of price rise based on direction of 5-day and 20-day trend yesterday

	5-day trend	20-day trend
Yesterday rose more than +0.1%	59%	67%
Little change *(+0.1% to -0.1%)*	67%	47%
Yesterday fell more than -0.1%	39%	36%

Odds of rise based upon distance between trend and yesterday s closing price

	5-day trend	20-day trend
Yesterday more than +0.5% above trend	58%	68%
Yesterday near trend *(+0.5% to -0.5%)*	59%	64%
Yesterday more than -0.5% below trend	44%	29%

Looking ahead: odds of rise in future

	Next 3 days	Next 5 days
Today rose over +0.25%	50%	44%
Today small swing *(+0.25% to -0.25%)*	67%	60%
Today fell below -0.25%	25%	50%

FEBRUARY 11 ODDS OF A PRICE RISE: 42%

Odds of different size price shift

	1935 to present
Large rise *(above +0.25%)*	29%
Small swing *(+0.25% to -0.25%)*	31%
Large fall *(below -0.25%)*	40%

Odds of rise based on yesterday

	1935 to present
Large rise yesterday *(above +0.25%)*	38%
Small swing yesterday *(+0.25% to -0.25%)*	47%
Large fall yesterday *(below -0.25%)*	40%

DIAGNOSTICS

Odds of price rise based on direction of 5-day and 20-day trend yesterday

	5-day trend	20-day trend
Yesterday rose more than +0.1%	50%	48%
Little change *(+0.1% to -0.1%)*	*33%	42%
Yesterday fell more than -0.1%	39%	30%

Odds of rise based upon distance between trend and yesterday s closing price

	5-day trend	20-day trend
Yesterday more than +0.5% above trend	46%	52%
Yesterday near trend *(+0.5% to -0.5%)*	45%	*25%
Yesterday more than -0.5% below trend	33%	38%

Looking ahead: odds of rise in future

	Next 3 days	Next 5 days
Today rose over +0.25%	62%	54%
Today small swing *(+0.25% to -0.25%)*	36%	50%
Today fell below -0.25%	56%	50%

* *Per cent based on fewer than 10 observations*

FEBRUARY 12 ODDS OF A PRICE RISE: 36%

Odds of different size price shift

	1935 to present
Large rise *(above +0.25%)*	29%
Small swing *(+0.25% to -0.25%)*	24%
Large fall (*below -0.25%)*	47%

Odds of rise based on yesterday

	1935 to present
Large rise yesterday *(above +0.25%)*	55%
Small swing yesterday *(+0.25% to -0.25%)*	32%
Large fall yesterday (*below -0.25%)*	27%

DIAGNOSTICS

Odds of price rise based on direction of 5-day and 20-day trend yesterday

	5-day trend	20-day trend
Yesterday rose more than +0.1%	47%	42%
Little change *(+0.1% to -0.1%)*	45%	31%
Yesterday fell more than -0.1%	21%	30%

Odds of rise based upon distance between trend and yesterday s closing price

	5-day trend	20-day trend
Yesterday more than +0.5% above trend	60%	37%
Yesterday near trend *(+0.5% to -0.5%)*	40%	60%
Yesterday more than -0.5% below trend	0%	19%

Looking ahead: odds of rise in future

	Next 3 days	Next 5 days
Today rose over +0.25%	54%	54%
Today small swing *(+0.25% to -0.25%)*	64%	73%
Today fell below -0.25%	62%	48%

FEBRUARY 13 ODDS OF A PRICE RISE: 58%

Odds of different size price shift

	1935 to present
Large rise *(above +0.25%)*	38%
Small swing *(+0.25% to -0.25%)*	40%
Large fall *(below -0.25%)*	22%

Odds of rise based on yesterday

	1935 to present
Large rise yesterday *(above +0.25%)*	58%
Small swing yesterday *(+0.25% to -0.25%)*	*67%
Large fall yesterday *(below -0.25%)*	54%

DIAGNOSTICS

Odds of price rise based on direction of 5-day and 20-day trend yesterday

	5-day trend	20-day trend
Yesterday rose more than +0.1%	61%	72%
Little change *(+0.1% to -0.1%)*	50%	58%
Yesterday fell more than -0.1%	59%	40%

Odds of rise based upon distance between trend and yesterday s closing price

	5-day trend	20-day trend
Yesterday more than +0.5% above trend	57%	67%
Yesterday near trend *(+0.5% to -0.5%)*	50%	55%
Yesterday more than -0.5% below trend	65%	50%

Looking ahead: odds of rise in future

	Next 3 days	Next 5 days
Today rose over +0.25%	59%	47%
Today small swing *(+0.25% to -0.25%)*	72%	56%
Today fell below -0.25%	40%	40%

* *Per cent based on fewer than 10 observations*

FEBRUARY 14 ODDS OF A PRICE RISE: 42%

Odds of different size price shift

	1935 to present
Large rise *(above +0.25%)*	31%
Small swing *(+0.25% to -0.25%)*	31%
Large fall (*below -0.25%)*	38%

Odds of rise based on yesterday

	1935 to present
Large rise yesterday *(above +0.25%)*	50%
Small swing yesterday *(+0.25% to -0.25%)*	56%
Large fall yesterday (*below -0.25%)*	15%

DIAGNOSTICS

Odds of price rise based on direction of 5-day and 20-day trend yesterday

	5-day trend	20-day trend
Yesterday rose more than +0.1%	38%	29%
Little change *(+0.1% to -0.1%)*	54%	50%
Yesterday fell more than -0.1%	38%	50%

Odds of rise based upon distance between trend and yesterday s closing price

	5-day trend	20-day trend
Yesterday more than +0.5% above trend	50%	40%
Yesterday near trend *(+0.5% to -0.5%)*	36%	50%
Yesterday more than -0.5% below trend	46%	40%

Looking ahead: odds of rise in future

	Next 3 days	Next 5 days
Today rose over +0.25%	64%	79%
Today small swing *(+0.25% to -0.25%)*	50%	36%
Today fell below -0.25%	35%	29%

FEBRUARY 15 ODDS OF A PRICE RISE: 59%

Odds of different size price shift

	1935 to present
Large rise *(above +0.25%)*	32%
Small swing *(+0.25% to -0.25%)*	39%
Large fall *(below -0.25%)*	30%

Odds of rise based on yesterday

	1935 to present
Large rise yesterday *(above +0.25%)*	71%
Small swing yesterday *(+0.25% to -0.25%)*	57%
Large fall yesterday *(below -0.25%)*	50%

DIAGNOSTICS

Odds of price rise based on direction of 5-day and 20-day trend yesterday

	5-day trend	20-day trend
Yesterday rose more than +0.1%	71%	40%
Little change *(+0.1% to -0.1%)*	67%	75%
Yesterday fell more than -0.1%	40%	*56%

Odds of rise based upon distance between trend and yesterday s closing price

	5-day trend	20-day trend
Yesterday more than +0.5% above trend	75%	53%
Yesterday near trend *(+0.5% to -0.5%)*	59%	75%
Yesterday more than -0.5% below trend	47%	54%

Looking ahead: odds of rise in future

	Next 3 days	Next 5 days
Today rose over +0.25%	43%	57%
Today small swing *(+0.25% to -0.25%)*	53%	41%
Today fell below -0.25%	31%	54%

* *Per cent based on fewer than 10 observations*

FEBRUARY 16 ODDS OF A PRICE RISE: 48%

Odds of different size price shift

	1935 to present
Large rise *(above +0.25%)*	39%
Small swing *(+0.25% to -0.25%)*	28%
Large fall (*below -0.25%)*	33%

Odds of rise based on yesterday

	1935 to present
Large rise yesterday *(above +0.25%)*	59%
Small swing yesterday *(+0.25% to -0.25%)*	39%
Large fall yesterday (*below -0.25%)*	45%

DIAGNOSTICS

Odds of price rise based on direction of 5-day and 20-day trend yesterday

	5-day trend	20-day trend
Yesterday rose more than +0.1%	43%	53%
Little change *(+0.1% to -0.1%)*	42%	33%
Yesterday fell more than -0.1%	55%	70%

Odds of rise based upon distance between trend and yesterday s closing price

	5-day trend	20-day trend
Yesterday more than +0.5% above trend	*44%	44%
Yesterday near trend *(+0.5% to -0.5%)*	48%	42%
Yesterday more than -0.5% below trend	50%	56%

Looking ahead: odds of rise in future

	Next 3 days	Next 5 days
Today rose over +0.25%	50%	61%
Today small swing *(+0.25% to -0.25%)*	62%	46%
Today fell below -0.25%	47%	53%

FEBRUARY 17 ODDS OF A PRICE RISE: 55%

Odds of different size price shift

	1935 to present
Large rise *(above +0.25%)*	38%
Small swing *(+0.25% to -0.25%)*	30%
Large fall *(below -0.25%)*	32%

Odds of rise based on yesterday

	1935 to present
Large rise yesterday *(above +0.25%)*	65%
Small swing yesterday *(+0.25% to -0.25%)*	62%
Large fall yesterday *(below -0.25%)*	41%

DIAGNOSTICS

Odds of price rise based on direction of 5-day and 20-day trend yesterday

	5-day trend	20-day trend
Yesterday rose more than +0.1%	50%	61%
Little change *(+0.1% to -0.1%)*	*78%	63%
Yesterday fell more than -0.1%	50%	30%

Odds of rise based upon distance between trend and yesterday s closing price

	5-day trend	20-day trend
Yesterday more than +0.5% above trend	62%	55%
Yesterday near trend *(+0.5% to -0.5%)*	67%	*63%
Yesterday more than -0.5% below trend	31%	53%

Looking ahead: odds of rise in future

	Next 3 days	Next 5 days
Today rose over +0.25%	61%	50%
Today small swing *(+0.25% to -0.25%)*	64%	50%
Today fell below -0.25%	33%	33%

* *Per cent based on fewer than 10 observations*

FEBRUARY 18 ODDS OF A PRICE RISE: 52%

Odds of different size price shift

	1935 to present
Large rise *(above +0.25%)*	30%
Small swing *(+0.25% to -0.25%)*	37%
Large fall (*below -0.25%)*	33%

Odds of rise based on yesterday

	1935 to present
Large rise yesterday *(above +0.25%)*	67%
Small swing yesterday *(+0.25% to -0.25%)*	54%
Large fall yesterday (*below -0.25%)*	39%

DIAGNOSTICS

Odds of price rise based on direction of 5-day and 20-day trend yesterday

	5-day trend	20-day trend
Yesterday rose more than +0.1%	61%	81%
Little change *(+0.1% to -0.1%)*	50%	38%
Yesterday fell more than -0.1%	44%	*33%

Odds of rise based upon distance between trend and yesterday s closing price

	5-day trend	20-day trend
Yesterday more than +0.5% above trend	56%	70%
Yesterday near trend *(+0.5% to -0.5%)*	53%	50%
Yesterday more than -0.5% below trend	47%	29%

Looking ahead: odds of rise in future

	Next 3 days	Next 5 days
Today rose over +0.25%	36%	64%
Today small swing *(+0.25% to -0.25%)*	47%	53%
Today fell below -0.25%	40%	33%

FEBRUARY 19 ODDS OF A PRICE RISE: 41%

Odds of different size price shift

	1935 to present
Large rise *(above +0.25%)*	13%
Small swing *(+0.25% to -0.25%)*	48%
Large fall (*below -0.25%)*	39%

Odds of rise based on yesterday

	1935 to present
Large rise yesterday *(above +0.25%)*	57%
Small swing yesterday *(+0.25% to -0.25%)*	44%
Large fall yesterday (*below -0.25%)*	21%

DIAGNOSTICS

Odds of price rise based on direction of 5-day and 20-day trend yesterday

	5-day trend	20-day trend
Yesterday rose more than +0.1%	45%	63%
Little change *(+0.1% to -0.1%)*	42%	40%
Yesterday fell more than -0.1%	36%	10%

Odds of rise based upon distance between trend and yesterday s closing price

	5-day trend	20-day trend
Yesterday more than +0.5% above trend	25%	52%
Yesterday near trend *(+0.5% to -0.5%)*	53%	50%
Yesterday more than -0.5% below trend	40%	20%

Looking ahead: odds of rise in future

	Next 3 days	Next 5 days
Today rose over +0.25%	*50%	*67%
Today small swing *(+0.25% to -0.25%)*	45%	64%
Today fell below -0.25%	44%	44%

* *Per cent based on fewer than 10 observations*

FEBRUARY 20 ODDS OF A PRICE RISE: 44%

Odds of different size price shift

	1935 to present
Large rise *(above +0.25%)*	29%
Small swing *(+0.25% to -0.25%)*	27%
Large fall (*below -0.25%)*	44%

Odds of rise based on yesterday

	1935 to present
Large rise yesterday *(above +0.25%)*	55%
Small swing yesterday *(+0.25% to -0.25%)*	50%
Large fall yesterday (*below -0.25%)*	31%

DIAGNOSTICS

Odds of price rise based on direction of 5-day and 20-day trend yesterday

	5-day trend	20-day trend
Yesterday rose more than +0.1%	65%	53%
Little change *(+0.1% to -0.1%)*	30%	39%
Yesterday fell more than -0.1%	27%	42%

Odds of rise based upon distance between trend and yesterday s closing price

	5-day trend	20-day trend
Yesterday more than +0.5% above trend	55%	65%
Yesterday near trend *(+0.5% to -0.5%)*	50%	36%
Yesterday more than -0.5% below trend	29%	21%

Looking ahead: odds of rise in future

	Next 3 days	Next 5 days
Today rose over +0.25%	77%	77%
Today small swing *(+0.25% to -0.25%)*	58%	58%
Today fell below -0.25%	45%	45%

FEBRUARY 21 ODDS OF A PRICE RISE: 31%

Odds of different size price shift

	1935 to present
Large rise *(above +0.25%)*	20%
Small swing *(+0.25% to -0.25%)*	36%
Large fall (*below -0.25%)*	44%

Odds of rise based on yesterday

	1935 to present
Large rise yesterday *(above +0.25%)*	25%
Small swing yesterday *(+0.25% to -0.25%)*	40%
Large fall yesterday (*below -0.25%)*	28%

DIAGNOSTICS

Odds of price rise based on direction of 5-day and 20-day trend yesterday

	5-day trend	20-day trend
Yesterday rose more than +0.1%	40%	43%
Little change *(+0.1% to -0.1%)*	*33%	32%
Yesterday fell more than -0.1%	21%	17%

Odds of rise based upon distance between trend and yesterday s closing price

	5-day trend	20-day trend
Yesterday more than +0.5% above trend	31%	37%
Yesterday near trend *(+0.5% to -0.5%)*	33%	*38%
Yesterday more than -0.5% below trend	29%	22%

Looking ahead: odds of rise in future

	Next 3 days	Next 5 days
Today rose over +0.25%	*78%	*89%
Today small swing *(+0.25% to -0.25%)*	69%	69%
Today fell below -0.25%	35%	30%

* *Per cent based on fewer than 10 observations*

FEBRUARY 22 ODDS OF A PRICE RISE: 53%

Odds of different size price shift

	1935 to present
Large rise *(above +0.25%)*	40%
Small swing *(+0.25% to -0.25%)*	27%
Large fall (*below -0.25%)*	33%

Odds of rise based on yesterday

	1935 to present
Large rise yesterday *(above +0.25%)*	*71%
Small swing yesterday *(+0.25% to -0.25%)*	48%
Large fall yesterday (*below -0.25%)*	53%

DIAGNOSTICS

Odds of price rise based on direction of 5-day and 20-day trend yesterday

	5-day trend	20-day trend
Yesterday rose more than +0.1%	67%	53%
Little change *(+0.1% to -0.1%)*	42%	52%
Yesterday fell more than -0.1%	50%	*56%

Odds of rise based upon distance between trend and yesterday s closing price

	5-day trend	20-day trend
Yesterday more than +0.5% above trend	60%	50%
Yesterday near trend *(+0.5% to -0.5%)*	61%	*50%
Yesterday more than -0.5% below trend	33%	58%

Looking ahead: odds of rise in future

	Next 3 days	Next 5 days
Today rose over +0.25%	50%	39%
Today small swing *(+0.25% to -0.25%)*	42%	58%
Today fell below -0.25%	40%	47%

FEBRUARY 23 ODDS OF A PRICE RISE: 46%

Odds of different size price shift

	1935 to present
Large rise *(above +0.25%)*	28%
Small swing *(+0.25% to -0.25%)*	37%
Large fall (*below -0.25%)*	35%

Odds of rise based on yesterday

	1935 to present
Large rise yesterday *(above +0.25%)*	57%
Small swing yesterday *(+0.25% to -0.25%)*	*33%
Large fall yesterday (*below -0.25%)*	38%

DIAGNOSTICS

Odds of price rise based on direction of 5-day and 20-day trend yesterday

	5-day trend	20-day trend
Yesterday rose more than +0.1%	53%	41%
Little change *(+0.1% to -0.1%)*	*25%	40%
Yesterday fell more than -0.1%	47%	57%

Odds of rise based upon distance between trend and yesterday s closing price

	5-day trend	20-day trend
Yesterday more than +0.5% above trend	50%	46%
Yesterday near trend *(+0.5% to -0.5%)*	56%	40%
Yesterday more than -0.5% below trend	33%	50%

Looking ahead: odds of rise in future

	Next 3 days	Next 5 days
Today rose over +0.25%	62%	46%
Today small swing *(+0.25% to -0.25%)*	47%	53%
Today fell below -0.25%	50%	63%

* *Per cent based on fewer than 10 observations*

FEBRUARY 24 ODDS OF A PRICE RISE: 49%

Odds of different size price shift

	1935 to present
Large rise *(above +0.25%)*	36%
Small swing *(+0.25% to -0.25%)*	34%
Large fall (*below -0.25%)*	30%

Odds of rise based on yesterday

	1935 to present
Large rise yesterday *(above +0.25%)*	67%
Small swing yesterday *(+0.25% to -0.25%)*	60%
Large fall yesterday (*below -0.25%)*	30%

DIAGNOSTICS

Odds of price rise based on direction of 5-day and 20-day trend yesterday

	5-day trend	20-day trend
Yesterday rose more than +0.1%	75%	63%
Little change *(+0.1% to -0.1%)*	27%	44%
Yesterday fell more than -0.1%	44%	40%

Odds of rise based upon distance between trend and yesterday s closing price

	5-day trend	20-day trend
Yesterday more than +0.5% above trend	90%	63%
Yesterday near trend *(+0.5% to -0.5%)*	42%	45%
Yesterday more than -0.5% below trend	31%	40%

Looking ahead: odds of rise in future

	Next 3 days	Next 5 days
Today rose over +0.25%	65%	65%
Today small swing *(+0.25% to -0.25%)*	56%	63%
Today fell below -0.25%	50%	50%

FEBRUARY 25 ODDS OF A PRICE RISE: 57%

Odds of different size price shift

	1935 to present
Large rise *(above +0.25%)*	43%
Small swing *(+0.25% to -0.25%)*	28%
Large fall (*below -0.25%)*	28%

Odds of rise based on yesterday

	1935 to present
Large rise yesterday *(above +0.25%)*	50%
Small swing yesterday *(+0.25% to -0.25%)*	80%
Large fall yesterday (*below -0.25%)*	40%

DIAGNOSTICS

Odds of price rise based on direction of 5-day and 20-day trend yesterday

	5-day trend	20-day trend
Yesterday rose more than +0.1%	38%	69%
Little change *(+0.1% to -0.1%)*	80%	50%
Yesterday fell more than -0.1%	60%	50%

Odds of rise based upon distance between trend and yesterday s closing price

	5-day trend	20-day trend
Yesterday more than +0.5% above trend	42%	56%
Yesterday near trend *(+0.5% to -0.5%)*	60%	*56%
Yesterday more than -0.5% below trend	63%	58%

Looking ahead: odds of rise in future

	Next 3 days	Next 5 days
Today rose over +0.25%	60%	75%
Today small swing *(+0.25% to -0.25%)*	69%	62%
Today fell below -0.25%	46%	54%

* *Per cent based on fewer than 10 observations*

FEBRUARY 26 ODDS OF A PRICE RISE: 57%

Odds of different size price shift

	1935 to present
Large rise *(above +0.25%)*	39%
Small swing *(+0.25% to -0.25%)*	30%
Large fall (*below -0.25%)*	30%

Odds of rise based on yesterday

	1935 to present
Large rise yesterday *(above +0.25%)*	60%
Small swing yesterday *(+0.25% to -0.25%)*	60%
Large fall yesterday (*below -0.25%)*	45%

DIAGNOSTICS

Odds of price rise based on direction of 5-day and 20-day trend yesterday

	5-day trend	20-day trend
Yesterday rose more than +0.1%	67%	75%
Little change *(+0.1% to -0.1%)*	*78%	42%
Yesterday fell more than -0.1%	37%	55%

Odds of rise based upon distance between trend and yesterday s closing price

	5-day trend	20-day trend
Yesterday more than +0.5% above trend	64%	71%
Yesterday near trend *(+0.5% to -0.5%)*	59%	64%
Yesterday more than -0.5% below trend	40%	39%

Looking ahead: odds of rise in future

	Next 3 days	Next 5 days
Today rose over +0.25%	61%	61%
Today small swing *(+0.25% to -0.25%)*	71%	79%
Today fell below -0.25%	43%	71%

FEBRUARY 27 ODDS OF A PRICE RISE: 67%

Odds of different size price shift

	1935 to present
Large rise *(above +0.25%)*	47%
Small swing *(+0.25% to -0.25%)*	27%
Large fall (*below -0.25%)*	27%

Odds of rise based on yesterday

	1935 to present
Large rise yesterday *(above +0.25%)*	88%
Small swing yesterday *(+0.25% to -0.25%)*	50%
Large fall yesterday (*below -0.25%)*	60%

DIAGNOSTICS

Odds of price rise based on direction of 5-day and 20-day trend yesterday

	5-day trend	20-day trend
Yesterday rose more than +0.1%	76%	88%
Little change *(+0.1% to -0.1%)*	*67%	44%
Yesterday fell more than -0.1%	56%	67%

Odds of rise based upon distance between trend and yesterday s closing price

	5-day trend	20-day trend
Yesterday more than +0.5% above trend	80%	87%
Yesterday near trend *(+0.5% to -0.5%)*	55%	*67%
Yesterday more than -0.5% below trend	70%	50%

Looking ahead: odds of rise in future

	Next 3 days	Next 5 days
Today rose over +0.25%	71%	71%
Today small swing *(+0.25% to -0.25%)*	83%	67%
Today fell below -0.25%	58%	58%

* *Per cent based on fewer than 10 observations*

FEBRUARY 28 ODDS OF A PRICE RISE: 64%

Odds of different size price shift

	1935 to present
Large rise *(above +0.25%)*	49%
Small swing *(+0.25% to -0.25%)*	27%
Large fall (*below -0.25%)*	24%

Odds of rise based on yesterday

	1935 to present
Large rise yesterday *(above +0.25%)*	85%
Small swing yesterday *(+0.25% to -0.25%)*	67%
Large fall yesterday (*below -0.25%)*	31%

DIAGNOSTICS

Odds of price rise based on direction of 5-day and 20-day trend yesterday

	5-day trend	20-day trend
Yesterday rose more than +0.1%	84%	85%
Little change *(+0.1% to -0.1%)*	*44%	56%
Yesterday fell more than -0.1%	53%	57%

Odds of rise based upon distance between trend and yesterday s closing price

	5-day trend	20-day trend
Yesterday more than +0.5% above trend	93%	84%
Yesterday near trend *(+0.5% to -0.5%)*	57%	*67%
Yesterday more than -0.5% below trend	40%	45%

Looking ahead: odds of rise in future

	Next 3 days	Next 5 days
Today rose over +0.25%	68%	59%
Today small swing *(+0.25% to -0.25%)*	42%	42%
Today fell below -0.25%	64%	64%

MARCH

PROFIT ODDS SUMMARY FOR THE MONTH

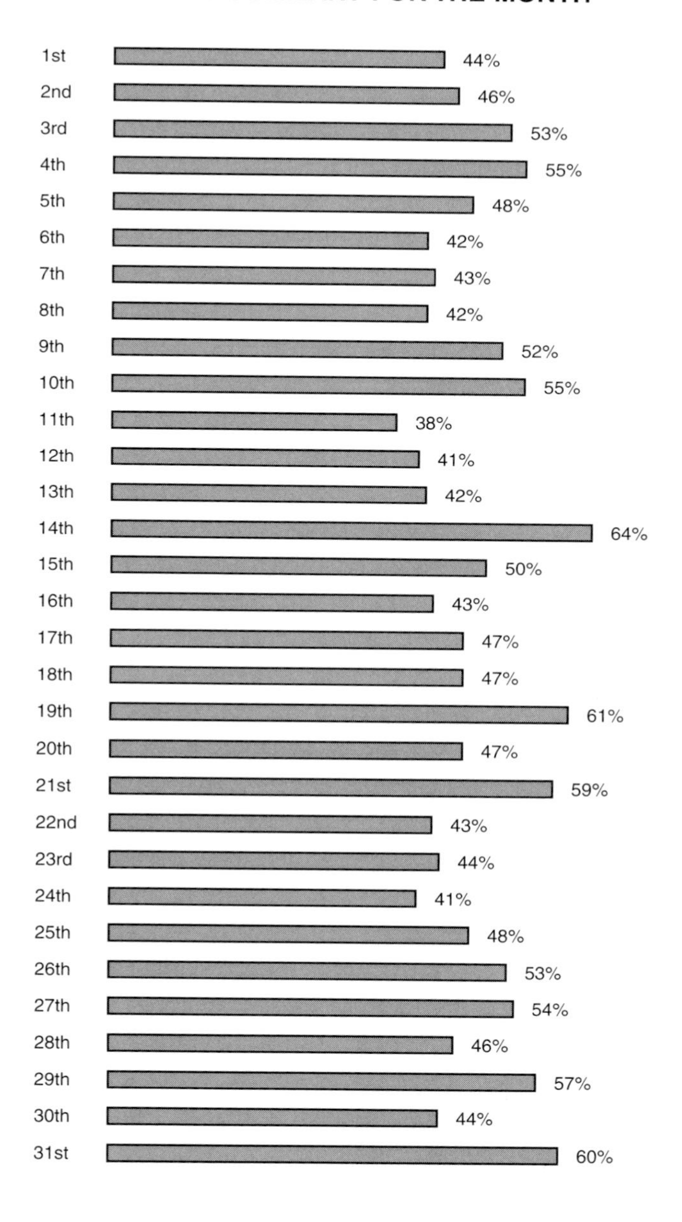

MARCH 1 ODDS OF A PRICE RISE: 44%

Odds of different size price shift

	1935 to present
Large rise *(above +0.25%)*	33%
Small swing *(+0.25% to -0.25%)*	29%
Large fall (*below -0.25%)*	38%

Odds of rise based on yesterday

	1935 to present
Large rise yesterday *(above +0.25%)*	59%
Small swing yesterday *(+0.25% to -0.25%)*	46%
Large fall yesterday (*below -0.25%)*	27%

DIAGNOSTICS

Odds of price rise based on direction of 5-day and 20-day trend yesterday

	5-day trend	20-day trend
Yesterday rose more than +0.1%	44%	42%
Little change *(+0.1% to -0.1%)*	50%	61%
Yesterday fell more than -0.1%	41%	27%

Odds of rise based upon distance between trend and yesterday s closing price

	5-day trend	20-day trend
Yesterday more than +0.5% above trend	57%	50%
Yesterday near trend *(+0.5% to -0.5%)*	40%	*43%
Yesterday more than -0.5% below trend	36%	41%

Looking ahead: odds of rise in future

	Next 3 days	Next 5 days
Today rose over +0.25%	80%	60%
Today small swing *(+0.25% to -0.25%)*	46%	46%
Today fell below -0.25%	47%	47%

* *Per cent based on fewer than 10 observations*

MARCH 2 ODDS OF A PRICE RISE: 46%

Odds of different size price shift

	1935 to present
Large rise *(above +0.25%)*	37%
Small swing *(+0.25% to -0.25%)*	35%
Large fall (*below -0.25%)*	28%

Odds of rise based on yesterday

	1935 to present
Large rise yesterday *(above +0.25%)*	47%
Small swing yesterday *(+0.25% to -0.25%)*	33%
Large fall yesterday (*below -0.25%)*	53%

DIAGNOSTICS

Odds of price rise based on direction of 5-day and 20-day trend yesterday

	5-day trend	20-day trend
Yesterday rose more than +0.1%	44%	55%
Little change *(+0.1% to -0.1%)*	40%	50%
Yesterday fell more than -0.1%	50%	37%

Odds of rise based upon distance between trend and yesterday s closing price

	5-day trend	20-day trend
Yesterday more than +0.5% above trend	38%	53%
Yesterday near trend *(+0.5% to -0.5%)*	44%	*25%
Yesterday more than -0.5% below trend	53%	43%

Looking ahead: odds of rise in future

	Next 3 days	Next 5 days
Today rose over +0.25%	53%	59%
Today small swing *(+0.25% to -0.25%)*	56%	56%
Today fell below -0.25%	54%	38%

MARCH 3 ODDS OF A PRICE RISE: 53%

Odds of different size price shift

	1935 to present
Large rise *(above +0.25%)*	40%
Small swing *(+0.25% to -0.25%)*	32%
Large fall *(below -0.25%)*	28%

Odds of rise based on yesterday

	1935 to present
Large rise yesterday *(above +0.25%)*	53%
Small swing yesterday *(+0.25% to -0.25%)*	46%
Large fall yesterday *(below -0.25%)*	60%

DIAGNOSTICS

Odds of price rise based on direction of 5-day and 20-day trend yesterday

	5-day trend	20-day trend
Yesterday rose more than +0.1%	68%	54%
Little change *(+0.1% to -0.1%)*	27%	53%
Yesterday fell more than -0.1%	53%	53%

Odds of rise based upon distance between trend and yesterday s closing price

	5-day trend	20-day trend
Yesterday more than +0.5% above trend	67%	56%
Yesterday near trend *(+0.5% to -0.5%)*	41%	*50%
Yesterday more than -0.5% below trend	50%	52%

Looking ahead: odds of rise in future

	Next 3 days	Next 5 days
Today rose over +0.25%	58%	68%
Today small swing *(+0.25% to -0.25%)*	73%	67%
Today fell below -0.25%	38%	38%

* *Per cent based on fewer than 10 observations*

MARCH 4 ODDS OF A PRICE RISE: 55%

Odds of different size price shift

	1935 to present
Large rise *(above +0.25%)*	40%
Small swing *(+0.25% to -0.25%)*	34%
Large fall (*below -0.25%)*	26%

Odds of rise based on yesterday

	1935 to present
Large rise yesterday *(above +0.25%)*	61%
Small swing yesterday *(+0.25% to -0.25%)*	47%
Large fall yesterday (*below -0.25%)*	58%

DIAGNOSTICS

Odds of price rise based on direction of 5-day and 20-day trend yesterday

	5-day trend	20-day trend
Yesterday rose more than +0.1%	45%	69%
Little change *(+0.1% to -0.1%)*	60%	40%
Yesterday fell more than -0.1%	67%	58%

Odds of rise based upon distance between trend and yesterday s closing price

	5-day trend	20-day trend
Yesterday more than +0.5% above trend	53%	50%
Yesterday near trend *(+0.5% to -0.5%)*	56%	*50%
Yesterday more than -0.5% below trend	60%	62%

Looking ahead: odds of rise in future

	Next 3 days	Next 5 days
Today rose over +0.25%	68%	58%
Today small swing *(+0.25% to -0.25%)*	38%	50%
Today fell below -0.25%	25%	25%

MARCH 5 ODDS OF A PRICE RISE: 48%

Odds of different size price shift

	1935 to present
Large rise *(above +0.25%)*	35%
Small swing *(+0.25% to -0.25%)*	39%
Large fall (*below -0.25%)*	26%

Odds of rise based on yesterday

	1935 to present
Large rise yesterday *(above +0.25%)*	72%
Small swing yesterday *(+0.25% to -0.25%)*	32%
Large fall yesterday (*below -0.25%)*	*33%

DIAGNOSTICS

Odds of price rise based on direction of 5-day and 20-day trend yesterday

	5-day trend	20-day trend
Yesterday rose more than +0.1%	50%	63%
Little change *(+0.1% to -0.1%)*	40%	42%
Yesterday fell more than -0.1%	50%	39%

Odds of rise based upon distance between trend and yesterday s closing price

	5-day trend	20-day trend
Yesterday more than +0.5% above trend	87%	52%
Yesterday near trend *(+0.5% to -0.5%)*	26%	*38%
Yesterday more than -0.5% below trend	*50%	47%

Looking ahead: odds of rise in future

	Next 3 days	Next 5 days
Today rose over +0.25%	63%	50%
Today small swing *(+0.25% to -0.25%)*	44%	39%
Today fell below -0.25%	58%	25%

* *Per cent based on fewer than 10 observations*

MARCH 6 ODDS OF A PRICE RISE: 42%

Odds of different size price shift

	1935 to present
Large rise *(above +0.25%)*	31%
Small swing *(+0.25% to -0.25%)*	31%
Large fall (*below -0.25%)*	38%

Odds of rise based on yesterday

	1935 to present
Large rise yesterday *(above +0.25%)*	53%
Small swing yesterday *(+0.25% to -0.25%)*	44%
Large fall yesterday (*below -0.25%)*	29%

DIAGNOSTICS

Odds of price rise based on direction of 5-day and 20-day trend yesterday

	5-day trend	20-day trend
Yesterday rose more than +0.1%	52%	41%
Little change *(+0.1% to -0.1%)*	29%	50%
Yesterday fell more than -0.1%	40%	33%

Odds of rise based upon distance between trend and yesterday s closing price

	5-day trend	20-day trend
Yesterday more than +0.5% above trend	67%	50%
Yesterday near trend *(+0.5% to -0.5%)*	27%	60%
Yesterday more than -0.5% below trend	*38%	15%

Looking ahead: odds of rise in future

	Next 3 days	Next 5 days
Today rose over +0.25%	64%	64%
Today small swing *(+0.25% to -0.25%)*	43%	36%
Today fell below -0.25%	35%	47%

MARCH 7 ODDS OF A PRICE RISE: 43%

Odds of different size price shift

	1935 to present
Large rise *(above +0.25%)*	32%
Small swing *(+0.25% to -0.25%)*	36%
Large fall (*below -0.25%)*	32%

Odds of rise based on yesterday

	1935 to present
Large rise yesterday *(above +0.25%)*	56%
Small swing yesterday *(+0.25% to -0.25%)*	50%
Large fall yesterday (*below -0.25%)*	25%

DIAGNOSTICS

Odds of price rise based on direction of 5-day and 20-day trend yesterday

	5-day trend	20-day trend
Yesterday rose more than +0.1%	62%	50%
Little change *(+0.1% to -0.1%)*	*33%	53%
Yesterday fell more than -0.1%	21%	27%

Odds of rise based upon distance between trend and yesterday s closing price

	5-day trend	20-day trend
Yesterday more than +0.5% above trend	61%	59%
Yesterday near trend *(+0.5% to -0.5%)*	38%	*75%
Yesterday more than -0.5% below trend	23%	17%

Looking ahead: odds of rise in future

	Next 3 days	Next 5 days
Today rose over +0.25%	50%	64%
Today small swing *(+0.25% to -0.25%)*	50%	38%
Today fell below -0.25%	57%	43%

* *Per cent based on fewer than 10 observations*

MARCH 8 ODDS OF A PRICE RISE: 42%

Odds of different size price shift

	1935 to present
Large rise *(above +0.25%)*	24%
Small swing *(+0.25% to -0.25%)*	51%
Large fall (*below -0.25%)*	24%

Odds of rise based on yesterday

	1935 to present
Large rise yesterday *(above +0.25%)*	71%
Small swing yesterday *(+0.25% to -0.25%)*	28%
Large fall yesterday (*below -0.25%)*	31%

DIAGNOSTICS

Odds of price rise based on direction of 5-day and 20-day trend yesterday

	5-day trend	20-day trend
Yesterday rose more than +0.1%	63%	54%
Little change *(+0.1% to -0.1%)*	*33%	33%
Yesterday fell more than -0.1%	30%	40%

Odds of rise based upon distance between trend and yesterday s closing price

	5-day trend	20-day trend
Yesterday more than +0.5% above trend	67%	44%
Yesterday near trend *(+0.5% to -0.5%)*	24%	*60%
Yesterday more than -0.5% below trend	*44%	36%

Looking ahead: odds of rise in future

	Next 3 days	Next 5 days
Today rose over +0.25%	55%	55%
Today small swing *(+0.25% to -0.25%)*	61%	65%
Today fell below -0.25%	36%	36%

MARCH 9 ODDS OF A PRICE RISE: 52%

Odds of different size price shift

	1935 to present
Large rise *(above +0.25%)*	28%
Small swing *(+0.25% to -0.25%)*	39%
Large fall (*below -0.25%)*	33%

Odds of rise based on yesterday

	1935 to present
Large rise yesterday *(above +0.25%)*	55%
Small swing yesterday *(+0.25% to -0.25%)*	61%
Large fall yesterday (*below -0.25%)*	33%

DIAGNOSTICS

Odds of price rise based on direction of 5-day and 20-day trend yesterday

	5-day trend	20-day trend
Yesterday rose more than +0.1%	70%	69%
Little change *(+0.1% to -0.1%)*	50%	46%
Yesterday fell more than -0.1%	31%	41%

Odds of rise based upon distance between trend and yesterday s closing price

	5-day trend	20-day trend
Yesterday more than +0.5% above trend	75%	71%
Yesterday near trend *(+0.5% to -0.5%)*	52%	*43%
Yesterday more than -0.5% below trend	27%	41%

Looking ahead: odds of rise in future

	Next 3 days	Next 5 days
Today rose over +0.25%	69%	69%
Today small swing *(+0.25% to -0.25%)*	56%	61%
Today fell below -0.25%	53%	47%

* *Per cent based on fewer than 10 observations*

MARCH 10 ODDS OF A PRICE RISE: 55%

Odds of different size price shift

	1935 to present
Large rise *(above +0.25%)*	36%
Small swing *(+0.25% to -0.25%)*	43%
Large fall (*below -0.25%)*	21%

Odds of rise based on yesterday

	1935 to present
Large rise yesterday *(above +0.25%)*	60%
Small swing yesterda y*(+0.25% to -0.25%)*	65%
Large fall yesterday (*below -0.25%)*	40%

DIAGNOSTICS

Odds of price rise based on direction of 5-day and 20-day trend yesterday

	5-day trend	20-day trend
Yesterday rose more than +0.1%	70%	71%
Little change *(+0.1% to -0.1%)*	64%	50%
Yesterday fell more than -0.1%	23%	47%

Odds of rise based upon distance between trend and yesterday s closing price

	5-day trend	20-day trend
Yesterday more than +0.5% above trend	64%	62%
Yesterday near trend *(+0.5% to -0.5%)*	62%	*88%
Yesterday more than -0.5% below trend	33%	33%

Looking ahead: odds of rise in future

	Next 3 days	Next 5 days
Today rose over +0.25%	65%	41%
Today small swing *(+0.25% to -0.25%)*	45%	55%
Today fell below -0.25%	30%	20%

MARCH 11 ODDS OF A PRICE RISE: 38%

Odds of different size price shift

	1935 to present
Large rise *(above +0.25%)*	19%
Small swing *(+0.25% to -0.25%)*	40%
Large fall (*below -0.25%)*	40%

Odds of rise based on yesterday

	1935 to present
Large rise yesterday *(above +0.25%)*	38%
Small swing yesterday *(+0.25% to -0.25%)*	47%
Large fall yesterday (*below -0.25%)*	29%

DIAGNOSTICS

Odds of price rise based on direction of 5-day and 20-day trend yesterday

	5-day trend	20-day trend
Yesterday rose more than +0.1%	47%	38%
Little change *(+0.1% to -0.1%)*	45%	44%
Yesterday fell more than -0.1%	24%	33%

Odds of rise based upon distance between trend and yesterday s closing price

	5-day trend	20-day trend
Yesterday more than +0.5% above trend	40%	41%
Yesterday near trend *(+0.5% to -0.5%)*	47%	*38%
Yesterday more than -0.5% below trend	23%	35%

Looking ahead: odds of rise in future

	Next 3 days	Next 5 days
Today rose over +0.25%	*33%	*33%
Today small swing *(+0.25% to -0.25%)*	37%	47%
Today fell below -0.25%	58%	47%

* *Per cent based on fewer than 10 observations*

MARCH 12 ODDS OF A PRICE RISE: 41%

Odds of different size price shift

	1935 to present
Large rise *(above +0.25%)*	30%
Small swing *(+0.25% to -0.25%)*	33%
Large fall (*below -0.25%)*	37%

Odds of rise based on yesterday

	1935 to present
Large rise yesterday *(above +0.25%)*	50%
Small swing yesterday *(+0.25% to -0.25%)*	40%
Large fall yesterday (*below -0.25%)*	36%

DIAGNOSTICS

Odds of price rise based on direction of 5-day and 20-day trend yesterday

	5-day trend	20-day trend
Yesterday rose more than +0.1%	47%	25%
Little change *(+0.1% to -0.1%)*	*33%	59%
Yesterday fell more than -0.1%	38%	38%

Odds of rise based upon distance between trend and yesterday s closing price

	5-day trend	20-day trend
Yesterday more than +0.5% above trend	50%	42%
Yesterday near trend *(+0.5% to -0.5%)*	42%	*50%
Yesterday more than -0.5% below trend	33%	37%

Looking ahead: odds of rise in future

	Next 3 days	Next 5 days
Today rose over +0.25%	71%	71%
Today small swing *(+0.25% to -0.25%)*	27%	40%
Today fell below -0.25%	41%	47%

MARCH 13 ODDS OF A PRICE RISE: 42%

Odds of different size price shift

	1935 to present
Large rise *(above +0.25%)*	33%
Small swing *(+0.25% to -0.25%)*	33%
Large fall (*below -0.25%)*	33%

Odds of rise based on yesterday

	1935 to present
Large rise yesterday *(above +0.25%)*	50%
Small swing yesterday *(+0.25% to -0.25%)*	39%
Large fall yesterday (*below -0.25%)*	38%

DIAGNOSTICS

Odds of price rise based on direction of 5-day and 20-day trend yesterday

	5-day trend	20-day trend
Yesterday rose more than +0.1%	29%	33%
Little change *(+0.1% to -0.1%)*	60%	40%
Yesterday fell more than -0.1%	43%	53%

Odds of rise based upon distance between trend and yesterday s closing price

	5-day trend	20-day trend
Yesterday more than +0.5% above trend	*33%	44%
Yesterday near trend *(+0.5% to -0.5%)*	42%	*38%
Yesterday more than -0.5% below trend	50%	42%

Looking ahead: odds of rise in future

	Next 3 days	Next 5 days
Today rose over +0.25%	80%	60%
Today small swing *(+0.25% to -0.25%)*	60%	67%
Today fell below -0.25%	47%	40%

* *Per cent based on fewer than 10 observations*

MARCH 14 ODDS OF A PRICE RISE: 64%

Odds of different size price shift

	1935 to present
Large rise *(above +0.25%)*	48%
Small swing *(+0.25% to -0.25%)*	30%
Large fall (*below -0.25%)*	23%

Odds of rise based on yesterday

	1935 to present
Large rise yesterday *(above +0.25%)*	92%
Small swing yesterday *(+0.25% to -0.25%)*	47%
Large fall yesterday (*below -0.25%)*	59%

DIAGNOSTICS

Odds of price rise based on direction of 5-day and 20-day trend yesterday

	5-day trend	20-day trend
Yesterday rose more than +0.1%	82%	73%
Little change *(+0.1% to -0.1%)*	67%	50%
Yesterday fell more than -0.1%	50%	65%

Odds of rise based upon distance between trend and yesterday s closing price

	5-day trend	20-day trend
Yesterday more than +0.5% above trend	91%	83%
Yesterday near trend *(+0.5% to -0.5%)*	61%	*50%
Yesterday more than -0.5% below trend	47%	50%

Looking ahead: odds of rise in future

	Next 3 days	Next 5 days
Today rose over +0.25%	62%	52%
Today small swing *(+0.25% to -0.25%)*	62%	69%
Today fell below -0.25%	40%	40%

MARCH 15 ODDS OF A PRICE RISE: 50%

Odds of different size price shift

	1935 to present
Large rise *(above +0.25%)*	34%
Small swing *(+0.25% to -0.25%)*	36%
Large fall (*below -0.25%)*	30%

Odds of rise based on yesterday

	1935 to present
Large rise yesterday *(above +0.25%)*	74%
Small swing yesterday *(+0.25% to -0.25%)*	33%
Large fall yesterday (*below -0.25%)*	30%

DIAGNOSTICS

Odds of price rise based on direction of 5-day and 20-day trend yesterday

	5-day trend	20-day trend
Yesterday rose more than +0.1%	60%	64%
Little change *(+0.1% to -0.1%)*	50%	44%
Yesterday fell more than -0.1%	36%	42%

Odds of rise based upon distance between trend and yesterday s closing price

	5-day trend	20-day trend
Yesterday more than +0.5% above trend	59%	57%
Yesterday near trend *(+0.5% to -0.5%)*	56%	*50%
Yesterday more than -0.5% below trend	27%	41%

Looking ahead: odds of rise in future

	Next 3 days	Next 5 days
Today rose over +0.25%	67%	67%
Today small swing *(+0.25% to -0.25%)*	50%	50%
Today fell below -0.25%	38%	69%

* *Per cent based on fewer than 10 observations*

MARCH 16 ODDS OF A PRICE RISE: 43%

Odds of different size price shift

	1935 to present
Large rise *(above +0.25%)*	28%
Small swing *(+0.25% to -0.25%)*	41%
Large fall (*below -0.25%)*	30%

Odds of rise based on yesterday

	1935 to present
Large rise yesterday *(above +0.25%)*	56%
Small swing yesterday *(+0.25% to -0.25%)*	50%
Large fall yesterday (*below -0.25%)*	25%

DIAGNOSTICS

Odds of price rise based on direction of 5-day and 20-day trend yesterday

	5-day trend	20-day trend
Yesterday rose more than +0.1%	54%	23%
Little change *(+0.1% to -0.1%)*	*43%	47%
Yesterday fell more than -0.1%	27%	57%

Odds of rise based upon distance between trend and yesterday s closing price

	5-day trend	20-day trend
Yesterday more than +0.5% above trend	44%	43%
Yesterday near trend *(+0.5% to -0.5%)*	47%	*44%
Yesterday more than -0.5% below trend	38%	43%

Looking ahead: odds of rise in future

	Next 3 days	Next 5 days
Today rose over +0.25%	69%	77%
Today small swing *(+0.25% to -0.25%)*	63%	68%
Today fell below -0.25%	43%	50%

MARCH 17 ODDS OF A PRICE RISE: 47%

Odds of different size price shift

	1935 to present
Large rise *(above +0.25%)*	32%
Small swing *(+0.25% to -0.25%)*	32%
Large fall (*below -0.25%)*	36%

Odds of rise based on yesterday

	1935 to present
Large rise yesterday *(above +0.25%)*	54%
Small swing yesterday *(+0.25% to -0.25%)*	38%
Large fall yesterday (*below -0.25%)*	50%

DIAGNOSTICS

Odds of price rise based on direction of 5-day and 20-day trend yesterday

	5-day trend	20-day trend
Yesterday rose more than +0.1%	53%	47%
Little change *(+0.1% to -0.1%)*	36%	38%
Yesterday fell more than -0.1%	47%	56%

Odds of rise based upon distance between trend and yesterday s closing price

	5-day trend	20-day trend
Yesterday more than +0.5% above trend	60%	46%
Yesterday near trend *(+0.5% to -0.5%)*	42%	*0%
Yesterday more than -0.5% below trend	46%	52%

Looking ahead: odds of rise in future

	Next 3 days	Next 5 days
Today rose over +0.25%	73%	67%
Today small swing *(+0.25% to -0.25%)*	80%	67%
Today fell below -0.25%	41%	35%

* *Per cent based on fewer than 10 observations*

MARCH 18 ODDS OF A PRICE RISE: 47%

Odds of different size price shift

	1935 to present
Large rise *(above +0.25%)*	36%
Small swing *(+0.25% to -0.25%)*	26%
Large fall (*below -0.25%)*	38%

Odds of rise based on yesterday

	1935 to present
Large rise yesterday *(above +0.25%)*	59%
Small swing yesterday *(+0.25% to -0.25%)*	50%
Large fall yesterday (*below -0.25%)*	31%

DIAGNOSTICS

Odds of price rise based on direction of 5-day and 20-day trend yesterday

	5-day trend	20-day trend
Yesterday rose more than +0.1%	47%	25%
Little change *(+0.1% to -0.1%)*	*71%	53%
Yesterday fell more than -0.1%	40%	55%

Odds of rise based upon distance between trend and yesterday s closing price

	5-day trend	20-day trend
Yesterday more than +0.5% above trend	53%	38%
Yesterday near trend *(+0.5% to -0.5%)*	64%	*50%
Yesterday more than -0.5% below trend	28%	52%

Looking ahead: odds of rise in future

	Next 3 days	Next 5 days
Today rose over +0.25%	71%	59%
Today small swing *(+0.25% to -0.25%)*	42%	58%
Today fell below -0.25%	28%	28%

MARCH 19 ODDS OF A PRICE RISE: 61%

Odds of different size price shift

	1935 to present
Large rise *(above +0.25%)*	41%
Small swing *(+0.25% to -0.25%)*	30%
Large fall *(below -0.25%)*	28%

Odds of rise based on yesterday

	1935 to present
Large rise yesterday *(above +0.25%)*	75%
Small swing yesterday *(+0.25% to -0.25%)*	50%
Large fall yesterday *(below -0.25%)*	56%

DIAGNOSTICS

Odds of price rise based on direction of 5-day and 20-day trend yesterday

	5-day trend	20-day trend
Yesterday rose more than +0.1%	59%	46%
Little change *(+0.1% to -0.1%)*	*56%	71%
Yesterday fell more than -0.1%	65%	58%

Odds of rise based upon distance between trend and yesterday s closing price

	5-day trend	20-day trend
Yesterday more than +0.5% above trend	75%	56%
Yesterday near trend *(+0.5% to -0.5%)*	55%	80%
Yesterday more than -0.5% below trend	57%	56%

Looking ahead: odds of rise in future

	Next 3 days	Next 5 days
Today rose over +0.25%	63%	47%
Today small swing *(+0.25% to -0.25%)*	36%	50%
Today fell below -0.25%	46%	46%

* *Per cent based on fewer than 10 observations*

MARCH 20 ODDS OF A PRICE RISE: 47%

Odds of different size price shift

	1935 to present
Large rise *(above +0.25%)*	31%
Small swing *(+0.25% to -0.25%)*	38%
Large fall (*below -0.25%)*	31%

Odds of rise based on yesterday

	1935 to present
Large rise yesterday *(above +0.25%)*	67%
Small swing yesterday *(+0.25% to -0.25%)*	44%
Large fall yesterday (*below -0.25%)*	29%

DIAGNOSTICS

Odds of price rise based on direction of 5-day and 20-day trend yesterday

	5-day trend	20-day trend
Yesterday rose more than +0.1%	56%	53%
Little change *(+0.1% to -0.1%)*	58%	45%
Yesterday fell more than -0.1%	29%	40%

Odds of rise based upon distance between trend and yesterday s closing price

	5-day trend	20-day trend
Yesterday more than +0.5% above trend	60%	60%
Yesterday near trend *(+0.5% to -0.5%)*	47%	50%
Yesterday more than -0.5% below trend	31%	23%

Looking ahead: odds of rise in future

	Next 3 days	Next 5 days
Today rose over +0.25%	57%	57%
Today small swing *(+0.25% to -0.25%)*	53%	53%
Today fell below -0.25%	57%	50%

MARCH 21 ODDS OF A PRICE RISE: 59%

Odds of different size price shift

	1935 to present
Large rise *(above +0.25%)*	36%
Small swing *(+0.25% to -0.25%)*	36%
Large fall (*below -0.25%)*	27%

Odds of rise based on yesterday

	1935 to present
Large rise yesterday *(above +0.25%)*	69%
Small swing yesterday *(+0.25% to -0.25%)*	47%
Large fall yesterday (*below -0.25%)*	62%

DIAGNOSTICS

Odds of price rise based on direction of 5-day and 20-day trend yesterday

	5-day trend	20-day trend
Yesterday rose more than +0.1%	58%	64%
Little change *(+0.1% to -0.1%)*	*56%	50%
Yesterday fell more than -0.1%	63%	70%

Odds of rise based upon distance between trend and yesterday s closing price

	5-day trend	20-day trend
Yesterday more than +0.5% above trend	67%	68%
Yesterday near trend *(+0.5% to -0.5%)*	56%	*44%
Yesterday more than -0.5% below trend	57%	56%

Looking ahead: odds of rise in future

	Next 3 days	Next 5 days
Today rose over +0.25%	38%	38%
Today small swing *(+0.25% to -0.25%)*	56%	50%
Today fell below -0.25%	42%	33%

* *Per cent based on fewer than 10 observations*

MARCH 22 ODDS OF A PRICE RISE: 43%

Odds of different size price shift

	1935 to present
Large rise *(above +0.25%)*	32%
Small swing *(+0.25% to -0.25%)*	39%
Large fall (*below -0.25%)*	30%

Odds of rise based on yesterday

	1935 to present
Large rise yesterday *(above +0.25%)*	43%
Small swing yesterday *(+0.25% to -0.25%)*	33%
Large fall yesterday (*below -0.25%)*	55%

DIAGNOSTICS

Odds of price rise based on direction of 5-day and 20-day trend yesterday

	5-day trend	20-day trend
Yesterday rose more than +0.1%	47%	40%
Little change *(+0.1% to -0.1%)*	38%	33%
Yesterday fell more than -0.1%	43%	*75%

Odds of rise based upon distance between trend and yesterday s closing price

	5-day trend	20-day trend
Yesterday more than +0.5% above trend	41%	42%
Yesterday near trend *(+0.5% to -0.5%)*	41%	30%
Yesterday more than -0.5% below trend	50%	53%

Looking ahead: odds of rise in future

	Next 3 days	Next 5 days
Today rose over +0.25%	50%	43%
Today small swing *(+0.25% to -0.25%)*	47%	65%
Today fell below -0.25%	69%	54%

MARCH 23 ODDS OF A PRICE RISE: 44%

Odds of different size price shift

	1935 to present
Large rise *(above +0.25%)*	31%
Small swing *(+0.25% to -0.25%)*	38%
Large fall (*below -0.25%)*	31%

Odds of rise based on yesterday

	1935 to present
Large rise yesterday *(above +0.25%)*	50%
Small swing yesterday *(+0.25% to -0.25%)*	32%
Large fall yesterday (*below -0.25%)*	58%

DIAGNOSTICS

Odds of price rise based on direction of 5-day and 20-day trend yesterday

	5-day trend	20-day trend
Yesterday rose more than +0.1%	48%	36%
Little change *(+0.1% to -0.1%)*	*56%	50%
Yesterday fell more than -0.1%	31%	*44%

Odds of rise based upon distance between trend and yesterday s closing price

	5-day trend	20-day trend
Yesterday more than +0.5% above trend	38%	48%
Yesterday near trend *(+0.5% to -0.5%)*	45%	45%
Yesterday more than -0.5% below trend	*56%	38%

Looking ahead: odds of rise in future

	Next 3 days	Next 5 days
Today rose over +0.25%	50%	57%
Today small swing *(+0.25% to -0.25%)*	47%	59%
Today fell below -0.25%	57%	50%

* *Per cent based on fewer than 10 observations*

MARCH 24 ODDS OF A PRICE RISE: 41%

Odds of different size price shift

	1935 to present
Large rise *(above +0.25%)*	32%
Small swing *(+0.25% to -0.25%)*	30%
Large fall (*below -0.25%)*	39%

Odds of rise based on yesterday

	1935 to present
Large rise yesterday *(above +0.25%)*	*78%
Small swing yesterday *(+0.25% to -0.25%)*	30%
Large fall yesterday (*below -0.25%)*	33%

DIAGNOSTICS

Odds of price rise based on direction of 5-day and 20-day trend yesterday

	5-day trend	20-day trend
Yesterday rose more than +0.1%	48%	46%
Little change *(+0.1% to -0.1%)*	*14%	28%
Yesterday fell more than -0.1%	44%	54%

Odds of rise based upon distance between trend and yesterday s closing price

	5-day trend	20-day trend
Yesterday more than +0.5% above trend	50%	42%
Yesterday near trend *(+0.5% to -0.5%)*	43%	*57%
Yesterday more than -0.5% below trend	*22%	33%

Looking ahead: odds of rise in future

	Next 3 days	Next 5 days
Today rose over +0.25%	57%	57%
Today small swing *(+0.25% to -0.25%)*	62%	77%
Today fell below -0.25%	47%	65%

MARCH 25 ODDS OF A PRICE RISE: 48%

Odds of different size price shift

	1935 to present
Large rise *(above +0.25%)*	33%
Small swing *(+0.25% to -0.25%)*	37%
Large fall (*below -0.25%)*	30%

Odds of rise based on yesterday

	1935 to present
Large rise yesterday *(above +0.25%)*	58%
Small swing yesterday *(+0.25% to -0.25%)*	57%
Large fall yesterday (*below -0.25%)*	35%

DIAGNOSTICS

Odds of price rise based on direction of 5-day and 20-day trend yesterday

	5-day trend	20-day trend
Yesterday rose more than +0.1%	42%	27%
Little change *(+0.1% to -0.1%)*	*40%	36%
Yesterday fell more than -0.1%	55%	85%

Odds of rise based upon distance between trend and yesterday s closing price

	5-day trend	20-day trend
Yesterday more than +0.5% above trend	55%	29%
Yesterday near trend *(+0.5% to -0.5%)*	43%	45%
Yesterday more than -0.5% below trend	50%	62%

Looking ahead: odds of rise in future

	Next 3 days	Next 5 days
Today rose over +0.25%	53%	47%
Today small swing *(+0.25% to -0.25%)*	59%	76%
Today fell below -0.25%	64%	71%

* *Per cent based on fewer than 10 observations*

MARCH 26 ODDS OF A PRICE RISE: 53%

Odds of different size price shift

	1935 to present
Large rise *(above +0.25%)*	33%
Small swing *(+0.25% to -0.25%)*	47%
Large fall (*below -0.25%)*	21%

Odds of rise based on yesterday

	1935 to present
Large rise yesterday *(above +0.25%)*	69%
Small swing yesterday *(+0.25% to -0.25%)*	40%
Large fall yesterday (*below -0.25%)*	50%

DIAGNOSTICS

Odds of price rise based on direction of 5-day and 20-day trend yesterday

	5-day trend	20-day trend
Yesterday rose more than +0.1%	47%	30%
Little change *(+0.1% to -0.1%)*	54%	52%
Yesterday fell more than -0.1%	62%	*88%

Odds of rise based upon distance between trend and yesterday s closing price

	5-day trend	20-day trend
Yesterday more than +0.5% above trend	60%	35%
Yesterday near trend *(+0.5% to -0.5%)*	43%	60%
Yesterday more than -0.5% below trend	67%	69%

Looking ahead: odds of rise in future

	Next 3 days	Next 5 days
Today rose over +0.25%	50%	50%
Today small swing *(+0.25% to -0.25%)*	70%	70%
Today fell below -0.25%	*67%	*78%

MARCH 27 ODDS OF A PRICE RISE: 54%

Odds of different size price shift

	1935 to present
Large rise *(above +0.25%)*	36%
Small swing *(+0.25% to -0.25%)*	46%
Large fall *(below -0.25%)*	18%

Odds of rise based on yesterday

	1935 to present
Large rise yesterday *(above +0.25%)*	50%
Small swing yesterday *(+0.25% to -0.25%)*	56%
Large fall yesterday *(below -0.25%)*	*56%

DIAGNOSTICS

Odds of price rise based on direction of 5-day and 20-day trend yesterday

	5-day trend	20-day trend
Yesterday rose more than +0.1%	62%	58%
Little change *(+0.1% to -0.1%)*	27%	57%
Yesterday fell more than -0.1%	67%	*33%

Odds of rise based upon distance between trend and yesterday s closing price

	5-day trend	20-day trend
Yesterday more than +0.5% above trend	75%	56%
Yesterday near trend *(+0.5% to -0.5%)*	37%	*43%
Yesterday more than -0.5% below trend	*63%	56%

Looking ahead: odds of rise in future

	Next 3 days	Next 5 days
Today rose over +0.25%	71%	79%
Today small swing *(+0.25% to -0.25%)*	61%	72%
Today fell below -0.25%	*57%	*43%

* *Per cent based on fewer than 10 observations*

MARCH 28 ODDS OF A PRICE RISE: 46%

Odds of different size price shift

	1935 to present
Large rise *(above +0.25%)*	27%
Small swing *(+0.25% to -0.25%)*	41%
Large fall (*below -0.25%)*	32%

Odds of rise based on yesterday

	1935 to present
Large rise yesterday *(above +0.25%)*	57%
Small swing yesterday *(+0.25% to -0.25%)*	47%
Large fall yesterday (*below -0.25%)*	30%

DIAGNOSTICS

Odds of price rise based on direction of 5-day and 20-day trend yesterday

	5-day trend	20-day trend
Yesterday rose more than +0.1%	42%	31%
Little change *(+0.1% to -0.1%)*	57%	53%
Yesterday fell more than -0.1%	40%	*56%

Odds of rise based upon distance between trend and yesterday s closing price

	5-day trend	20-day trend
Yesterday more than +0.5% above trend	*56%	40%
Yesterday near trend *(+0.5% to -0.5%)*	50%	50%
Yesterday more than -0.5% below trend	*25%	50%

Looking ahead: odds of rise in future

	Next 3 days	Next 5 days
Today rose over +0.25%	73%	64%
Today small swing *(+0.25% to -0.25%)*	65%	71%
Today fell below -0.25%	46%	77%

MARCH 29 ODDS OF A PRICE RISE: 57%

Odds of different size price shift

	1935 to present
Large rise *(above +0.25%)*	40%
Small swing *(+0.25% to -0.25%)*	31%
Large fall (*below -0.25%)*	29%

Odds of rise based on yesterday

	1935 to present
Large rise yesterday *(above +0.25%)*	80%
Small swing yesterday *(+0.25% to -0.25%)*	60%
Large fall yesterday (*below -0.25%)*	33%

DIAGNOSTICS

Odds of price rise based on direction of 5-day and 20-day trend yesterday

	5-day trend	20-day trend
Yesterday rose more than +0.1%	58%	80%
Little change *(+0.1% to -0.1%)*	65%	52%
Yesterday fell more than -0.1%	46%	*43%

Odds of rise based upon distance between trend and yesterday s closing price

	5-day trend	20-day trend
Yesterday more than +0.5% above trend	*71%	65%
Yesterday near trend *(+0.5% to -0.5%)*	59%	64%
Yesterday more than -0.5% below trend	*38%	43%

Looking ahead: odds of rise in future

	Next 3 days	Next 5 days
Today rose over +0.25%	59%	65%
Today small swing *(+0.25% to -0.25%)*	77%	69%
Today fell below -0.25%	75%	67%

* *Per cent based on fewer than 10 observations*

MARCH 30 ODDS OF A PRICE RISE: 44%

Odds of different size price shift

	1935 to present
Large rise *(above +0.25%)*	27%
Small swing *(+0.25% to -0.25%)*	37%
Large fall (*below -0.25%)*	37%

Odds of rise based on yesterday

	1935 to present
Large rise yesterday *(above +0.25%)*	53%
Small swing yesterday *(+0.25% to -0.25%)*	38%
Large fall yesterday (*below -0.25%)*	40%

DIAGNOSTICS

Odds of price rise based on direction of 5-day and 20-day trend yesterday

	5-day trend	20-day trend
Yesterday rose more than +0.1%	47%	38%
Little change *(+0.1% to -0.1%)*	40%	38%
Yesterday fell more than -0.1%	45%	*71%

Odds of rise based upon distance between trend and yesterday s closing price

	5-day trend	20-day trend
Yesterday more than +0.5% above trend	*50%	35%
Yesterday near trend *(+0.5% to -0.5%)*	40%	42%
Yesterday more than -0.5% below trend	*50%	58%

Looking ahead: odds of rise in future

	Next 3 days	Next 5 days
Today rose over +0.25%	91%	64%
Today small swing *(+0.25% to -0.25%)*	73%	80%
Today fell below -0.25%	60%	67%

MARCH 31 ODDS OF A PRICE RISE: 60%

Odds of different size price shift

	1935 to present
Large rise *(above +0.25%)*	40%
Small swing *(+0.25% to -0.25%)*	33%
Large fall (*below -0.25%)*	26%

Odds of rise based on yesterday

	1935 to present
Large rise yesterday *(above +0.25%)*	67%
Small swing yesterday *(+0.25% to -0.25%)*	57%
Large fall yesterday (*below -0.25%)*	54%

DIAGNOSTICS

Odds of price rise based on direction of 5-day and 20-day trend yesterday

	5-day trend	20-day trend
Yesterday rose more than +0.1%	69%	67%
Little change *(+0.1% to -0.1%)*	55%	58%
Yesterday fell more than -0.1%	53%	55%

Odds of rise based upon distance between trend and yesterday s closing price

	5-day trend	20-day trend
Yesterday more than +0.5% above trend	58%	63%
Yesterday near trend *(+0.5% to -0.5%)*	64%	62%
Yesterday more than -0.5% below trend	*50%	54%

Looking ahead: odds of rise in future

	Next 3 days	Next 5 days
Today rose over +0.25%	76%	71%
Today small swing *(+0.25% to -0.25%)*	93%	64%
Today fell below -0.25%	64%	55%

* *Per cent based on fewer than 10 observations*

APRIL

PROFIT ODDS SUMMARY FOR THE MONTH

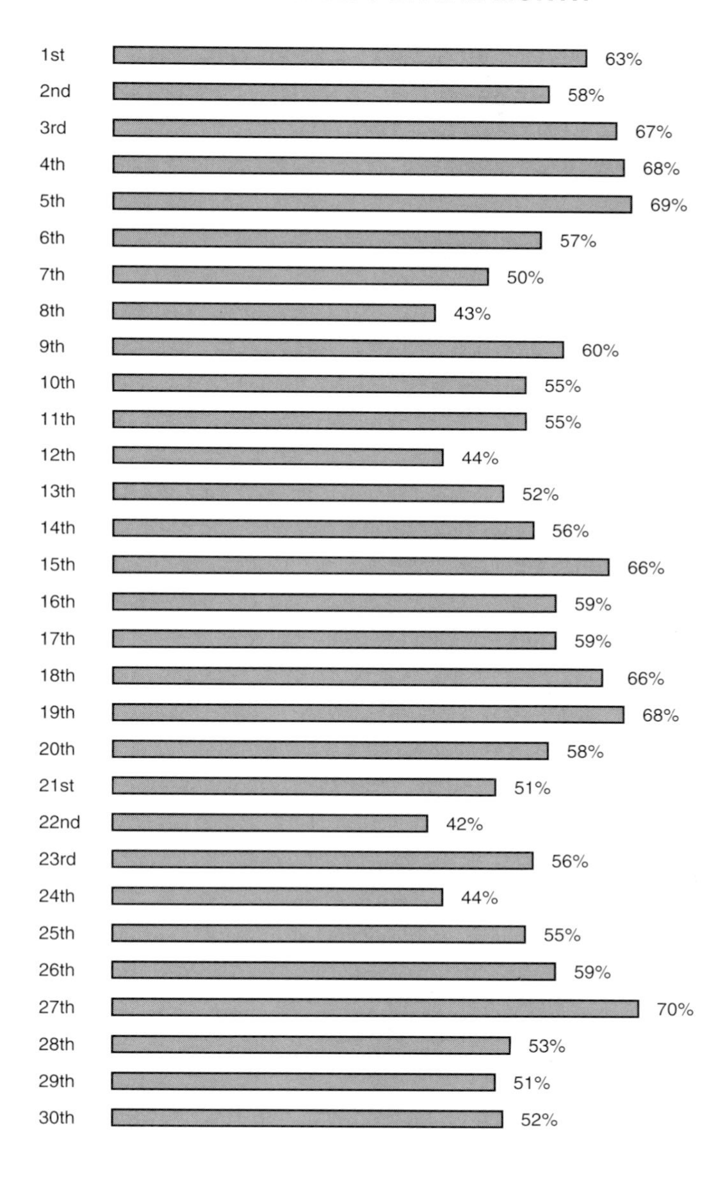

APRIL 1 ODDS OF A PRICE RISE: 63%

Odds of different size price shift

	1935 to present
Large rise *(above +0.25%)*	47%
Small swing *(+0.25% to -0.25%)*	26%
Large fall (*below -0.25%)*	28%

Odds of rise based on yesterday

	1935 to present
Large rise yesterday *(above +0.25%)*	83%
Small swing yesterday *(+0.25% to -0.25%)*	56%
Large fall yesterday (*below -0.25%)*	*33%

DIAGNOSTICS

Odds of price rise based on direction of 5-day and 20-day trend yesterday

	5-day trend	20-day trend
Yesterday rose more than +0.1%	68%	80%
Little change *(+0.1% to -0.1%)*	55%	54%
Yesterday fell more than -0.1%	62%	*67%

Odds of rise based upon distance between trend and yesterday s closing price

	5-day trend	20-day trend
Yesterday more than +0.5% above trend	65%	83%
Yesterday near trend *(+0.5% to -0.5%)*	71%	40%
Yesterday more than -0.5% below trend	*44%	53%

Looking ahead: odds of rise in future

	Next 3 days	Next 5 days
Today rose over +0.25%	70%	60%
Today small swing *(+0.25% to -0.25%)*	64%	64%
Today fell below -0.25%	58%	58%

* *Per cent based on fewer than 10 observations*

APRIL 2 ODDS OF A PRICE RISE: 58%

Odds of different size price shift

	1935 to present
Large rise *(above +0.25%)*	47%
Small swing *(+0.25% to -0.25%)*	37%
Large fall (*below -0.25%)*	16%

Odds of rise based on yesterday

	1935 to present
Large rise yesterday *(above +0.25%)*	73%
Small swing yesterday *(+0.25% to -0.25%)*	54%
Large fall yesterday (*below -0.25%)*	47%

DIAGNOSTICS

Odds of price rise based on direction of 5-day and 20-day trend yesterday

	5-day trend	20-day trend
Yesterday rose more than +0.1%	62%	62%
Little change *(+0.1% to -0.1%)*	*67%	65%
Yesterday fell more than -0.1%	46%	40%

Odds of rise based upon distance between trend and yesterday s closing price

	5-day trend	20-day trend
Yesterday more than +0.5% above trend	67%	61%
Yesterday near trend *(+0.5% to -0.5%)*	67%	73%
Yesterday more than -0.5% below trend	30%	43%

Looking ahead: odds of rise in future

	Next 3 days	Next 5 days
Today rose over +0.25%	60%	65%
Today small swing *(+0.25% to -0.25%)*	56%	63%
Today fell below -0.25%	*57%	*86%

APRIL 3 ODDS OF A PRICE RISE: 67%

Odds of different size price shift

	1935 to present
Large rise *(above +0.25%)*	43%
Small swing *(+0.25% to -0.25%)*	38%
Large fall *(below -0.25%)*	19%

Odds of rise based on yesterday

	1935 to present
Large rise yesterday *(above +0.25%)*	68%
Small swing yesterday *(+0.25% to -0.25%)*	64%
Large fall yesterday *(below -0.25%)*	*67%

DIAGNOSTICS

Odds of price rise based on direction of 5-day and 20-day trend yesterday

	5-day trend	20-day trend
Yesterday rose more than +0.1%	65%	60%
Little change *(+0.1% to -0.1%)*	69%	67%
Yesterday fell more than -0.1%	*67%	*78%

Odds of rise based upon distance between trend and yesterday s closing price

	5-day trend	20-day trend
Yesterday more than +0.5% above trend	71%	57%
Yesterday near trend *(+0.5% to -0.5%)*	70%	*100%
Yesterday more than -0.5% below trend	*50%	64%

Looking ahead: odds of rise in future

	Next 3 days	Next 5 days
Today rose over +0.25%	50%	56%
Today small swing *(+0.25% to -0.25%)*	69%	94%
Today fell below -0.25%	*50%	*63%

* *Per cent based on fewer than 10 observations*

APRIL 4 ODDS OF A PRICE RISE: 68%

Odds of different size price shift

	1935 to present
Large rise *(above +0.25%)*	49%
Small swing *(+0.25% to -0.25%)*	32%
Large fall (*below -0.25%)*	19%

Odds of rise based on yesterday

	1935 to present
Large rise yesterday *(above +0.25%)*	62%
Small swing yesterday *(+0.25% to -0.25%)*	*100%
Large fall yesterday (*below -0.25%)*	*43%

DIAGNOSTICS

Odds of price rise based on direction of 5-day and 20-day trend yesterday

	5-day trend	20-day trend
Yesterday rose more than +0.1%	65%	79%
Little change *(+0.1% to -0.1%)*	*100%	59%
Yesterday fell more than -0.1%	50%	*67%

Odds of rise based upon distance between trend and yesterday s closing price

	5-day trend	20-day trend
Yesterday more than +0.5% above trend	73%	74%
Yesterday near trend *(+0.5% to -0.5%)*	71%	*67%
Yesterday more than -0.5% below trend	*40%	*50%

Looking ahead: odds of rise in future

	Next 3 days	Next 5 days
Today rose over +0.25%	78%	89%
Today small swing *(+0.25% to -0.25%)*	75%	75%
Today fell below -0.25%	*14%	*29%

APRIL 5 ODDS OF A PRICE RISE: 69%

Odds of different size price shift

	1935 to present
Large rise *(above +0.25%)*	52%
Small swing *(+0.25% to -0.25%)*	29%
Large fall (*below -0.25%)*	19%

Odds of rise based on yesterday

	1935 to present
Large rise yesterday *(above +0.25%)*	89%
Small swing yesterday *(+0.25% to -0.25%)*	54%
Large fall yesterday (*below -0.25%)*	55%

DIAGNOSTICS

Odds of price rise based on direction of 5-day and 20-day trend yesterday

	5-day trend	20-day trend
Yesterday rose more than +0.1%	76%	82%
Little change *(+0.1% to -0.1%)*	58%	58%
Yesterday fell more than -0.1%	*67%	*67%

Odds of rise based upon distance between trend and yesterday s closing price

	5-day trend	20-day trend
Yesterday more than +0.5% above trend	83%	83%
Yesterday near trend *(+0.5% to -0.5%)*	53%	*43%
Yesterday more than -0.5% below trend	*71%	55%

Looking ahead: odds of rise in future

	Next 3 days	Next 5 days
Today rose over +0.25%	77%	68%
Today small swing *(+0.25% to -0.25%)*	75%	58%
Today fell below -0.25%	*50%	*63%

* *Per cent based on fewer than 10 observations*

APRIL 6 ODDS OF A PRICE RISE: 57%

Odds of different size price shift

	1935 to present
Large rise *(above +0.25%)*	39%
Small swing *(+0.25% to -0.25%)*	30%
Large fall (*below -0.25%)*	32%

Odds of rise based on yesterday

	1935 to present
Large rise yesterday *(above +0.25%)*	62%
Small swing yesterday *(+0.25% to -0.25%)*	62%
Large fall yesterday (*below -0.25%)*	40%

DIAGNOSTICS

Odds of price rise based on direction of 5-day and 20-day trend yesterday

	5-day trend	20-day trend
Yesterday rose more than +0.1%	58%	50%
Little change *(+0.1% to -0.1%)*	*50%	60%
Yesterday fell more than -0.1%	60%	*67%

Odds of rise based upon distance between trend and yesterday s closing price

	5-day trend	20-day trend
Yesterday more than +0.5% above trend	68%	59%
Yesterday near trend *(+0.5% to -0.5%)*	44%	*44%
Yesterday more than -0.5% below trend	*57%	*63%

Looking ahead: odds of rise in future

	Next 3 days	Next 5 days
Today rose over +0.25%	59%	71%
Today small swing *(+0.25% to -0.25%)*	77%	62%
Today fell below -0.25%	50%	36%

APRIL 7 ODDS OF A PRICE RISE: 50%

Odds of different size price shift

	1935 to present
Large rise *(above +0.25%)*	48%
Small swing *(+0.25% to -0.25%)*	25%
Large fall (*below -0.25%)*	28%

Odds of rise based on yesterday

	1935 to present
Large rise yesterday *(above +0.25%)*	71%
Small swing yesterday *(+0.25% to -0.25%)*	42%
Large fall yesterday (*below -0.25%)*	27%

DIAGNOSTICS

Odds of price rise based on direction of 5-day and 20-day trend yesterday

	5-day trend	20-day trend
Yesterday rose more than +0.1%	57%	60%
Little change *(+0.1% to -0.1%)*	30%	38%
Yesterday fell more than -0.1%	*56%	*56%

Odds of rise based upon distance between trend and yesterday s closing price

	5-day trend	20-day trend
Yesterday more than +0.5% above trend	63%	55%
Yesterday near trend *(+0.5% to -0.5%)*	36%	*17%
Yesterday more than -0.5% below trend	*43%	58%

Looking ahead: odds of rise in future

	Next 3 days	Next 5 days
Today rose over +0.25%	47%	47%
Today small swing *(+0.25% to -0.25%)*	70%	40%
Today fell below -0.25%	55%	55%

* *Per cent based on fewer than 10 observations*

APRIL 8 ODDS OF A PRICE RISE: 43%

Odds of different size price shift

	1935 to present
Large rise *(above +0.25%)*	38%
Small swing *(+0.25% to -0.25%)*	29%
Large fall (*below -0.25%)*	33%

Odds of rise based on yesterday

	1935 to present
Large rise yesterday *(above +0.25%)*	50%
Small swing yesterday *(+0.25% to -0.25%)*	40%
Large fall yesterday (*below -0.25%)*	*33%

DIAGNOSTICS

Odds of price rise based on direction of 5-day and 20-day trend yesterday

	5-day trend	20-day trend
Yesterday rose more than +0.1%	48%	54%
Little change *(+0.1% to -0.1%)*	46%	44%
Yesterday fell more than -0.1%	*25%	27%

Odds of rise based upon distance between trend and yesterday s closing price

	5-day trend	20-day trend
Yesterday more than +0.5% above trend	47%	50%
Yesterday near trend *(+0.5% to -0.5%)*	35%	*29%
Yesterday more than -0.5% below trend	*50%	36%

Looking ahead: odds of rise in future

	Next 3 days	Next 5 days
Today rose over +0.25%	50%	56%
Today small swing *(+0.25% to -0.25%)*	67%	83%
Today fell below -0.25%	57%	71%

APRIL 9 ODDS OF A PRICE RISE: 60%

Odds of different size price shift

	1935 to present
Large rise *(above +0.25%)*	42%
Small swing *(+0.25% to -0.25%)*	30%
Large fall *(below -0.25%)*	28%

Odds of rise based on yesterday

	1935 to present
Large rise yesterday *(above +0.25%)*	64%
Small swing yesterday *(+0.25% to -0.25%)*	62%
Large fall yesterday *(below -0.25%)*	56%

DIAGNOSTICS

Odds of price rise based on direction of 5-day and 20-day trend yesterday

	5-day trend	20-day trend
Yesterday rose more than +0.1%	59%	65%
Little change *(+0.1% to -0.1%)*	54%	53%
Yesterday fell more than -0.1%	*75%	*67%

Odds of rise based upon distance between trend and yesterday s closing price

	5-day trend	20-day trend
Yesterday more than +0.5% above trend	67%	60%
Yesterday near trend *(+0.5% to -0.5%)*	55%	*50%
Yesterday more than -0.5% below trend	*67%	67%

Looking ahead: odds of rise in future

	Next 3 days	Next 5 days
Today rose over +0.25%	67%	72%
Today small swing *(+0.25% to -0.25%)*	54%	62%
Today fell below -0.25%	67%	75%

* *Per cent based on fewer than 10 observations*

APRIL 10 ODDS OF A PRICE RISE: 55%

Odds of different size price shift

	1935 to present
Large rise *(above +0.25%)*	43%
Small swing *(+0.25% to -0.25%)*	38%
Large fall (*below -0.25%)*	20%

Odds of rise based on yesterday

	1935 to present
Large rise yesterday *(above +0.25%)*	82%
Small swing yesterda y*(+0.25% to -0.25%)*	36%
Large fall yesterday (*below -0.25%)*	33%

DIAGNOSTICS

Odds of price rise based on direction of 5-day and 20-day trend yesterday

	5-day trend	20-day trend
Yesterday rose more than +0.1%	68%	78%
Little change *(+0.1% to -0.1%)*	*57%	36%
Yesterday fell more than -0.1%	27%	*38%

Odds of rise based upon distance between trend and yesterday s closing price

	5-day trend	20-day trend
Yesterday more than +0.5% above trend	88%	68%
Yesterday near trend *(+0.5% to -0.5%)*	36%	*33%
Yesterday more than -0.5% below trend	*22%	42%

Looking ahead: odds of rise in future

	Next 3 days	Next 5 days
Today rose over +0.25%	65%	71%
Today small swing *(+0.25% to -0.25%)*	87%	67%
Today fell below -0.25%	*50%	*63%

APRIL 11 ODDS OF A PRICE RISE: 55%

Odds of different size price shift

	1935 to present
Large rise *(above +0.25%)*	43%
Small swing *(+0.25% to -0.25%)*	30%
Large fall *(below -0.25%)*	28%

Odds of rise based on yesterday

	1935 to present
Large rise yesterday *(above +0.25%)*	63%
Small swing yesterday *(+0.25% to -0.25%)*	50%
Large fall yesterday *(below -0.25%)*	50%

DIAGNOSTICS

Odds of price rise based on direction of 5-day and 20-day trend yesterday

	5-day trend	20-day trend
Yesterday rose more than +0.1%	58%	53%
Little change *(+0.1% to -0.1%)*	40%	50%
Yesterday fell more than -0.1%	*67%	*67%

Odds of rise based upon distance between trend and yesterday s closing price

	5-day trend	20-day trend
Yesterday more than +0.5% above trend	56%	52%
Yesterday near trend *(+0.5% to -0.5%)*	56%	*63%
Yesterday more than -0.5% below trend	*50%	*56%

Looking ahead: odds of rise in future

	Next 3 days	Next 5 days
Today rose over +0.25%	59%	76%
Today small swing *(+0.25% to -0.25%)*	58%	67%
Today fell below -0.25%	64%	64%

* *Per cent based on fewer than 10 observations*

APRIL 12 ODDS OF A PRICE RISE: 44%

Odds of different size price shift

	1935 to present
Large rise *(above +0.25%)*	28%
Small swing *(+0.25% to -0.25%)*	36%
Large fall (*below -0.25%)*	36%

Odds of rise based on yesterday

	1935 to present
Large rise yesterday *(above +0.25%)*	56%
Small swing yesterday *(+0.25% to -0.25%)*	36%
Large fall yesterday (*below -0.25%)*	30%

DIAGNOSTICS

Odds of price rise based on direction of 5-day and 20-day trend yesterday

	5-day trend	20-day trend
Yesterday rose more than +0.1%	45%	43%
Little change *(+0.1% to -0.1%)*	*38%	*25%
Yesterday fell more than -0.1%	*44%	*63%

Odds of rise based upon distance between trend and yesterday s closing price

	5-day trend	20-day trend
Yesterday more than +0.5% above trend	47%	39%
Yesterday near trend *(+0.5% to -0.5%)*	50%	*40%
Yesterday more than -0.5% below trend	*17%	55%

Looking ahead: odds of rise in future

	Next 3 days	Next 5 days
Today rose over +0.25%	73%	73%
Today small swing *(+0.25% to -0.25%)*	64%	71%
Today fell below -0.25%	57%	57%

APRIL 13 ODDS OF A PRICE RISE: 52%

Odds of different size price shift

	1935 to present
Large rise *(above +0.25%)*	40%
Small swing *(+0.25% to -0.25%)*	31%
Large fall (*below -0.25%)*	29%

Odds of rise based on yesterday

	1935 to present
Large rise yesterday *(above +0.25%)*	67%
Small swing yesterday *(+0.25% to -0.25%)*	71%
Large fall yesterday (*below -0.25%)*	15%

DIAGNOSTICS

Odds of price rise based on direction of 5-day and 20-day trend yesterday

	5-day trend	20-day trend
Yesterday rose more than +0.1%	63%	53%
Little change *(+0.1% to -0.1%)*	*44%	45%
Yesterday fell more than -0.1%	47%	*71%

Odds of rise based upon distance between trend and yesterday s closing price

	5-day trend	20-day trend
Yesterday more than +0.5% above trend	69%	62%
Yesterday near trend *(+0.5% to -0.5%)*	53%	*33%
Yesterday more than -0.5% below trend	33%	50%

Looking ahead: odds of rise in future

	Next 3 days	Next 5 days
Today rose over +0.25%	53%	65%
Today small swing *(+0.25% to -0.25%)*	77%	92%
Today fell below -0.25%	67%	83%

* *Per cent based on fewer than 10 observations*

APRIL 14 ODDS OF A PRICE RISE: 56%

Odds of different size price shift

	1935 to present
Large rise *(above +0.25%)*	40%
Small swing *(+0.25% to -0.25%)*	27%
Large fall (*below -0.25%)*	33%

Odds of rise based on yesterday

	1935 to present
Large rise yesterday *(above +0.25%)*	56%
Small swing yesterday *(+0.25% to -0.25%)*	64%
Large fall yesterday (*below -0.25%)*	46%

DIAGNOSTICS

Odds of price rise based on direction of 5-day and 20-day trend yesterday

	5-day trend	20-day trend
Yesterday rose more than +0.1%	53%	42%
Little change *(+0.1% to -0.1%)*	62%	74%
Yesterday fell more than -0.1%	53%	*43%

Odds of rise based upon distance between trend and yesterday s closing price

	5-day trend	20-day trend
Yesterday more than +0.5% above trend	54%	48%
Yesterday near trend *(+0.5% to -0.5%)*	62%	*89%
Yesterday more than -0.5% below trend	45%	46%

Looking ahead: odds of rise in future

	Next 3 days	Next 5 days
Today rose over +0.25%	78%	61%
Today small swing *(+0.25% to -0.25%)*	75%	83%
Today fell below -0.25%	73%	67%

APRIL 15 ODDS OF A PRICE RISE: 66%

Odds of different size price shift

	1935 to present
Large rise *(above +0.25%)*	49%
Small swing *(+0.25% to -0.25%)*	34%
Large fall *(below -0.25%)*	17%

Odds of rise based on yesterday

	1935 to present
Large rise yesterday *(above +0.25%)*	72%
Small swing yesterday *(+0.25% to -0.25%)*	50%
Large fall yesterday *(below -0.25%)*	69%

DIAGNOSTICS

Odds of price rise based on direction of 5-day and 20-day trend yesterday

	5-day trend	20-day trend
Yesterday rose more than +0.1%	71%	71%
Little change *(+0.1% to -0.1%)*	67%	63%
Yesterday fell more than -0.1%	58%	*63%

Odds of rise based upon distance between trend and yesterday s closing price

	5-day trend	20-day trend
Yesterday more than +0.5% above trend	77%	68%
Yesterday near trend *(+0.5% to -0.5%)*	59%	*80%
Yesterday more than -0.5% below trend	*67%	55%

Looking ahead: odds of rise in future

	Next 3 days	Next 5 days
Today rose over +0.25%	50%	55%
Today small swing *(+0.25% to -0.25%)*	71%	64%
Today fell below -0.25%	*71%	*71%

* *Per cent based on fewer than 10 observations*

APRIL 16 ODDS OF A PRICE RISE: 59%

Odds of different size price shift

	1935 to present
Large rise *(above +0.25%)*	37%
Small swing *(+0.25% to -0.25%)*	37%
Large fall (*below -0.25%)*	27%

Odds of rise based on yesterday

	1935 to present
Large rise yesterday *(above +0.25%)*	70%
Small swing yesterday *(+0.25% to -0.25%)*	47%
Large fall yesterday (*below -0.25%)*	*50%

DIAGNOSTICS

Odds of price rise based on direction of 5-day and 20-day trend yesterday

	5-day trend	20-day trend
Yesterday rose more than +0.1%	59%	65%
Little change *(+0.1% to -0.1%)*	*44%	47%
Yesterday fell more than -0.1%	70%	*71%

Odds of rise based upon distance between trend and yesterday s closing price

	5-day trend	20-day trend
Yesterday more than +0.5% above trend	63%	57%
Yesterday near trend *(+0.5% to -0.5%)*	50%	64%
Yesterday more than -0.5% below trend	*75%	*57%

Looking ahead: odds of rise in future

	Next 3 days	Next 5 days
Today rose over +0.25%	87%	67%
Today small swing *(+0.25% to -0.25%)*	60%	73%
Today fell below -0.25%	45%	55%

APRIL 17 ODDS OF A PRICE RISE: 59%

Odds of different size price shift

	1935 to present
Large rise *(above +0.25%)*	37%
Small swing *(+0.25% to -0.25%)*	41%
Large fall *(below -0.25%)*	22%

Odds of rise based on yesterday

	1935 to present
Large rise yesterday *(above +0.25%)*	69%
Small swing yesterday *(+0.25% to -0.25%)*	46%
Large fall yesterday *(below -0.25%)*	58%

DIAGNOSTICS

Odds of price rise based on direction of 5-day and 20-day trend yesterday

	5-day trend	20-day trend
Yesterday rose more than +0.1%	70%	67%
Little change *(+0.1% to -0.1%)*	50%	44%
Yesterday fell more than -0.1%	*43%	*80%

Odds of rise based upon distance between trend and yesterday s closing price

	5-day trend	20-day trend
Yesterday more than +0.5% above trend	65%	67%
Yesterday near trend *(+0.5% to -0.5%)*	50%	50%
Yesterday more than -0.5% below trend	*67%	*43%

Looking ahead: odds of rise in future

	Next 3 days	Next 5 days
Today rose over +0.25%	60%	60%
Today small swing *(+0.25% to -0.25%)*	71%	88%
Today fell below -0.25%	*33%	*22%

* *Per cent based on fewer than 10 observations*

APRIL 18 ODDS OF A PRICE RISE: 66%

Odds of different size price shift

	1935 to present
Large rise *(above +0.25%)*	44%
Small swing *(+0.25% to -0.25%)*	29%
Large fall (*below -0.25%)*	27%

Odds of rise based on yesterday

	1935 to present
Large rise yesterday *(above +0.25%)*	72%
Small swing yesterday *(+0.25% to -0.25%)*	73%
Large fall yesterday (*below -0.25%)*	*38%

DIAGNOSTICS

Odds of price rise based on direction of 5-day and 20-day trend yesterday

	5-day trend	20-day trend
Yesterday rose more than +0.1%	71%	80%
Little change *(+0.1% to -0.1%)*	62%	53%
Yesterday fell more than -0.1%	*50%	*50%

Odds of rise based upon distance between trend and yesterday s closing price

	5-day trend	20-day trend
Yesterday more than +0.5% above trend	89%	76%
Yesterday near trend *(+0.5% to -0.5%)*	42%	*78%
Yesterday more than -0.5% below trend	*75%	*14%

Looking ahead: odds of rise in future

	Next 3 days	Next 5 days
Today rose over +0.25%	67%	56%
Today small swing *(+0.25% to -0.25%)*	58%	58%
Today fell below -0.25%	73%	55%

APRIL 19 ODDS OF A PRICE RISE: 68%

Odds of different size price shift

	1935 to present
Large rise *(above +0.25%)*	45%
Small swing *(+0.25% to -0.25%)*	30%
Large fall (*below -0.25%)*	25%

Odds of rise based on yesterday

	1935 to present
Large rise yesterday *(above +0.25%)*	69%
Small swing yesterday *(+0.25% to -0.25%)*	91%
Large fall yesterday (*below -0.25%)*	46%

DIAGNOSTICS

Odds of price rise based on direction of 5-day and 20-day trend yesterday

	5-day trend	20-day trend
Yesterday rose more than +0.1%	69%	74%
Little change *(+0.1% to -0.1%)*	69%	67%
Yesterday fell more than -0.1%	64%	*50%

Odds of rise based upon distance between trend and yesterday s closing price

	5-day trend	20-day trend
Yesterday more than +0.5% above trend	80%	67%
Yesterday near trend *(+0.5% to -0.5%)*	60%	*78%
Yesterday more than -0.5% below trend	*60%	60%

Looking ahead: odds of rise in future

	Next 3 days	Next 5 days
Today rose over +0.25%	44%	56%
Today small swing *(+0.25% to -0.25%)*	67%	83%
Today fell below -0.25%	50%	50%

* *Per cent based on fewer than 10 observations*

APRIL 20 ODDS OF A PRICE RISE: 58%

Odds of different size price shift

	1935 to present
Large rise *(above +0.25%)*	43%
Small swing *(+0.25% to -0.25%)*	30%
Large fall (*below -0.25%)*	28%

Odds of rise based on yesterday

	1935 to present
Large rise yesterday *(above +0.25%)*	53%
Small swing yesterday *(+0.25% to -0.25%)*	67%
Large fall yesterday (*below -0.25%)*	55%

DIAGNOSTICS

Odds of price rise based on direction of 5-day and 20-day trend yesterday

	5-day trend	20-day trend
Yesterday rose more than +0.1%	44%	67%
Little change *(+0.1% to -0.1%)*	71%	58%
Yesterday fell more than -0.1%	60%	*33%

Odds of rise based upon distance between trend and yesterday s closing price

	5-day trend	20-day trend
Yesterday more than +0.5% above trend	50%	59%
Yesterday near trend *(+0.5% to -0.5%)*	53%	*44%
Yesterday more than -0.5% below trend	*86%	*67%

Looking ahead: odds of rise in future

	Next 3 days	Next 5 days
Today rose over +0.25%	41%	53%
Today small swing *(+0.25% to -0.25%)*	75%	83%
Today fell below -0.25%	64%	73%

APRIL 21 ODDS OF A PRICE RISE: 51%

Odds of different size price shift

	1935 to present
Large rise *(above +0.25%)*	32%
Small swing *(+0.25% to -0.25%)*	49%
Large fall (*below -0.25%)*	19%

Odds of rise based on yesterday

	1935 to present
Large rise yesterday *(above +0.25%)*	50%
Small swing yesterday *(+0.25% to -0.25%)*	50%
Large fall yesterday (*below -0.25%)*	55%

DIAGNOSTICS

Odds of price rise based on direction of 5-day and 20-day trend yesterday

	5-day trend	20-day trend
Yesterday rose more than +0.1%	52%	52%
Little change *(+0.1% to -0.1%)*	55%	48%
Yesterday fell more than -0.1%	46%	*60%

Odds of rise based upon distance between trend and yesterday s closing price

	5-day trend	20-day trend
Yesterday more than +0.5% above trend	48%	50%
Yesterday near trend *(+0.5% to -0.5%)*	56%	64%
Yesterday more than -0.5% below trend	*50%	40%

Looking ahead: odds of rise in future

	Next 3 days	Next 5 days
Today rose over +0.25%	73%	73%
Today small swing *(+0.25% to -0.25%)*	57%	70%
Today fell below -0.25%	*44%	*44%

* *Per cent based on fewer than 10 observations*

APRIL 22 ODDS OF A PRICE RISE: 42%

Odds of different size price shift

	1935 to present
Large rise *(above +0.25%)*	36%
Small swing *(+0.25% to -0.25%)*	29%
Large fall (*below -0.25%)*	36%

Odds of rise based on yesterday

	1935 to present
Large rise yesterday *(above +0.25%)*	56%
Small swing yesterday *(+0.25% to -0.25%)*	39%
Large fall yesterday (*below -0.25%)*	27%

DIAGNOSTICS

Odds of price rise based on direction of 5-day and 20-day trend yesterday

	5-day trend	20-day trend
Yesterday rose more than +0.1%	50%	38%
Little change *(+0.1% to -0.1%)*	20%	50%
Yesterday fell more than -0.1%	45%	*33%

Odds of rise based upon distance between trend and yesterday s closing price

	5-day trend	20-day trend
Yesterday more than +0.5% above trend	53%	41%
Yesterday near trend *(+0.5% to -0.5%)*	33%	*60%
Yesterday more than -0.5% below trend	*43%	36%

Looking ahead: odds of rise in future

	Next 3 days	Next 5 days
Today rose over +0.25%	63%	50%
Today small swing *(+0.25% to -0.25%)*	46%	46%
Today fell below -0.25%	44%	56%

APRIL 23 ODDS OF A PRICE RISE: 56%

Odds of different size price shift

	1935 to present
Large rise *(above +0.25%)*	37%
Small swing *(+0.25% to -0.25%)*	33%
Large fall (*below -0.25%)*	30%

Odds of rise based on yesterday

	1935 to present
Large rise yesterday *(above +0.25%)*	87%
Small swing yesterday *(+0.25% to -0.25%)*	33%
Large fall yesterday (*below -0.25%)*	46%

DIAGNOSTICS

Odds of price rise based on direction of 5-day and 20-day trend yesterday

	5-day trend	20-day trend
Yesterday rose more than +0.1%	54%	65%
Little change *(+0.1% to -0.1%)*	80%	53%
Yesterday fell more than -0.1%	*33%	*25%

Odds of rise based upon distance between trend and yesterday s closing price

	5-day trend	20-day trend
Yesterday more than +0.5% above trend	60%	59%
Yesterday near trend *(+0.5% to -0.5%)*	58%	*67%
Yesterday more than -0.5% below trend	*44%	40%

Looking ahead: odds of rise in future

	Next 3 days	Next 5 days
Today rose over +0.25%	44%	63%
Today small swing *(+0.25% to -0.25%)*	57%	64%
Today fell below -0.25%	38%	46%

* *Per cent based on fewer than 10 observations*

APRIL 24 ODDS OF A PRICE RISE: 44%

Odds of different size price shift

	1935 to present
Large rise *(above +0.25%)*	27%
Small swing *(+0.25% to -0.25%)*	40%
Large fall (*below -0.25%)*	33%

Odds of rise based on yesterday

	1935 to present
Large rise yesterday *(above +0.25%)*	47%
Small swing yesterday *(+0.25% to -0.25%)*	47%
Large fall yesterday (*below -0.25%)*	36%

DIAGNOSTICS

Odds of price rise based on direction of 5-day and 20-day trend yesterday

	5-day trend	20-day trend
Yesterday rose more than +0.1%	45%	48%
Little change *(+0.1% to -0.1%)*	73%	41%
Yesterday fell more than -0.1%	17%	*40%

Odds of rise based upon distance between trend and yesterday s closing price

	5-day trend	20-day trend
Yesterday more than +0.5% above trend	45%	50%
Yesterday near trend *(+0.5% to -0.5%)*	50%	*57%
Yesterday more than -0.5% below trend	*25%	20%

Looking ahead: odds of rise in future

	Next 3 days	Next 5 days
Today rose over +0.25%	92%	83%
Today small swing *(+0.25% to -0.25%)*	50%	61%
Today fell below -0.25%	53%	67%

APRIL 25 ODDS OF A PRICE RISE: 55%

Odds of different size price shift

	1935 to present
Large rise *(above +0.25%)*	36%
Small swing *(+0.25% to -0.25%)*	32%
Large fall (*below -0.25%)*	32%

Odds of rise based on yesterday

	1935 to present
Large rise yesterday *(above +0.25%)*	75%
Small swing yesterday *(+0.25% to -0.25%)*	47%
Large fall yesterday (*below -0.25%)*	47%

DIAGNOSTICS

Odds of price rise based on direction of 5-day and 20-day trend yesterday

	5-day trend	20-day trend
Yesterday rose more than +0.1%	45%	45%
Little change *(+0.1% to -0.1%)*	*88%	71%
Yesterday fell more than -0.1%	50%	*40%

Odds of rise based upon distance between trend and yesterday s closing price

	5-day trend	20-day trend
Yesterday more than +0.5% above trend	70%	52%
Yesterday near trend *(+0.5% to -0.5%)*	52%	*67%
Yesterday more than -0.5% below trend	45%	*50%

Looking ahead: odds of rise in future

	Next 3 days	Next 5 days
Today rose over +0.25%	75%	75%
Today small swing *(+0.25% to -0.25%)*	71%	79%
Today fell below -0.25%	79%	79%

* *Per cent based on fewer than 10 observations*

APRIL 26 ODDS OF A PRICE RISE: 59%

Odds of different size price shift

	1935 to present
Large rise *(above +0.25%)*	36%
Small swing *(+0.25% to -0.25%)*	36%
Large fall (*below -0.25%)*	27%

Odds of rise based on yesterday

	1935 to present
Large rise yesterday *(above +0.25%)*	69%
Small swing yesterday *(+0.25% to -0.25%)*	71%
Large fall yesterday (*below -0.25%)*	36%

DIAGNOSTICS

Odds of price rise based on direction of 5-day and 20-day trend yesterday

	5-day trend	20-day trend
Yesterday rose more than +0.1%	52%	55%
Little change *(+0.1% to -0.1%)*	69%	72%
Yesterday fell more than -0.1%	60%	*25%

Odds of rise based upon distance between trend and yesterday s closing price

	5-day trend	20-day trend
Yesterday more than +0.5% above trend	64%	61%
Yesterday near trend *(+0.5% to -0.5%)*	63%	*75%
Yesterday more than -0.5% below trend	45%	*38%

Looking ahead: odds of rise in future

	Next 3 days	Next 5 days
Today rose over +0.25%	75%	81%
Today small swing *(+0.25% to -0.25%)*	81%	69%
Today fell below -0.25%	50%	67%

APRIL 27 ODDS OF A PRICE RISE: 70%

Odds of different size price shift

	1935 to present
Large rise *(above +0.25%)*	48%
Small swing *(+0.25% to -0.25%)*	33%
Large fall (*below -0.25%)*	20%

Odds of rise based on yesterday

	1935 to present
Large rise yesterday *(above +0.25%)*	78%
Small swing yesterday *(+0.25% to -0.25%)*	72%
Large fall yesterday (*below -0.25%)*	50%

DIAGNOSTICS

Odds of price rise based on direction of 5-day and 20-day trend yesterday

	5-day trend	20-day trend
Yesterday rose more than +0.1%	68%	70%
Little change *(+0.1% to -0.1%)*	79%	88%
Yesterday fell more than -0.1%	*50%	*29%

Odds of rise based upon distance between trend and yesterday s closing price

	5-day trend	20-day trend
Yesterday more than +0.5% above trend	74%	72%
Yesterday near trend *(+0.5% to -0.5%)*	75%	*89%
Yesterday more than -0.5% below trend	55%	*38%

Looking ahead: odds of rise in future

	Next 3 days	Next 5 days
Today rose over +0.25%	59%	55%
Today small swing *(+0.25% to -0.25%)*	60%	67%
Today fell below -0.25%	*89%	*67%

* *Per cent based on fewer than 10 observations*

APRIL 28 ODDS OF A PRICE RISE: 53%

Odds of different size price shift

	1935 to present
Large rise *(above +0.25%)*	32%
Small swing *(+0.25% to -0.25%)*	47%
Large fall (*below -0.25%)*	21%

Odds of rise based on yesterday

	1935 to present
Large rise yesterday *(above +0.25%)*	57%
Small swing yesterday *(+0.25% to -0.25%)*	40%
Large fall yesterday (*below -0.25%)*	64%

DIAGNOSTICS

Odds of price rise based on direction of 5-day and 20-day trend yesterday

	5-day trend	20-day trend
Yesterday rose more than +0.1%	58%	52%
Little change *(+0.1% to -0.1%)*	42%	44%
Yesterday fell more than -0.1%	55%	*75%

Odds of rise based upon distance between trend and yesterday s closing price

	5-day trend	20-day trend
Yesterday more than +0.5% above trend	71%	55%
Yesterday near trend *(+0.5% to -0.5%)*	38%	*20%
Yesterday more than -0.5% below trend	*56%	64%

Looking ahead: odds of rise in future

	Next 3 days	Next 5 days
Today rose over +0.25%	80%	80%
Today small swing *(+0.25% to -0.25%)*	73%	73%
Today fell below -0.25%	60%	30%

APRIL 29 ODDS OF A PRICE RISE: 51%

Odds of different size price shift

	1935 to present
Large rise *(above +0.25%)*	43%
Small swing *(+0.25% to -0.25%)*	28%
Large fall *(below -0.25%)*	30%

Odds of rise based on yesterday

	1935 to present
Large rise yesterday *(above +0.25%)*	64%
Small swing yesterday *(+0.25% to -0.25%)*	58%
Large fall yesterday *(below -0.25%)*	29%

DIAGNOSTICS

Odds of price rise based on direction of 5-day and 20-day trend yesterday

	5-day trend	20-day trend
Yesterday rose more than +0.1%	63%	52%
Little change *(+0.1% to -0.1%)*	43%	63%
Yesterday fell more than -0.1%	47%	*17%

Odds of rise based upon distance between trend and yesterday s closing price

	5-day trend	20-day trend
Yesterday more than +0.5% above trend	70%	54%
Yesterday near trend *(+0.5% to -0.5%)*	41%	*57%
Yesterday more than -0.5% below trend	60%	42%

Looking ahead: odds of rise in future

	Next 3 days	Next 5 days
Today rose over +0.25%	80%	80%
Today small swing *(+0.25% to -0.25%)*	69%	69%
Today fell below -0.25%	43%	50%

* *Per cent based on fewer than 10 observations*

APRIL 30 ODDS OF A PRICE RISE: 52%

Odds of different size price shift

	1935 to present
Large rise *(above +0.25%)*	35%
Small swing *(+0.25% to -0.25%)*	41%
Large fall (*below -0.25%)*	24%

Odds of rise based on yesterday

	1935 to present
Large rise yesterday *(above +0.25%)*	67%
Small swing yesterday *(+0.25% to -0.25%)*	36%
Large fall yesterday (*below -0.25%)*	45%

DIAGNOSTICS

Odds of price rise based on direction of 5-day and 20-day trend yesterday

	5-day trend	20-day trend
Yesterday rose more than +0.1%	53%	52%
Little change *(+0.1% to -0.1%)*	60%	67%
Yesterday fell more than -0.1%	47%	*17%

Odds of rise based upon distance between trend and yesterday s closing price

	5-day trend	20-day trend
Yesterday more than +0.5% above trend	60%	57%
Yesterday near trend *(+0.5% to -0.5%)*	50%	*50%
Yesterday more than -0.5% below trend	46%	42%

Looking ahead: odds of rise in future

	Next 3 days	Next 5 days
Today rose over +0.25%	69%	75%
Today small swing *(+0.25% to -0.25%)*	68%	63%
Today fell below -0.25%	64%	55%

MAY

PROFIT ODDS SUMMARY FOR THE MONTH

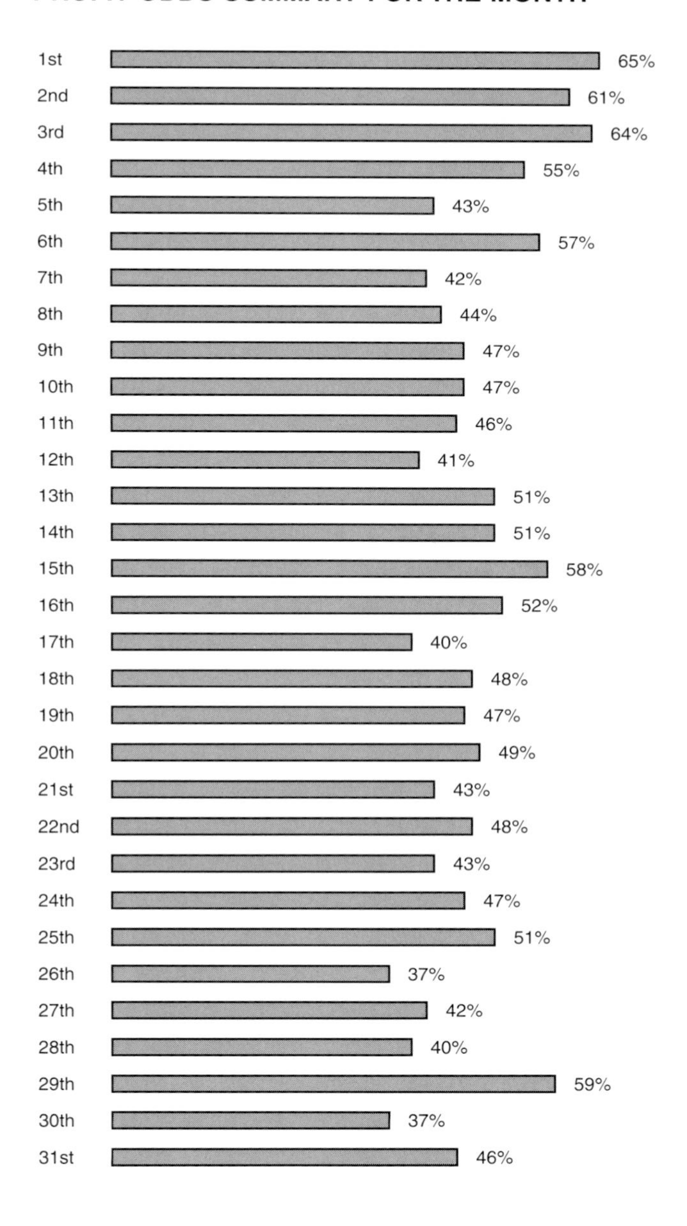

MAY 1 ODDS OF A PRICE RISE: 65%

Odds of different size price shift

	1935 to present
Large rise *(above +0.25%)*	49%
Small swing *(+0.25% to -0.25%)*	35%
Large fall (*below -0.25%)*	16%

Odds of rise based on yesterday

	1935 to present
Large rise yesterday *(above +0.25%)*	55%
Small swing yesterday *(+0.25% to -0.25%)*	68%
Large fall yesterday (*below -0.25%)*	70%

DIAGNOSTICS

Odds of price rise based on direction of 5-day and 20-day trend yesterday

	5-day trend	20-day trend
Yesterday rose more than +0.1%	60%	67%
Little change *(+0.1% to -0.1%)*	70%	77%
Yesterday fell more than -0.1%	69%	*33%

Odds of rise based upon distance between trend and yesterday s closing price

	5-day trend	20-day trend
Yesterday more than +0.5% above trend	50%	66%
Yesterday near trend *(+0.5% to -0.5%)*	70%	*67%
Yesterday more than -0.5% below trend	*86%	*63%

Looking ahead: odds of rise in future

	Next 3 days	Next 5 days
Today rose over +0.25%	76%	71%
Today small swing *(+0.25% to -0.25%)*	53%	40%
Today fell below -0.25%	*29%	*29%

* *Per cent based on fewer than 10 observations*

MAY 2 ODDS OF A PRICE RISE: 61%

Odds of different size price shift

	1935 to present
Large rise *(above +0.25%)*	46%
Small swing *(+0.25% to -0.25%)*	37%
Large fall (*below -0.25%)*	17%

Odds of rise based on yesterday

	1935 to present
Large rise yesterday *(above +0.25%)*	74%
Small swing yesterday *(+0.25% to -0.25%)*	46%
Large fall yesterday (*below -0.25%)*	*56%

DIAGNOSTICS

Odds of price rise based on direction of 5-day and 20-day trend yesterday

	5-day trend	20-day trend
Yesterday rose more than +0.1%	62%	52%
Little change *(+0.1% to -0.1%)*	58%	71%
Yesterday fell more than -0.1%	*63%	*67%

Odds of rise based upon distance between trend and yesterday s closing price

	5-day trend	20-day trend
Yesterday more than +0.5% above trend	55%	57%
Yesterday near trend *(+0.5% to -0.5%)*	65%	*75%
Yesterday more than -0.5% below trend	*75%	*71%

Looking ahead: odds of rise in future

	Next 3 days	Next 5 days
Today rose over +0.25%	68%	58%
Today small swing *(+0.25% to -0.25%)*	47%	47%
Today fell below -0.25%	*14%	*29%

MAY 3 ODDS OF A PRICE RISE: 64%

Odds of different size price shift

	1935 to present
Large rise *(above +0.25%)*	48%
Small swing *(+0.25% to -0.25%)*	24%
Large fall *(below -0.25%)*	29%

Odds of rise based on yesterday

	1935 to present
Large rise yesterday *(above +0.25%)*	86%
Small swing yesterday *(+0.25% to -0.25%)*	50%
Large fall yesterday *(below -0.25%)*	*17%

DIAGNOSTICS

Odds of price rise based on direction of 5-day and 20-day trend yesterday

	5-day trend	20-day trend
Yesterday rose more than +0.1%	72%	72%
Little change *(+0.1% to -0.1%)*	60%	58%
Yesterday fell more than -0.1%	*43%	*40%

Odds of rise based upon distance between trend and yesterday s closing price

	5-day trend	20-day trend
Yesterday more than +0.5% above trend	75%	73%
Yesterday near trend *(+0.5% to -0.5%)*	63%	*43%
Yesterday more than -0.5% below trend	*0%	*40%

Looking ahead: odds of rise in future

	Next 3 days	Next 5 days
Today rose over +0.25%	65%	65%
Today small swing *(+0.25% to -0.25%)*	50%	60%
Today fell below -0.25%	25%	17%

* *Per cent based on fewer than 10 observations*

MAY 4 ODDS OF A PRICE RISE: 55%

Odds of different size price shift

	1935 to present
Large rise *(above +0.25%)*	26%
Small swing *(+0.25% to -0.25%)*	45%
Large fall (*below -0.25%)*	29%

Odds of rise based on yesterday

	1935 to present
Large rise yesterday *(above +0.25%)*	62%
Small swing yesterday *(+0.25% to -0.25%)*	55%
Large fall yesterday (*below -0.25%)*	40%

DIAGNOSTICS

Odds of price rise based on direction of 5-day and 20-day trend yesterday

	5-day trend	20-day trend
Yesterday rose more than +0.1%	57%	55%
Little change *(+0.1% to -0.1%)*	70%	57%
Yesterday fell more than -0.1%	*33%	*50%

Odds of rise based upon distance between trend and yesterday s closing price

	5-day trend	20-day trend
Yesterday more than +0.5% above trend	71%	63%
Yesterday near trend *(+0.5% to -0.5%)*	59%	*33%
Yesterday more than -0.5% below trend	*13%	*44%

Looking ahead: odds of rise in future

	Next 3 days	Next 5 days
Today rose over +0.25%	64%	55%
Today small swing *(+0.25% to -0.25%)*	58%	68%
Today fell below -0.25%	42%	50%

MAY 5 ODDS OF A PRICE RISE: 43%

Odds of different size price shift

	1935 to present
Large rise *(above +0.25%)*	32%
Small swing *(+0.25% to -0.25%)*	34%
Large fall *(below -0.25%)*	34%

Odds of rise based on yesterday

	1935 to present
Large rise yesterday *(above +0.25%)*	73%
Small swing yesterday *(+0.25% to -0.25%)*	38%
Large fall yesterday *(below -0.25%)*	25%

DIAGNOSTICS

Odds of price rise based on direction of 5-day and 20-day trend yesterday

	5-day trend	20-day trend
Yesterday rose more than +0.1%	48%	33%
Little change *(+0.1% to -0.1%)*	30%	50%
Yesterday fell more than -0.1%	45%	*67%

Odds of rise based upon distance between trend and yesterday s closing price

	5-day trend	20-day trend
Yesterday more than +0.5% above trend	38%	37%
Yesterday near trend *(+0.5% to -0.5%)*	50%	40%
Yesterday more than -0.5% below trend	*33%	*71%

Looking ahead: odds of rise in future

	Next 3 days	Next 5 days
Today rose over +0.25%	43%	50%
Today small swing *(+0.25% to -0.25%)*	87%	80%
Today fell below -0.25%	53%	60%

* *Per cent based on fewer than 10 observations*

MAY 6 ODDS OF A PRICE RISE: 57%

Odds of different size price shift

	1935 to present
Large rise *(above +0.25%)*	41%
Small swing *(+0.25% to -0.25%)*	27%
Large fall (*below -0.25%)*	32%

Odds of rise based on yesterday

	1935 to present
Large rise yesterday *(above +0.25%)*	43%
Small swing yesterday *(+0.25% to -0.25%)*	88%
Large fall yesterday (*below -0.25%)*	36%

DIAGNOSTICS

Odds of price rise based on direction of 5-day and 20-day trend yesterday

	5-day trend	20-day trend
Yesterday rose more than +0.1%	74%	50%
Little change *(+0.1% to -0.1%)*	*50%	73%
Yesterday fell more than -0.1%	33%	*40%

Odds of rise based upon distance between trend and yesterday s closing price

	5-day trend	20-day trend
Yesterday more than +0.5% above trend	65%	67%
Yesterday near trend *(+0.5% to -0.5%)*	60%	*75%
Yesterday more than -0.5% below trend	*29%	31%

Looking ahead: odds of rise in future

	Next 3 days	Next 5 days
Today rose over +0.25%	72%	61%
Today small swing *(+0.25% to -0.25%)*	50%	58%
Today fell below -0.25%	21%	21%

MAY 7 ODDS OF A PRICE RISE: 42%

Odds of different size price shift

	1935 to present
Large rise *(above +0.25%)*	21%
Small swing *(+0.25% to -0.25%)*	35%
Large fall (*below -0.25%)*	44%

Odds of rise based on yesterday

	1935 to present
Large rise yesterday *(above +0.25%)*	65%
Small swing yesterday *(+0.25% to -0.25%)*	27%
Large fall yesterday (*below -0.25%)*	27%

DIAGNOSTICS

Odds of price rise based on direction of 5-day and 20-day trend yesterday

	5-day trend	20-day trend
Yesterday rose more than +0.1%	50%	45%
Little change *(+0.1% to -0.1%)*	*43%	44%
Yesterday fell more than -0.1%	20%	*0%

Odds of rise based upon distance between trend and yesterday s closing price

	5-day trend	20-day trend
Yesterday more than +0.5% above trend	67%	48%
Yesterday near trend *(+0.5% to -0.5%)*	25%	*33%
Yesterday more than -0.5% below trend	*22%	30%

Looking ahead: odds of rise in future

	Next 3 days	Next 5 days
Today rose over +0.25%	*67%	*67%
Today small swing *(+0.25% to -0.25%)*	47%	53%
Today fell below -0.25%	32%	37%

* *Per cent based on fewer than 10 observations*

MAY 8 ODDS OF A PRICE RISE: 44%

Odds of different size price shift

	1935 to present
Large rise *(above +0.25%)*	33%
Small swing *(+0.25% to -0.25%)*	26%
Large fall (*below -0.25%)*	42%

Odds of rise based on yesterday

	1935 to present
Large rise yesterday *(above +0.25%)*	64%
Small swing yesterday *(+0.25% to -0.25%)*	10%
Large fall yesterday (*below -0.25%)*	47%

DIAGNOSTICS

Odds of price rise based on direction of 5-day and 20-day trend yesterday

	5-day trend	20-day trend
Yesterday rose more than +0.1%	52%	52%
Little change *(+0.1% to -0.1%)*	*17%	38%
Yesterday fell more than -0.1%	42%	*29%

Odds of rise based upon distance between trend and yesterday s closing price

	5-day trend	20-day trend
Yesterday more than +0.5% above trend	44%	46%
Yesterday near trend *(+0.5% to -0.5%)*	50%	*56%
Yesterday more than -0.5% below trend	40%	30%

Looking ahead: odds of rise in future

	Next 3 days	Next 5 days
Today rose over +0.25%	50%	57%
Today small swing *(+0.25% to -0.25%)*	64%	73%
Today fell below -0.25%	39%	28%

MAY 9 ODDS OF A PRICE RISE: 47%

Odds of different size price shift

	1935 to present
Large rise *(above +0.25%)*	30%
Small swing *(+0.25% to -0.25%)*	33%
Large fall (*below -0.25%)*	37%

Odds of rise based on yesterday

	1935 to present
Large rise yesterday *(above +0.25%)*	58%
Small swing yesterda y*(+0.25% to -0.25%)*	42%
Large fall yesterday (*below -0.25%)*	42%

DIAGNOSTICS

Odds of price rise based on direction of 5-day and 20-day trend yesterday

	5-day trend	20-day trend
Yesterday rose more than +0.1%	60%	55%
Little change *(+0.1% to -0.1%)*	*40%	40%
Yesterday fell more than -0.1%	33%	*33%

Odds of rise based upon distance between trend and yesterday s closing price

	5-day trend	20-day trend
Yesterday more than +0.5% above trend	55%	50%
Yesterday near trend *(+0.5% to -0.5%)*	50%	*38%
Yesterday more than -0.5% below trend	38%	45%

Looking ahead: odds of rise in future

	Next 3 days	Next 5 days
Today rose over +0.25%	77%	85%
Today small swing *(+0.25% to -0.25%)*	50%	50%
Today fell below -0.25%	44%	56%

* *Per cent based on fewer than 10 observations*

MAY 10 ODDS OF A PRICE RISE: 47%

Odds of different size price shift

	1935 to present
Large rise *(above +0.25%)*	36%
Small swing *(+0.25% to -0.25%)*	31%
Large fall *(below -0.25%)*	33%

Odds of rise based on yesterday

	1935 to present
Large rise yesterday *(above +0.25%)*	73%
Small swing yesterday *(+0.25% to -0.25%)*	47%
Large fall yesterday *(below -0.25%)*	29%

DIAGNOSTICS

Odds of price rise based on direction of 5-day and 20-day trend yesterday

	5-day trend	20-day trend
Yesterday rose more than +0.1%	52%	58%
Little change *(+0.1% to -0.1%)*	*50%	41%
Yesterday fell more than -0.1%	38%	*25%

Odds of rise based upon distance between trend and yesterday s closing price

	5-day trend	20-day trend
Yesterday more than +0.5% above trend	*63%	58%
Yesterday near trend *(+0.5% to -0.5%)*	54%	*20%
Yesterday more than -0.5% below trend	18%	36%

Looking ahead: odds of rise in future

	Next 3 days	Next 5 days
Today rose over +0.25%	56%	50%
Today small swing *(+0.25% to -0.25%)*	71%	50%
Today fell below -0.25%	40%	47%

MAY 11 ODDS OF A PRICE RISE: 46%

Odds of different size price shift

	1935 to present
Large rise *(above +0.25%)*	28%
Small swing *(+0.25% to -0.25%)*	39%
Large fall (*below -0.25%)*	33%

Odds of rise based on yesterday

	1935 to present
Large rise yesterday *(above +0.25%)*	59%
Small swing yesterday *(+0.25% to -0.25%)*	63%
Large fall yesterday (*below -0.25%)*	8%

DIAGNOSTICS

Odds of price rise based on direction of 5-day and 20-day trend yesterday

	5-day trend	20-day trend
Yesterday rose more than +0.1%	55%	60%
Little change *(+0.1% to -0.1%)*	*50%	35%
Yesterday fell more than -0.1%	31%	*33%

Odds of rise based upon distance between trend and yesterday s closing price

	5-day trend	20-day trend
Yesterday more than +0.5% above trend	50%	63%
Yesterday near trend *(+0.5% to -0.5%)*	54%	*22%
Yesterday more than -0.5% below trend	20%	31%

Looking ahead: odds of rise in future

	Next 3 days	Next 5 days
Today rose over +0.25%	54%	46%
Today small swing *(+0.25% to -0.25%)*	44%	33%
Today fell below -0.25%	53%	53%

* *Per cent based on fewer than 10 observations*

MAY 12 ODDS OF A PRICE RISE: 41%

Odds of different size price shift

	1935 to present
Large rise *(above +0.25%)*	26%
Small swing *(+0.25% to -0.25%)*	39%
Large fall (*below -0.25%)*	35%

Odds of rise based on yesterday

	1935 to present
Large rise yesterday *(above +0.25%)*	38%
Small swing yesterday *(+0.25% to -0.25%)*	53%
Large fall yesterday (*below -0.25%)*	27%

DIAGNOSTICS

Odds of price rise based on direction of 5-day and 20-day trend yesterday

	5-day trend	20-day trend
Yesterday rose more than +0.1%	46%	43%
Little change *(+0.1% to -0.1%)*	*50%	42%
Yesterday fell more than -0.1%	29%	*33%

Odds of rise based upon distance between trend and yesterday s closing price

	5-day trend	20-day trend
Yesterday more than +0.5% above trend	47%	42%
Yesterday near trend *(+0.5% to -0.5%)*	43%	*43%
Yesterday more than -0.5% below trend	30%	38%

Looking ahead: odds of rise in future

	Next 3 days	Next 5 days
Today rose over +0.25%	50%	50%
Today small swing *(+0.25% to -0.25%)*	50%	44%
Today fell below -0.25%	38%	31%

MAY 13 ODDS OF A PRICE RISE: 51%

Odds of different size price shift

	1935 to present
Large rise *(above +0.25%)*	34%
Small swing *(+0.25% to -0.25%)*	32%
Large fall *(below -0.25%)*	34%

Odds of rise based on yesterday

	1935 to present
Large rise yesterday *(above +0.25%)*	46%
Small swing yesterday *(+0.25% to -0.25%)*	64%
Large fall yesterday *(below -0.25%)*	45%

DIAGNOSTICS

Odds of price rise based on direction of 5-day and 20-day trend yesterday

	5-day trend	20-day trend
Yesterday rose more than +0.1%	56%	50%
Little change *(+0.1% to -0.1%)*	46%	53%
Yesterday fell more than -0.1%	50%	*50%

Odds of rise based upon distance between trend and yesterday s closing price

	5-day trend	20-day trend
Yesterday more than +0.5% above trend	46%	61%
Yesterday near trend *(+0.5% to -0.5%)*	60%	*50%
Yesterday more than -0.5% below trend	43%	38%

Looking ahead: odds of rise in future

	Next 3 days	Next 5 days
Today rose over +0.25%	56%	38%
Today small swing *(+0.25% to -0.25%)*	67%	53%
Today fell below -0.25%	44%	38%

* *Per cent based on fewer than 10 observations*

MAY 14 ODDS OF A PRICE RISE: 51%

Odds of different size price shift

	1935 to present
Large rise *(above +0.25%)*	36%
Small swing *(+0.25% to -0.25%)*	29%
Large fall (*below -0.25%)*	36%

Odds of rise based on yesterday

	1935 to present
Large rise yesterday *(above +0.25%)*	54%
Small swing yesterday *(+0.25% to -0.25%)*	57%
Large fall yesterday (*below -0.25%)*	44%

DIAGNOSTICS

Odds of price rise based on direction of 5-day and 20-day trend yesterday

	5-day trend	20-day trend
Yesterday rose more than +0.1%	64%	59%
Little change *(+0.1% to -0.1%)*	64%	41%
Yesterday fell more than -0.1%	35%	55%

Odds of rise based upon distance between trend and yesterday s closing price

	5-day trend	20-day trend
Yesterday more than +0.5% above trend	50%	60%
Yesterday near trend *(+0.5% to -0.5%)*	69%	*40%
Yesterday more than -0.5% below trend	35%	45%

Looking ahead: odds of rise in future

	Next 3 days	Next 5 days
Today rose over +0.25%	63%	63%
Today small swing *(+0.25% to -0.25%)*	54%	54%
Today fell below -0.25%	50%	44%

MAY 15 ODDS OF A PRICE RISE: 58%

Odds of different size price shift

	1935 to present
Large rise *(above +0.25%)*	40%
Small swing *(+0.25% to -0.25%)*	36%
Large fall *(below -0.25%)*	24%

Odds of rise based on yesterday

	1935 to present
Large rise yesterday *(above +0.25%)*	87%
Small swing yesterday *(+0.25% to -0.25%)*	47%
Large fall yesterday *(below -0.25%)*	40%

DIAGNOSTICS

Odds of price rise based on direction of 5-day and 20-day trend yesterday

	5-day trend	20-day trend
Yesterday rose more than +0.1%	63%	65%
Little change *(+0.1% to -0.1%)*	55%	57%
Yesterday fell more than -0.1%	56%	45%

Odds of rise based upon distance between trend and yesterday s closing price

	5-day trend	20-day trend
Yesterday more than +0.5% above trend	69%	52%
Yesterday near trend *(+0.5% to -0.5%)*	58%	*75%
Yesterday more than -0.5% below trend	46%	60%

Looking ahead: odds of rise in future

	Next 3 days	Next 5 days
Today rose over +0.25%	72%	56%
Today small swing *(+0.25% to -0.25%)*	25%	19%
Today fell below -0.25%	45%	45%

* *Per cent based on fewer than 10 observations*

MAY 16 ODDS OF A PRICE RISE: 52%

Odds of different size price shift

	1935 to present
Large rise *(above +0.25%)*	34%
Small swing *(+0.25% to -0.25%)*	41%
Large fall (*below -0.25%)*	25%

Odds of rise based on yesterday

	1935 to present
Large rise yesterday *(above +0.25%)*	59%
Small swing yesterday *(+0.25% to -0.25%)*	59%
Large fall yesterday (*below -0.25%)*	30%

DIAGNOSTICS

Odds of price rise based on direction of 5-day and 20-day trend yesterday

	5-day trend	20-day trend
Yesterday rose more than +0.1%	45%	31%
Little change *(+0.1% to -0.1%)*	*43%	63%
Yesterday fell more than -0.1%	65%	*67%

Odds of rise based upon distance between trend and yesterday s closing price

	5-day trend	20-day trend
Yesterday more than +0.5% above trend	50%	38%
Yesterday near trend *(+0.5% to -0.5%)*	47%	*67%
Yesterday more than -0.5% below trend	*67%	64%

Looking ahead: odds of rise in future

	Next 3 days	Next 5 days
Today rose over +0.25%	53%	60%
Today small swing *(+0.25% to -0.25%)*	33%	28%
Today fell below -0.25%	45%	18%

MAY 17 ODDS OF A PRICE RISE: 40%

Odds of different size price shift

	1935 to present
Large rise *(above +0.25%)*	23%
Small swing *(+0.25% to -0.25%)*	42%
Large fall *(below -0.25%)*	35%

Odds of rise based on yesterday

	1935 to present
Large rise yesterday *(above +0.25%)*	41%
Small swing yesterday *(+0.25% to -0.25%)*	38%
Large fall yesterday *(below -0.25%)*	40%

DIAGNOSTICS

Odds of price rise based on direction of 5-day and 20-day trend yesterday

	5-day trend	20-day trend
Yesterday rose more than +0.1%	38%	25%
Little change *(+0.1% to -0.1%)*	*33%	48%
Yesterday fell more than -0.1%	46%	*50%

Odds of rise based upon distance between trend and yesterday s closing price

	5-day trend	20-day trend
Yesterday more than +0.5% above trend	42%	35%
Yesterday near trend *(+0.5% to -0.5%)*	40%	*29%
Yesterday more than -0.5% below trend	*33%	54%

Looking ahead: odds of rise in future

	Next 3 days	Next 5 days
Today rose over +0.25%	40%	40%
Today small swing *(+0.25% to -0.25%)*	39%	44%
Today fell below -0.25%	47%	33%

* *Per cent based on fewer than 10 observations*

MAY 18 ODDS OF A PRICE RISE: 48%

Odds of different size price shift

	1935 to present
Large rise *(above +0.25%)*	39%
Small swing *(+0.25% to -0.25%)*	32%
Large fall (*below -0.25%)*	30%

Odds of rise based on yesterday

	1935 to present
Large rise yesterday *(above +0.25%)*	64%
Small swing yesterday *(+0.25% to -0.25%)*	41%
Large fall yesterday (*below -0.25%)*	44%

DIAGNOSTICS

Odds of price rise based on direction of 5-day and 20-day trend yesterday

	5-day trend	20-day trend
Yesterday rose more than +0.1%	54%	47%
Little change *(+0.1% to -0.1%)*	35%	40%
Yesterday fell more than -0.1%	57%	*71%

Odds of rise based upon distance between trend and yesterday s closing price

	5-day trend	20-day trend
Yesterday more than +0.5% above trend	64%	48%
Yesterday near trend *(+0.5% to -0.5%)*	35%	30%
Yesterday more than -0.5% below trend	54%	64%

Looking ahead: odds of rise in future

	Next 3 days	Next 5 days
Today rose over +0.25%	53%	53%
Today small swing *(+0.25% to -0.25%)*	29%	36%
Today fell below -0.25%	46%	62%

MAY 19 ODDS OF A PRICE RISE: 47%

Odds of different size price shift

	1935 to present
Large rise *(above +0.25%)*	34%
Small swing *(+0.25% to -0.25%)*	30%
Large fall *(below -0.25%)*	36%

Odds of rise based on yesterday

	1935 to present
Large rise yesterday *(above +0.25%)*	53%
Small swing yesterday *(+0.25% to -0.25%)*	41%
Large fall yesterday *(below -0.25%)*	45%

DIAGNOSTICS

Odds of price rise based on direction of 5-day and 20-day trend yesterday

	5-day trend	20-day trend
Yesterday rose more than +0.1%	58%	47%
Little change *(+0.1% to -0.1%)*	*33%	39%
Yesterday fell more than -0.1%	42%	60%

Odds of rise based upon distance between trend and yesterday s closing price

	5-day trend	20-day trend
Yesterday more than +0.5% above trend	67%	48%
Yesterday near trend *(+0.5% to -0.5%)*	30%	*44%
Yesterday more than -0.5% below trend	50%	47%

Looking ahead: odds of rise in future

	Next 3 days	Next 5 days
Today rose over +0.25%	63%	63%
Today small swing *(+0.25% to -0.25%)*	57%	50%
Today fell below -0.25%	53%	53%

* *Per cent based on fewer than 10 observations*

MAY 20 ODDS OF A PRICE RISE: 49%

Odds of different size price shift

	1935 to present
Large rise *(above +0.25%)*	34%
Small swing *(+0.25% to -0.25%)*	28%
Large fall (*below -0.25%)*	38%

Odds of rise based on yesterday

	1935 to present
Large rise yesterday *(above +0.25%)*	60%
Small swing yesterday *(+0.25% to -0.25%)*	47%
Large fall yesterday (*below -0.25%)*	41%

DIAGNOSTICS

Odds of price rise based on direction of 5-day and 20-day trend yesterday

	5-day trend	20-day trend
Yesterday rose more than +0.1%	41%	57%
Little change *(+0.1% to -0.1%)*	45%	52%
Yesterday fell more than -0.1%	58%	30%

Odds of rise based upon distance between trend and yesterday s closing price

	5-day trend	20-day trend
Yesterday more than +0.5% above trend	38%	56%
Yesterday near trend *(+0.5% to -0.5%)*	59%	64%
Yesterday more than -0.5% below trend	42%	27%

Looking ahead: odds of rise in future

	Next 3 days	Next 5 days
Today rose over +0.25%	69%	63%
Today small swing *(+0.25% to -0.25%)*	31%	23%
Today fell below -0.25%	44%	33%

MAY 21 ODDS OF A PRICE RISE: 43%

Odds of different size price shift

	1935 to present
Large rise *(above +0.25%)*	34%
Small swing *(+0.25% to -0.25%)*	27%
Large fall *(below -0.25%)*	39%

Odds of rise based on yesterday

	1935 to present
Large rise yesterday *(above +0.25%)*	67%
Small swing yesterday *(+0.25% to -0.25%)*	17%
Large fall yesterday *(below -0.25%)*	41%

DIAGNOSTICS

Odds of price rise based on direction of 5-day and 20-day trend yesterday

	5-day trend	20-day trend
Yesterday rose more than +0.1%	41%	50%
Little change *(+0.1% to -0.1%)*	*50%	33%
Yesterday fell more than -0.1%	42%	50%

Odds of rise based upon distance between trend and yesterday s closing price

	5-day trend	20-day trend
Yesterday more than +0.5% above trend	50%	50%
Yesterday near trend *(+0.5% to -0.5%)*	53%	36%
Yesterday more than -0.5% below trend	29%	41%

Looking ahead: odds of rise in future

	Next 3 days	Next 5 days
Today rose over +0.25%	60%	67%
Today small swing *(+0.25% to -0.25%)*	25%	33%
Today fell below -0.25%	29%	41%

* *Per cent based on fewer than 10 observations*

MAY 22 ODDS OF A PRICE RISE: 48%

Odds of different size price shift

	1935 to present
Large rise *(above +0.25%)*	34%
Small swing *(+0.25% to -0.25%)*	23%
Large fall (*below -0.25%)*	43%

Odds of rise based on yesterday

	1935 to present
Large rise yesterday *(above +0.25%)*	50%
Small swing yesterday *(+0.25% to -0.25%)*	30%
Large fall yesterday (*below -0.25%)*	56%

DIAGNOSTICS

Odds of price rise based on direction of 5-day and 20-day trend yesterday

	5-day trend	20-day trend
Yesterday rose more than +0.1%	38%	56%
Little change *(+0.1% to -0.1%)*	58%	31%
Yesterday fell more than -0.1%	47%	58%

Odds of rise based upon distance between trend and yesterday s closing price

	5-day trend	20-day trend
Yesterday more than +0.5% above trend	60%	53%
Yesterday near trend *(+0.5% to -0.5%)*	42%	*43%
Yesterday more than -0.5% below trend	47%	44%

Looking ahead: odds of rise in future

	Next 3 days	Next 5 days
Today rose over +0.25%	47%	67%
Today small swing *(+0.25% to -0.25%)*	50%	60%
Today fell below -0.25%	26%	26%

MAY 23 ODDS OF A PRICE RISE: 43%

Odds of different size price shift

	1935 to present
Large rise *(above +0.25%)*	30%
Small swing *(+0.25% to -0.25%)*	20%
Large fall (*below -0.25%)*	50%

Odds of rise based on yesterday

	1935 to present
Large rise yesterday *(above +0.25%)*	64%
Small swing yesterday *(+0.25% to -0.25%)*	60%
Large fall yesterday (*below -0.25%)*	26%

DIAGNOSTICS

Odds of price rise based on direction of 5-day and 20-day trend yesterday

	5-day trend	20-day trend
Yesterday rose more than +0.1%	58%	53%
Little change *(+0.1% to -0.1%)*	36%	47%
Yesterday fell more than -0.1%	38%	25%

Odds of rise based upon distance between trend and yesterday s closing price

	5-day trend	20-day trend
Yesterday more than +0.5% above trend	*67%	59%
Yesterday near trend *(+0.5% to -0.5%)*	45%	*38%
Yesterday more than -0.5% below trend	31%	32%

Looking ahead: odds of rise in future

	Next 3 days	Next 5 days
Today rose over +0.25%	62%	62%
Today small swing *(+0.25% to -0.25%)*	*56%	*67%
Today fell below -0.25%	41%	36%

* *Per cent based on fewer than 10 observations*

MAY 24 ODDS OF A PRICE RISE: 47%

Odds of different size price shift

	1935 to present
Large rise *(above +0.25%)*	36%
Small swing *(+0.25% to -0.25%)*	22%
Large fall (*below -0.25%)*	42%

Odds of rise based on yesterday

	1935 to present
Large rise yesterday *(above +0.25%)*	57%
Small swing yesterday *(+0.25% to -0.25%)*	60%
Large fall yesterday (*below -0.25%)*	33%

DIAGNOSTICS

Odds of price rise based on direction of 5-day and 20-day trend yesterday

	5-day trend	20-day trend
Yesterday rose more than +0.1%	58%	56%
Little change *(+0.1% to -0.1%)*	38%	40%
Yesterday fell more than -0.1%	45%	*44%

Odds of rise based upon distance between trend and yesterday s closing price

	5-day trend	20-day trend
Yesterday more than +0.5% above trend	*56%	56%
Yesterday near trend *(+0.5% to -0.5%)*	47%	40%
Yesterday more than -0.5% below trend	42%	42%

Looking ahead: odds of rise in future

	Next 3 days	Next 5 days
Today rose over +0.25%	50%	69%
Today small swing *(+0.25% to -0.25%)*	50%	50%
Today fell below -0.25%	32%	42%

MAY 25 ODDS OF A PRICE RISE: 51%

Odds of different size price shift

	1935 to present
Large rise *(above +0.25%)*	33%
Small swing *(+0.25% to -0.25%)*	31%
Large fall (*below -0.25%)*	36%

Odds of rise based on yesterday

	1935 to present
Large rise yesterday *(above +0.25%)*	65%
Small swing yesterday *(+0.25% to -0.25%)*	*44%
Large fall yesterday (*below -0.25%)*	38%

DIAGNOSTICS

Odds of price rise based on direction of 5-day and 20-day trend yesterday

	5-day trend	20-day trend
Yesterday rose more than +0.1%	62%	64%
Little change *(+0.1% to -0.1%)*	*56%	56%
Yesterday fell more than -0.1%	41%	*22%

Odds of rise based upon distance between trend and yesterday s closing price

	5-day trend	20-day trend
Yesterday more than +0.5% above trend	83%	63%
Yesterday near trend *(+0.5% to -0.5%)*	36%	*88%
Yesterday more than -0.5% below trend	38%	20%

Looking ahead: odds of rise in future

	Next 3 days	Next 5 days
Today rose over +0.25%	69%	62%
Today small swing *(+0.25% to -0.25%)*	33%	42%
Today fell below -0.25%	36%	43%

* *Per cent based on fewer than 10 observations*

MAY 26 ODDS OF A PRICE RISE: 37%

Odds of different size price shift

	1935 to present
Large rise *(above +0.25%)*	34%
Small swing *(+0.25% to -0.25%)*	27%
Large fall (*below -0.25%)*	39%

Odds of rise based on yesterday

	1935 to present
Large rise yesterday *(above +0.25%)*	50%
Small swing yesterday *(+0.25% to -0.25%)*	25%
Large fall yesterday (*below -0.25%)*	31%

DIAGNOSTICS

Odds of price rise based on direction of 5-day and 20-day trend yesterday

	5-day trend	20-day trend
Yesterday rose more than +0.1%	44%	47%
Little change *(+0.1% to -0.1%)*	*50%	23%
Yesterday fell more than -0.1%	24%	36%

Odds of rise based upon distance between trend and yesterday s closing price

	5-day trend	20-day trend
Yesterday more than +0.5% above trend	57%	44%
Yesterday near trend *(+0.5% to -0.5%)*	24%	*38%
Yesterday more than -0.5% below trend	30%	27%

Looking ahead: odds of rise in future

	Next 3 days	Next 5 days
Today rose over +0.25%	50%	57%
Today small swing *(+0.25% to -0.25%)*	64%	64%
Today fell below -0.25%	44%	38%

MAY 27 ODDS OF A PRICE RISE: 42%

Odds of different size price shift

	1935 to present
Large rise *(above +0.25%)*	30%
Small swing *(+0.25% to -0.25%)*	30%
Large fall (*below -0.25%)*	40%

Odds of rise based on yesterday

	1935 to present
Large rise yesterday *(above +0.25%)*	64%
Small swing yesterday *(+0.25% to -0.25%)*	47%
Large fall yesterday (*below -0.25%)*	24%

DIAGNOSTICS

Odds of price rise based on direction of 5-day and 20-day trend yesterday

	5-day trend	20-day trend
Yesterday rose more than +0.1%	69%	59%
Little change *(+0.1% to -0.1%)*	*40%	38%
Yesterday fell more than -0.1%	23%	23%

Odds of rise based upon distance between trend and yesterday s closing price

	5-day trend	20-day trend
Yesterday more than +0.5% above trend	67%	61%
Yesterday near trend *(+0.5% to -0.5%)*	47%	*43%
Yesterday more than -0.5% below trend	19%	22%

Looking ahead: odds of rise in future

	Next 3 days	Next 5 days
Today rose over +0.25%	54%	62%
Today small swing *(+0.25% to -0.25%)*	46%	62%
Today fell below -0.25%	35%	59%

* *Per cent based on fewer than 10 observations*

MAY 28 ODDS OF A PRICE RISE: 40%

Odds of different size price shift

	1935 to present
Large rise *(above +0.25%)*	26%
Small swing *(+0.25% to -0.25%)*	43%
Large fall (*below -0.25%)*	31%

Odds of rise based on yesterday

	1935 to present
Large rise yesterday *(above +0.25%)*	36%
Small swing yesterday *(+0.25% to -0.25%)*	46%
Large fall yesterday (*below -0.25%)*	39%

DIAGNOSTICS

Odds of price rise based on direction of 5-day and 20-day trend yesterday

	5-day trend	20-day trend
Yesterday rose more than +0.1%	33%	36%
Little change *(+0.1% to -0.1%)*	*25%	31%
Yesterday fell more than -0.1%	50%	53%

Odds of rise based upon distance between trend and yesterday s closing price

	5-day trend	20-day trend
Yesterday more than +0.5% above trend	40%	38%
Yesterday near trend *(+0.5% to -0.5%)*	36%	30%
Yesterday more than -0.5% below trend	44%	47%

Looking ahead: odds of rise in future

	Next 3 days	Next 5 days
Today rose over +0.25%	73%	73%
Today small swing *(+0.25% to -0.25%)*	56%	56%
Today fell below -0.25%	46%	46%

MAY 29 ODDS OF A PRICE RISE: 59%

Odds of different size price shift

	1935 to present
Large rise *(above +0.25%)*	38%
Small swing *(+0.25% to -0.25%)*	43%
Large fall (*below -0.25%)*	19%

Odds of rise based on yesterday

	1935 to present
Large rise yesterday *(above +0.25%)*	70%
Small swing yesterday *(+0.25% to -0.25%)*	60%
Large fall yesterday (*below -0.25%)*	50%

DIAGNOSTICS

Odds of price rise based on direction of 5-day and 20-day trend yesterday

	5-day trend	20-day trend
Yesterday rose more than +0.1%	*56%	82%
Little change *(+0.1% to -0.1%)*	*71%	50%
Yesterday fell more than -0.1%	57%	50%

Odds of rise based upon distance between trend and yesterday s closing price

	5-day trend	20-day trend
Yesterday more than +0.5% above trend	*67%	64%
Yesterday near trend *(+0.5% to -0.5%)*	67%	*57%
Yesterday more than -0.5% below trend	50%	58%

Looking ahead: odds of rise in future

	Next 3 days	Next 5 days
Today rose over +0.25%	57%	64%
Today small swing *(+0.25% to -0.25%)*	44%	56%
Today fell below -0.25%	*71%	*86%

* *Per cent based on fewer than 10 observations*

MAY 30 ODDS OF A PRICE RISE: 37%

Odds of different size price shift

	1935 to present
Large rise *(above +0.25%)*	32%
Small swing *(+0.25% to -0.25%)*	16%
Large fall (*below -0.25%)*	53%

Odds of rise based on yesterday

	1935 to present
Large rise yesterday *(above +0.25%)*	53%
Small swing yesterday *(+0.25% to -0.25%)*	31%
Large fall yesterday (*below -0.25%)*	20%

DIAGNOSTICS

Odds of price rise based on direction of 5-day and 20-day trend yesterday

	5-day trend	20-day trend
Yesterday rose more than +0.1%	43%	54%
Little change *(+0.1% to -0.1%)*	*43%	42%
Yesterday fell more than -0.1%	29%	15%

Odds of rise based upon distance between trend and yesterday s closing price

	5-day trend	20-day trend
Yesterday more than +0.5% above trend	*67%	58%
Yesterday near trend *(+0.5% to -0.5%)*	33%	30%
Yesterday more than -0.5% below trend	18%	25%

Looking ahead: odds of rise in future

	Next 3 days	Next 5 days
Today rose over +0.25%	58%	67%
Today small swing *(+0.25% to -0.25%)*	*67%	*83%
Today fell below -0.25%	40%	55%

MAY 31 ODDS OF A PRICE RISE: 46%

Odds of different size price shift

	1935 to present
Large rise *(above +0.25%)*	23%
Small swing *(+0.25% to -0.25%)*	46%
Large fall (*below -0.25%)*	31%

Odds of rise based on yesterday

	1935 to present
Large rise yesterday *(above +0.25%)*	54%
Small swing yesterday *(+0.25% to -0.25%)*	*50%
Large fall yesterday (*below -0.25%)*	39%

DIAGNOSTICS

Odds of price rise based on direction of 5-day and 20-day trend yesterday

	5-day trend	20-day trend
Yesterday rose more than +0.1%	69%	57%
Little change *(+0.1% to -0.1%)*	50%	50%
Yesterday fell more than -0.1%	15%	31%

Odds of rise based upon distance between trend and yesterday s closing price

	5-day trend	20-day trend
Yesterday more than +0.5% above trend	50%	67%
Yesterday near trend *(+0.5% to -0.5%)*	63%	50%
Yesterday more than -0.5% below trend	*11%	27%

Looking ahead: odds of rise in future

	Next 3 days	Next 5 days
Today rose over +0.25%	*56%	*67%
Today small swing *(+0.25% to -0.25%)*	61%	67%
Today fell below -0.25%	33%	58%

* *Per cent based on fewer than 10 observations*

JUNE

PROFIT ODDS SUMMARY FOR THE MONTH

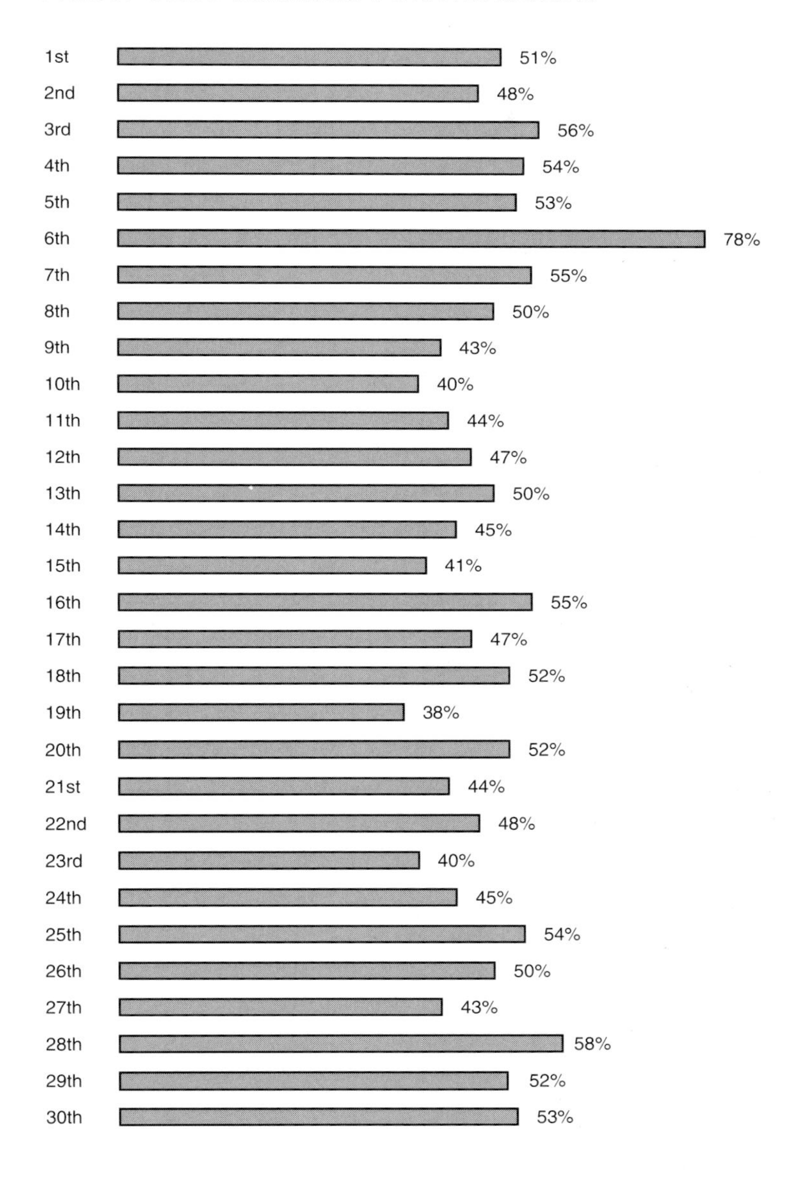

JUNE 1 ODDS OF A PRICE RISE: 51%

Odds of different size price shift

	1935 to present
Large rise *(above +0.25%)*	36%
Small swing *(+0.25% to -0.25%)*	20%
Large fall (*below -0.25%)*	44%

Odds of rise based on yesterday

	1935 to present
Large rise yesterday *(above +0.25%)*	71%
Small swing yesterday *(+0.25% to -0.25%)*	50%
Large fall yesterday (*below -0.25%)*	33%

DIAGNOSTICS

Odds of price rise based on direction of 5-day and 20-day trend yesterday

	5-day trend	20-day trend
Yesterday rose more than +0.1%	71%	67%
Little change *(+0.1% to -0.1%)*	*60%	46%
Yesterday fell more than -0.1%	26%	41%

Odds of rise based upon distance between trend and yesterday s closing price

	5-day trend	20-day trend
Yesterday more than +0.5% above trend	69%	67%
Yesterday near trend *(+0.5% to -0.5%)*	55%	*43%
Yesterday more than -0.5% below trend	25%	40%

Looking ahead: odds of rise in future

	Next 3 days	Next 5 days
Today rose over +0.25%	75%	69%
Today small swing *(+0.25% to -0.25%)*	*56%	*56%
Today fell below -0.25%	60%	60%

* *Per cent based on fewer than 10 observations*

JUNE 2 ODDS OF A PRICE RISE: 48%

Odds of different size price shift

	1935 to present
Large rise *(above +0.25%)*	27%
Small swing *(+0.25% to -0.25%)*	43%
Large fall (*below -0.25%)*	30%

Odds of rise based on yesterday

	1935 to present
Large rise yesterday *(above +0.25%)*	67%
Small swing yesterday *(+0.25% to -0.25%)*	*56%
Large fall yesterday (*below -0.25%)*	35%

DIAGNOSTICS

Odds of price rise based on direction of 5-day and 20-day trend yesterday

	5-day trend	20-day trend
Yesterday rose more than +0.1%	47%	36%
Little change *(+0.1% to -0.1%)*	*40%	63%
Yesterday fell more than -0.1%	50%	43%

Odds of rise based upon distance between trend and yesterday s closing price

	5-day trend	20-day trend
Yesterday more than +0.5% above trend	50%	44%
Yesterday near trend *(+0.5% to -0.5%)*	46%	*40%
Yesterday more than -0.5% below trend	47%	52%

Looking ahead: odds of rise in future

	Next 3 days	Next 5 days
Today rose over +0.25%	67%	83%
Today small swing *(+0.25% to -0.25%)*	74%	58%
Today fell below -0.25%	69%	54%

JUNE 3 ODDS OF A PRICE RISE: 56%

Odds of different size price shift

	1935 to present
Large rise *(above +0.25%)*	42%
Small swing *(+0.25% to -0.25%)*	29%
Large fall (*below -0.25%)*	29%

Odds of rise based on yesterday

	1935 to present
Large rise yesterday *(above +0.25%)*	62%
Small swing yesterday *(+0.25% to -0.25%)*	58%
Large fall yesterday (*below -0.25%)*	46%

DIAGNOSTICS

Odds of price rise based on direction of 5-day and 20-day trend yesterday

	5-day trend	20-day trend
Yesterday rose more than +0.1%	69%	60%
Little change *(+0.1% to -0.1%)*	*50%	55%
Yesterday fell more than -0.1%	48%	53%

Odds of rise based upon distance between trend and yesterday s closing price

	5-day trend	20-day trend
Yesterday more than +0.5% above trend	67%	69%
Yesterday near trend *(+0.5% to -0.5%)*	58%	62%
Yesterday more than -0.5% below trend	43%	42%

Looking ahead: odds of rise in future

	Next 3 days	Next 5 days
Today rose over +0.25%	74%	53%
Today small swing *(+0.25% to -0.25%)*	46%	62%
Today fell below -0.25%	46%	69%

* *Per cent based on fewer than 10 observations*

JUNE 4 ODDS OF A PRICE RISE: 54%

Odds of different size price shift

	1935 to present
Large rise *(above +0.25%)*	33%
Small swing *(+0.25% to -0.25%)*	33%
Large fall (*below -0.25%)*	35%

Odds of rise based on yesterday

	1935 to present
Large rise yesterday *(above +0.25%)*	65%
Small swing yesterday *(+0.25% to -0.25%)*	60%
Large fall yesterday (*below -0.25%)*	27%

DIAGNOSTICS

Odds of price rise based on direction of 5-day and 20-day trend yesterday

	5-day trend	20-day trend
Yesterday rose more than +0.1%	62%	64%
Little change *(+0.1% to -0.1%)*	*38%	50%
Yesterday fell more than -0.1%	53%	53%

Odds of rise based upon distance between trend and yesterday s closing price

	5-day trend	20-day trend
Yesterday more than +0.5% above trend	61%	64%
Yesterday near trend *(+0.5% to -0.5%)*	44%	45%
Yesterday more than -0.5% below trend	60%	52%

Looking ahead: odds of rise in future

	Next 3 days	Next 5 days
Today rose over +0.25%	60%	53%
Today small swing *(+0.25% to -0.25%)*	67%	47%
Today fell below -0.25%	63%	63%

JUNE 5 ODDS OF A PRICE RISE: 53%

Odds of different size price shift

	1935 to present
Large rise *(above +0.25%)*	36%
Small swing *(+0.25% to -0.25%)*	36%
Large fall (*below -0.25%)*	29%

Odds of rise based on yesterday

	1935 to present
Large rise yesterday *(above +0.25%)*	57%
Small swing yesterday *(+0.25% to -0.25%)*	50%
Large fall yesterday (*below -0.25%)*	53%

DIAGNOSTICS

Odds of price rise based on direction of 5-day and 20-day trend yesterday

	5-day trend	20-day trend
Yesterday rose more than +0.1%	52%	62%
Little change *(+0.1% to -0.1%)*	*38%	43%
Yesterday fell more than -0.1%	67%	56%

Odds of rise based upon distance between trend and yesterday s closing price

	5-day trend	20-day trend
Yesterday more than +0.5% above trend	56%	67%
Yesterday near trend *(+0.5% to -0.5%)*	42%	33%
Yesterday more than -0.5% below trend	70%	56%

Looking ahead: odds of rise in future

	Next 3 days	Next 5 days
Today rose over +0.25%	63%	50%
Today small swing *(+0.25% to -0.25%)*	56%	50%
Today fell below -0.25%	38%	31%

* *Per cent based on fewer than 10 observations*

JUNE 6 ODDS OF A PRICE RISE: 78%

Odds of different size price shift

	1935 to present
Large rise *(above +0.25%)*	48%
Small swing *(+0.25% to -0.25%)*	35%
Large fall (*below -0.25%)*	18%

Odds of rise based on yesterday

	1935 to present
Large rise yesterday *(above +0.25%)*	79%
Small swing yesterday *(+0.25% to -0.25%)*	81%
Large fall yesterday (*below -0.25%)*	70%

DIAGNOSTICS

Odds of price rise based on direction of 5-day and 20-day trend yesterday

	5-day trend	20-day trend
Yesterday rose more than +0.1%	80%	75%
Little change *(+0.1% to -0.1%)*	*100%	92%
Yesterday fell more than -0.1%	62%	67%

Odds of rise based upon distance between trend and yesterday s closing price

	5-day trend	20-day trend
Yesterday more than +0.5% above trend	78%	82%
Yesterday near trend *(+0.5% to -0.5%)*	69%	*83%
Yesterday more than -0.5% below trend	*89%	71%

Looking ahead: odds of rise in future

	Next 3 days	Next 5 days
Today rose over +0.25%	68%	79%
Today small swing *(+0.25% to -0.25%)*	43%	29%
Today fell below -0.25%	*43%	*43%

JUNE 7 ODDS OF A PRICE RISE: 55%

Odds of different size price shift

	1935 to present
Large rise *(above +0.25%)*	45%
Small swing *(+0.25% to -0.25%)*	29%
Large fall *(below -0.25%)*	26%

Odds of rise based on yesterday

	1935 to present
Large rise yesterday *(above +0.25%)*	69%
Small swing yesterday *(+0.25% to -0.25%)*	40%
Large fall yesterday *(below -0.25%)*	55%

DIAGNOSTICS

Odds of price rise based on direction of 5-day and 20-day trend yesterday

	5-day trend	20-day trend
Yesterday rose more than +0.1%	35%	50%
Little change *(+0.1% to -0.1%)*	*57%	57%
Yesterday fell more than -0.1%	80%	56%

Odds of rise based upon distance between trend and yesterday s closing price

	5-day trend	20-day trend
Yesterday more than +0.5% above trend	44%	56%
Yesterday near trend *(+0.5% to -0.5%)*	60%	*22%
Yesterday more than -0.5% below trend	*67%	71%

Looking ahead: odds of rise in future

	Next 3 days	Next 5 days
Today rose over +0.25%	63%	74%
Today small swing *(+0.25% to -0.25%)*	33%	50%
Today fell below -0.25%	45%	45%

* *Per cent based on fewer than 10 observations*

JUNE 8 ODDS OF A PRICE RISE: 50%

Odds of different size price shift

	1935 to present
Large rise *(above +0.25%)*	39%
Small swing *(+0.25% to -0.25%)*	30%
Large fall (*below -0.25%)*	30%

Odds of rise based on yesterday

	1935 to present
Large rise yesterday *(above +0.25%)*	55%
Small swing yesterday *(+0.25% to -0.25%)*	64%
Large fall yesterday (*below -0.25%)*	25%

DIAGNOSTICS

Odds of price rise based on direction of 5-day and 20-day trend yesterday

	5-day trend	20-day trend
Yesterday rose more than +0.1%	57%	60%
Little change *(+0.1% to -0.1%)*	42%	50%
Yesterday fell more than -0.1%	46%	41%

Odds of rise based upon distance between trend and yesterday s closing price

	5-day trend	20-day trend
Yesterday more than +0.5% above trend	58%	68%
Yesterday near trend *(+0.5% to -0.5%)*	48%	*13%
Yesterday more than -0.5% below trend	*33%	47%

Looking ahead: odds of rise in future

	Next 3 days	Next 5 days
Today rose over +0.25%	56%	50%
Today small swing *(+0.25% to -0.25%)*	57%	50%
Today fell below -0.25%	36%	29%

JUNE 9 ODDS OF A PRICE RISE: 43%

Odds of different size price shift

	1935 to present
Large rise *(above +0.25%)*	36%
Small swing *(+0.25% to -0.25%)*	30%
Large fall *(below -0.25%)*	34%

Odds of rise based on yesterday

	1935 to present
Large rise yesterday *(above +0.25%)*	62%
Small swing yesterday *(+0.25% to -0.25%)*	40%
Large fall yesterday *(below -0.25%)*	9%

DIAGNOSTICS

Odds of price rise based on direction of 5-day and 20-day trend yesterday

	5-day trend	20-day trend
Yesterday rose more than +0.1%	39%	57%
Little change *(+0.1% to -0.1%)*	54%	41%
Yesterday fell more than -0.1%	36%	31%

Odds of rise based upon distance between trend and yesterday s closing price

	5-day trend	20-day trend
Yesterday more than +0.5% above trend	50%	55%
Yesterday near trend *(+0.5% to -0.5%)*	47%	*50%
Yesterday more than -0.5% below trend	20%	26%

Looking ahead: odds of rise in future

	Next 3 days	Next 5 days
Today rose over +0.25%	82%	82%
Today small swing *(+0.25% to -0.25%)*	21%	14%
Today fell below -0.25%	38%	31%

* *Per cent based on fewer than 10 observations*

JUNE 10 ODDS OF A PRICE RISE: 40%

Odds of different size price shift

	1935 to present
Large rise *(above +0.25%)*	29%
Small swing *(+0.25% to -0.25%)*	31%
Large fall *(below -0.25%)*	40%

Odds of rise based on yesterday

	1935 to present
Large rise yesterday *(above +0.25%)*	59%
Small swing yesterda y*(+0.25% to -0.25%)*	17%
Large fall yesterday *(below -0.25%)*	38%

DIAGNOSTICS

Odds of price rise based on direction of 5-day and 20-day trend yesterday

	5-day trend	20-day trend
Yesterday rose more than +0.1%	38%	50%
Little change *(+0.1% to -0.1%)*	47%	37%
Yesterday fell more than -0.1%	*33%	38%

Odds of rise based upon distance between trend and yesterday s closing price

	5-day trend	20-day trend
Yesterday more than +0.5% above trend	44%	37%
Yesterday near trend *(+0.5% to -0.5%)*	54%	*43%
Yesterday more than -0.5% below trend	21%	42%

Looking ahead: odds of rise in future

	Next 3 days	Next 5 days
Today rose over +0.25%	77%	69%
Today small swing *(+0.25% to -0.25%)*	43%	43%
Today fell below -0.25%	33%	61%

JUNE 11 ODDS OF A PRICE RISE: 44%

Odds of different size price shift

	1935 to present
Large rise *(above +0.25%)*	38%
Small swing *(+0.25% to -0.25%)*	24%
Large fall (*below -0.25%)*	38%

Odds of rise based on yesterday

	1935 to present
Large rise yesterday *(above +0.25%)*	64%
Small swing yesterday *(+0.25% to -0.25%)*	54%
Large fall yesterday (*below -0.25%)*	29%

DIAGNOSTICS

Odds of price rise based on direction of 5-day and 20-day trend yesterday

	5-day trend	20-day trend
Yesterday rose more than +0.1%	44%	*56%
Little change *(+0.1% to -0.1%)*	62%	43%
Yesterday fell more than -0.1%	29%	40%

Odds of rise based upon distance between trend and yesterday s closing price

	5-day trend	20-day trend
Yesterday more than +0.5% above trend	50%	53%
Yesterday near trend *(+0.5% to -0.5%)*	53%	*44%
Yesterday more than -0.5% below trend	29%	38%

Looking ahead: odds of rise in future

	Next 3 days	Next 5 days
Today rose over +0.25%	53%	59%
Today small swing *(+0.25% to -0.25%)*	73%	64%
Today fell below -0.25%	53%	41%

* *Per cent based on fewer than 10 observations*

JUNE 12 ODDS OF A PRICE RISE: 47%

Odds of different size price shift

	1935 to present
Large rise *(above +0.25%)*	27%
Small swing *(+0.25% to -0.25%)*	36%
Large fall (*below -0.25%)*	38%

Odds of rise based on yesterday

	1935 to present
Large rise yesterday *(above +0.25%)*	47%
Small swing yesterday *(+0.25% to -0.25%)*	60%
Large fall yesterday (*below -0.25%)*	39%

DIAGNOSTICS

Odds of price rise based on direction of 5-day and 20-day trend yesterday

	5-day trend	20-day trend
Yesterday rose more than +0.1%	74%	73%
Little change *(+0.1% to -0.1%)*	20%	38%
Yesterday fell more than -0.1%	31%	38%

Odds of rise based upon distance between trend and yesterday s closing price

	5-day trend	20-day trend
Yesterday more than +0.5% above trend	67%	72%
Yesterday near trend *(+0.5% to -0.5%)*	41%	*22%
Yesterday more than -0.5% below trend	38%	33%

Looking ahead: odds of rise in future

	Next 3 days	Next 5 days
Today rose over +0.25%	58%	33%
Today small swing *(+0.25% to -0.25%)*	75%	81%
Today fell below -0.25%	29%	24%

JUNE 13 ODDS OF A PRICE RISE: 50%

Odds of different size price shift

	1935 to present
Large rise *(above +0.25%)*	27%
Small swing *(+0.25% to -0.25%)*	39%
Large fall (*below -0.25%)*	34%

Odds of rise based on yesterday

	1935 to present
Large rise yesterday *(above +0.25%)*	50%
Small swing yesterday *(+0.25% to -0.25%)*	73%
Large fall yesterday (*below -0.25%)*	23%

DIAGNOSTICS

Odds of price rise based on direction of 5-day and 20-day trend yesterday

	5-day trend	20-day trend
Yesterday rose more than +0.1%	74%	67%
Little change *(+0.1% to -0.1%)*	30%	56%
Yesterday fell more than -0.1%	33%	29%

Odds of rise based upon distance between trend and yesterday s closing price

	5-day trend	20-day trend
Yesterday more than +0.5% above trend	63%	69%
Yesterday near trend *(+0.5% to -0.5%)*	47%	*56%
Yesterday more than -0.5% below trend	38%	32%

Looking ahead: odds of rise in future

	Next 3 days	Next 5 days
Today rose over +0.25%	42%	42%
Today small swing *(+0.25% to -0.25%)*	53%	53%
Today fell below -0.25%	40%	40%

* *Per cent based on fewer than 10 observations*

JUNE 14 ODDS OF A PRICE RISE: 45%

Odds of different size price shift

	1935 to present
Large rise *(above +0.25%)*	36%
Small swing *(+0.25% to -0.25%)*	32%
Large fall (*below -0.25%)*	32%

Odds of rise based on yesterday

	1935 to present
Large rise yesterday *(above +0.25%)*	50%
Small swing yesterday *(+0.25% to -0.25%)*	41%
Large fall yesterday (*below -0.25%)*	47%

DIAGNOSTICS

Odds of price rise based on direction of 5-day and 20-day trend yesterday

	5-day trend	20-day trend
Yesterday rose more than +0.1%	56%	60%
Little change *(+0.1% to -0.1%)*	50%	47%
Yesterday fell more than -0.1%	31%	37%

Odds of rise based upon distance between trend and yesterday s closing price

	5-day trend	20-day trend
Yesterday more than +0.5% above trend	55%	59%
Yesterday near trend *(+0.5% to -0.5%)*	42%	*25%
Yesterday more than -0.5% below trend	43%	39%

Looking ahead: odds of rise in future

	Next 3 days	Next 5 days
Today rose over +0.25%	38%	56%
Today small swing *(+0.25% to -0.25%)*	50%	36%
Today fell below -0.25%	57%	36%

JUNE 15 ODDS OF A PRICE RISE: 41%

Odds of different size price shift

	1935 to present
Large rise *(above +0.25%)*	26%
Small swing *(+0.25% to -0.25%)*	30%
Large fall (*below -0.25%)*	43%

Odds of rise based on yesterday

	1935 to present
Large rise yesterday *(above +0.25%)*	50%
Small swing yesterday *(+0.25% to -0.25%)*	44%
Large fall yesterday (*below -0.25%)*	31%

DIAGNOSTICS

Odds of price rise based on direction of 5-day and 20-day trend yesterday

	5-day trend	20-day trend
Yesterday rose more than +0.1%	53%	33%
Little change *(+0.1% to -0.1%)*	*33%	53%
Yesterday fell more than -0.1%	33%	37%

Odds of rise based upon distance between trend and yesterday s closing price

	5-day trend	20-day trend
Yesterday more than +0.5% above trend	57%	47%
Yesterday near trend *(+0.5% to -0.5%)*	38%	40%
Yesterday more than -0.5% below trend	31%	37%

Looking ahead: odds of rise in future

	Next 3 days	Next 5 days
Today rose over +0.25%	75%	83%
Today small swing *(+0.25% to -0.25%)*	50%	57%
Today fell below -0.25%	40%	30%

* *Per cent based on fewer than 10 observations*

JUNE 16 ODDS OF A PRICE RISE: 55%

Odds of different size price shift

	1935 to present
Large rise *(above +0.25%)*	36%
Small swing *(+0.25% to -0.25%)*	36%
Large fall (*below -0.25%)*	28%

Odds of rise based on yesterday

	1935 to present
Large rise yesterday *(above +0.25%)*	75%
Small swing yesterday *(+0.25% to -0.25%)*	40%
Large fall yesterday (*below -0.25%)*	50%

DIAGNOSTICS

Odds of price rise based on direction of 5-day and 20-day trend yesterday

	5-day trend	20-day trend
Yesterday rose more than +0.1%	63%	54%
Little change *(+0.1% to -0.1%)*	50%	61%
Yesterday fell more than -0.1%	53%	50%

Odds of rise based upon distance between trend and yesterday s closing price

	5-day trend	20-day trend
Yesterday more than +0.5% above trend	62%	47%
Yesterday near trend *(+0.5% to -0.5%)*	55%	*63%
Yesterday more than -0.5% below trend	50%	60%

Looking ahead: odds of rise in future

	Next 3 days	Next 5 days
Today rose over +0.25%	65%	59%
Today small swing *(+0.25% to -0.25%)*	65%	65%
Today fell below -0.25%	31%	38%

JUNE 17 ODDS OF A PRICE RISE: 47%

Odds of different size price shift

	1935 to present
Large rise *(above +0.25%)*	34%
Small swing *(+0.25% to -0.25%)*	32%
Large fall (*below -0.25%)*	34%

Odds of rise based on yesterday

	1935 to present
Large rise yesterday *(above +0.25%)*	55%
Small swing yesterday *(+0.25% to -0.25%)*	60%
Large fall yesterday (*below -0.25%)*	17%

DIAGNOSTICS

Odds of price rise based on direction of 5-day and 20-day trend yesterday

	5-day trend	20-day trend
Yesterday rose more than +0.1%	60%	55%
Little change *(+0.1% to -0.1%)*	*17%	55%
Yesterday fell more than -0.1%	43%	31%

Odds of rise based upon distance between trend and yesterday s closing price

	5-day trend	20-day trend
Yesterday more than +0.5% above trend	62%	56%
Yesterday near trend *(+0.5% to -0.5%)*	50%	*44%
Yesterday more than -0.5% below trend	20%	40%

Looking ahead: odds of rise in future

	Next 3 days	Next 5 days
Today rose over +0.25%	56%	56%
Today small swing *(+0.25% to -0.25%)*	47%	40%
Today fell below -0.25%	31%	38%

* *Per cent based on fewer than 10 observations*

JUNE 18 ODDS OF A PRICE RISE: 52%

Odds of different size price shift

	1935 to present
Large rise *(above +0.25%)*	35%
Small swing *(+0.25% to -0.25%)*	30%
Large fall (*below -0.25%)*	35%

Odds of rise based on yesterday

	1935 to present
Large rise yesterday *(above +0.25%)*	79%
Small swing yesterday *(+0.25% to -0.25%)*	64%
Large fall yesterday (*below -0.25%)*	22%

DIAGNOSTICS

Odds of price rise based on direction of 5-day and 20-day trend yesterday

	5-day trend	20-day trend
Yesterday rose more than +0.1%	65%	50%
Little change *(+0.1% to -0.1%)*	64%	60%
Yesterday fell more than -0.1%	33%	44%

Odds of rise based upon distance between trend and yesterday s closing price

	5-day trend	20-day trend
Yesterday more than +0.5% above trend	75%	69%
Yesterday near trend *(+0.5% to -0.5%)*	55%	53%
Yesterday more than -0.5% below trend	25%	39%

Looking ahead: odds of rise in future

	Next 3 days	Next 5 days
Today rose over +0.25%	56%	69%
Today small swing *(+0.25% to -0.25%)*	50%	29%
Today fell below -0.25%	13%	31%

JUNE 19 ODDS OF A PRICE RISE: 38%

Odds of different size price shift

	1935 to present
Large rise *(above +0.25%)*	38%
Small swing *(+0.25% to -0.25%)*	20%
Large fall (*below -0.25%)*	42%

Odds of rise based on yesterday

	1935 to present
Large rise yesterday *(above +0.25%)*	58%
Small swing yesterday *(+0.25% to -0.25%)*	53%
Large fall yesterday (*below -0.25%)*	11%

DIAGNOSTICS

Odds of price rise based on direction of 5-day and 20-day trend yesterday

	5-day trend	20-day trend
Yesterday rose more than +0.1%	24%	31%
Little change *(+0.1% to -0.1%)*	*88%	44%
Yesterday fell more than -0.1%	30%	36%

Odds of rise based upon distance between trend and yesterday s closing price

	5-day trend	20-day trend
Yesterday more than +0.5% above trend	42%	47%
Yesterday near trend *(+0.5% to -0.5%)*	41%	31%
Yesterday more than -0.5% below trend	31%	33%

Looking ahead: odds of rise in future

	Next 3 days	Next 5 days
Today rose over +0.25%	47%	41%
Today small swing *(+0.25% to -0.25%)*	*44%	*44%
Today fell below -0.25%	47%	63%

* *Per cent based on fewer than 10 observations*

JUNE 20 ODDS OF A PRICE RISE: 52%

Odds of different size price shift

	1935 to present
Large rise *(above +0.25%)*	32%
Small swing *(+0.25% to -0.25%)*	36%
Large fall (*below -0.25%)*	32%

Odds of rise based on yesterday

	1935 to present
Large rise yesterday *(above +0.25%)*	73%
Small swing yesterday *(+0.25% to -0.25%)*	36%
Large fall yesterday (*below -0.25%)*	44%

DIAGNOSTICS

Odds of price rise based on direction of 5-day and 20-day trend yesterday

	5-day trend	20-day trend
Yesterday rose more than +0.1%	79%	60%
Little change *(+0.1% to -0.1%)*	46%	45%
Yesterday fell more than -0.1%	35%	50%

Odds of rise based upon distance between trend and yesterday s closing price

	5-day trend	20-day trend
Yesterday more than +0.5% above trend	83%	68%
Yesterday near trend *(+0.5% to -0.5%)*	38%	*33%
Yesterday more than -0.5% below trend	44%	42%

Looking ahead: odds of rise in future

	Next 3 days	Next 5 days
Today rose over +0.25%	43%	43%
Today small swing *(+0.25% to -0.25%)*	63%	50%
Today fell below -0.25%	29%	21%

JUNE 21 ODDS OF A PRICE RISE: 44%

Odds of different size price shift

	1935 to present
Large rise *(above +0.25%)*	29%
Small swing *(+0.25% to -0.25%)*	31%
Large fall *(below -0.25%)*	40%

Odds of rise based on yesterday

	1935 to present
Large rise yesterday *(above +0.25%)*	62%
Small swing yesterday *(+0.25% to -0.25%)*	41%
Large fall yesterday *(below -0.25%)*	33%

DIAGNOSTICS

Odds of price rise based on direction of 5-day and 20-day trend yesterday

	5-day trend	20-day trend
Yesterday rose more than +0.1%	67%	67%
Little change *(+0.1% to -0.1%)*	30%	50%
Yesterday fell more than -0.1%	35%	24%

Odds of rise based upon distance between trend and yesterday s closing price

	5-day trend	20-day trend
Yesterday more than +0.5% above trend	58%	74%
Yesterday near trend *(+0.5% to -0.5%)*	37%	*0%
Yesterday more than -0.5% below trend	43%	26%

Looking ahead: odds of rise in future

	Next 3 days	Next 5 days
Today rose over +0.25%	54%	38%
Today small swing *(+0.25% to -0.25%)*	29%	43%
Today fell below -0.25%	39%	33%

* *Per cent based on fewer than 10 observations*

JUNE 22 ODDS OF A PRICE RISE: 48%

Odds of different size price shift

	1935 to present
Large rise *(above +0.25%)*	28%
Small swing *(+0.25% to -0.25%)*	35%
Large fall (*below -0.25%)*	37%

Odds of rise based on yesterday

	1935 to present
Large rise yesterday *(above +0.25%)*	59%
Small swing yesterday *(+0.25% to -0.25%)*	64%
Large fall yesterday (*below -0.25%)*	28%

DIAGNOSTICS

Odds of price rise based on direction of 5-day and 20-day trend yesterday

	5-day trend	20-day trend
Yesterday rose more than +0.1%	53%	60%
Little change *(+0.1% to -0.1%)*	42%	53%
Yesterday fell more than -0.1%	47%	31%

Odds of rise based upon distance between trend and yesterday s closing price

	5-day trend	20-day trend
Yesterday more than +0.5% above trend	58%	58%
Yesterday near trend *(+0.5% to -0.5%)*	45%	*50%
Yesterday more than -0.5% below trend	43%	38%

Looking ahead: odds of rise in future

	Next 3 days	Next 5 days
Today rose over +0.25%	46%	31%
Today small swing *(+0.25% to -0.25%)*	44%	38%
Today fell below -0.25%	71%	47%

JUNE 23 ODDS OF A PRICE RISE: 40%

Odds of different size price shift

	1935 to present
Large rise *(above +0.25%)*	28%
Small swing *(+0.25% to -0.25%)*	36%
Large fall (*below -0.25%)*	36%

Odds of rise based on yesterday

	1935 to present
Large rise yesterday *(above +0.25%)*	31%
Small swing yesterday *(+0.25% to -0.25%)*	40%
Large fall yesterday (*below -0.25%)*	50%

DIAGNOSTICS

Odds of price rise based on direction of 5-day and 20-day trend yesterday

	5-day trend	20-day trend
Yesterday rose more than +0.1%	39%	44%
Little change *(+0.1% to -0.1%)*	31%	29%
Yesterday fell more than -0.1%	50%	47%

Odds of rise based upon distance between trend and yesterday s closing price

	5-day trend	20-day trend
Yesterday more than +0.5% above trend	43%	41%
Yesterday near trend *(+0.5% to -0.5%)*	28%	*20%
Yesterday more than -0.5% below trend	53%	45%

Looking ahead: odds of rise in future

	Next 3 days	Next 5 days
Today rose over +0.25%	38%	62%
Today small swing *(+0.25% to -0.25%)*	65%	65%
Today fell below -0.25%	29%	29%

* *Per cent based on fewer than 10 observations*

JUNE 24 ODDS OF A PRICE RISE: 45%

Odds of different size price shift

	1935 to present
Large rise *(above +0.25%)*	30%
Small swing *(+0.25% to -0.25%)*	28%
Large fall (*below -0.25%)*	43%

Odds of rise based on yesterday

	1935 to present
Large rise yesterday *(above +0.25%)*	67%
Small swing yesterday *(+0.25% to -0.25%)*	44%
Large fall yesterday (*below -0.25%)*	29%

DIAGNOSTICS

Odds of price rise based on direction of 5-day and 20-day trend yesterday

	5-day trend	20-day trend
Yesterday rose more than +0.1%	40%	36%
Little change *(+0.1% to -0.1%)*	*67%	53%
Yesterday fell more than -0.1%	39%	41%

Odds of rise based upon distance between trend and yesterday s closing price

	5-day trend	20-day trend
Yesterday more than +0.5% above trend	*33%	42%
Yesterday near trend *(+0.5% to -0.5%)*	52%	*63%
Yesterday more than -0.5% below trend	38%	40%

Looking ahead: odds of rise in future

	Next 3 days	Next 5 days
Today rose over +0.25%	71%	79%
Today small swing *(+0.25% to -0.25%)*	54%	69%
Today fell below -0.25%	40%	40%

JUNE 25 ODDS OF A PRICE RISE: 54%

Odds of different size price shift

	1935 to present
Large rise *(above +0.25%)*	33%
Small swing *(+0.25% to -0.25%)*	41%
Large fall (*below -0.25%)*	26%

Odds of rise based on yesterday

	1935 to present
Large rise yesterday *(above +0.25%)*	75%
Small swing yesterday *(+0.25% to -0.25%)*	53%
Large fall yesterday (*below -0.25%)*	42%

DIAGNOSTICS

Odds of price rise based on direction of 5-day and 20-day trend yesterday

	5-day trend	20-day trend
Yesterday rose more than +0.1%	67%	67%
Little change *(+0.1% to -0.1%)*	60%	47%
Yesterday fell more than -0.1%	46%	53%

Odds of rise based upon distance between trend and yesterday s closing price

	5-day trend	20-day trend
Yesterday more than +0.5% above trend	*40%	64%
Yesterday near trend *(+0.5% to -0.5%)*	70%	*67%
Yesterday more than -0.5% below trend	39%	43%

Looking ahead: odds of rise in future

	Next 3 days	Next 5 days
Today rose over +0.25%	53%	67%
Today small swing *(+0.25% to -0.25%)*	53%	74%
Today fell below -0.25%	42%	50%

* *Per cent based on fewer than 10 observations*

JUNE 26 ODDS OF A PRICE RISE: 50%

Odds of different size price shift

	1935 to present
Large rise *(above +0.25%)*	34%
Small swing *(+0.25% to -0.25%)*	25%
Large fall (*below -0.25%)*	41%

Odds of rise based on yesterday

	1935 to present
Large rise yesterday *(above +0.25%)*	63%
Small swing yesterday *(+0.25% to -0.25%)*	41%
Large fall yesterday (*below -0.25%)*	45%

DIAGNOSTICS

Odds of price rise based on direction of 5-day and 20-day trend yesterday

	5-day trend	20-day trend
Yesterday rose more than +0.1%	50%	75%
Little change *(+0.1% to -0.1%)*	60%	50%
Yesterday fell more than -0.1%	36%	29%

Odds of rise based upon distance between trend and yesterday s closing price

	5-day trend	20-day trend
Yesterday more than +0.5% above trend	*71%	71%
Yesterday near trend *(+0.5% to -0.5%)*	50%	50%
Yesterday more than -0.5% below trend	40%	33%

Looking ahead: odds of rise in future

	Next 3 days	Next 5 days
Today rose over +0.25%	80%	87%
Today small swing *(+0.25% to -0.25%)*	55%	82%
Today fell below -0.25%	56%	61%

JUNE 27 ODDS OF A PRICE RISE: 43%

Odds of different size price shift

	1935 to present
Large rise *(above +0.25%)*	30%
Small swing *(+0.25% to -0.25%)*	30%
Large fall *(below -0.25%)*	41%

Odds of rise based on yesterday

	1935 to present
Large rise yesterday *(above +0.25%)*	69%
Small swing yesterday *(+0.25% to -0.25%)*	*13%
Large fall yesterday *(below -0.25%)*	35%

DIAGNOSTICS

Odds of price rise based on direction of 5-day and 20-day trend yesterday

	5-day trend	20-day trend
Yesterday rose more than +0.1%	47%	46%
Little change *(+0.1% to -0.1%)*	*25%	42%
Yesterday fell more than -0.1%	47%	42%

Odds of rise based upon distance between trend and yesterday s closing price

	5-day trend	20-day trend
Yesterday more than +0.5% above trend	50%	47%
Yesterday near trend *(+0.5% to -0.5%)*	41%	*29%
Yesterday more than -0.5% below trend	41%	45%

Looking ahead: odds of rise in future

	Next 3 days	Next 5 days
Today rose over +0.25%	77%	77%
Today small swing *(+0.25% to -0.25%)*	62%	77%
Today fell below -0.25%	50%	56%

* *Per cent based on fewer than 10 observations*

JUNE 28 ODDS OF A PRICE RISE: 58%

Odds of different size price shift

	1935 to present
Large rise *(above +0.25%)*	38%
Small swing *(+0.25% to -0.25%)*	22%
Large fall (*below -0.25%)*	40%

Odds of rise based on yesterday

	1935 to present
Large rise yesterday *(above +0.25%)*	77%
Small swing yesterday *(+0.25% to -0.25%)*	53%
Large fall yesterday (*below -0.25%)*	47%

DIAGNOSTICS

Odds of price rise based on direction of 5-day and 20-day trend yesterday

	5-day trend	20-day trend
Yesterday rose more than +0.1%	*56%	*44%
Little change *(+0.1% to -0.1%)*	50%	61%
Yesterday fell more than -0.1%	64%	61%

Odds of rise based upon distance between trend and yesterday s closing price

	5-day trend	20-day trend
Yesterday more than +0.5% above trend	*88%	58%
Yesterday near trend *(+0.5% to -0.5%)*	45%	60%
Yesterday more than -0.5% below trend	59%	57%

Looking ahead: odds of rise in future

	Next 3 days	Next 5 days
Today rose over +0.25%	71%	59%
Today small swing *(+0.25% to -0.25%)*	60%	50%
Today fell below -0.25%	72%	56%

JUNE 29 ODDS OF A PRICE RISE: 52%

Odds of different size price shift

	1935 to present
Large rise *(above +0.25%)*	35%
Small swing *(+0.25% to -0.25%)*	30%
Large fall (*below -0.25%)*	35%

Odds of rise based on yesterday

	1935 to present
Large rise yesterday *(above +0.25%)*	67%
Small swing yesterday *(+0.25% to -0.25%)*	54%
Large fall yesterday (*below -0.25%)*	39%

DIAGNOSTICS

Odds of price rise based on direction of 5-day and 20-day trend yesterday

	5-day trend	20-day trend
Yesterday rose more than +0.1%	55%	38%
Little change *(+0.1% to -0.1%)*	53%	56%
Yesterday fell more than -0.1%	50%	60%

Odds of rise based upon distance between trend and yesterday s closing price

	5-day trend	20-day trend
Yesterday more than +0.5% above trend	55%	44%
Yesterday near trend *(+0.5% to -0.5%)*	57%	*50%
Yesterday more than -0.5% below trend	43%	59%

Looking ahead: odds of rise in future

	Next 3 days	Next 5 days
Today rose over +0.25%	56%	63%
Today small swing *(+0.25% to -0.25%)*	64%	71%
Today fell below -0.25%	44%	50%

* *Per cent based on fewer than 10 observations*

JUNE 30 ODDS OF A PRICE RISE: 53%

Odds of different size price shift

	1935 to present
Large rise *(above +0.25%)*	30%
Small swing *(+0.25% to -0.25%)*	40%
Large fall *(below -0.25%)*	30%

Odds of rise based on yesterday

	1935 to present
Large rise yesterday *(above +0.25%)*	54%
Small swing yesterday *(+0.25% to -0.25%)*	67%
Large fall yesterday *(below -0.25%)*	42%

DIAGNOSTICS

Odds of price rise based on direction of 5-day and 20-day trend yesterday

	5-day trend	20-day trend
Yesterday rose more than +0.1%	53%	53%
Little change *(+0.1% to -0.1%)*	67%	58%
Yesterday fell more than -0.1%	45%	46%

Odds of rise based upon distance between trend and yesterday s closing price

	5-day trend	20-day trend
Yesterday more than +0.5% above trend	50%	65%
Yesterday near trend *(+0.5% to -0.5%)*	57%	*40%
Yesterday more than -0.5% below trend	50%	42%

Looking ahead: odds of rise in future

	Next 3 days	Next 5 days
Today rose over +0.25%	64%	57%
Today small swing *(+0.25% to -0.25%)*	63%	68%
Today fell below -0.25%	57%	71%

JULY

PROFIT ODDS SUMMARY FOR THE MONTH

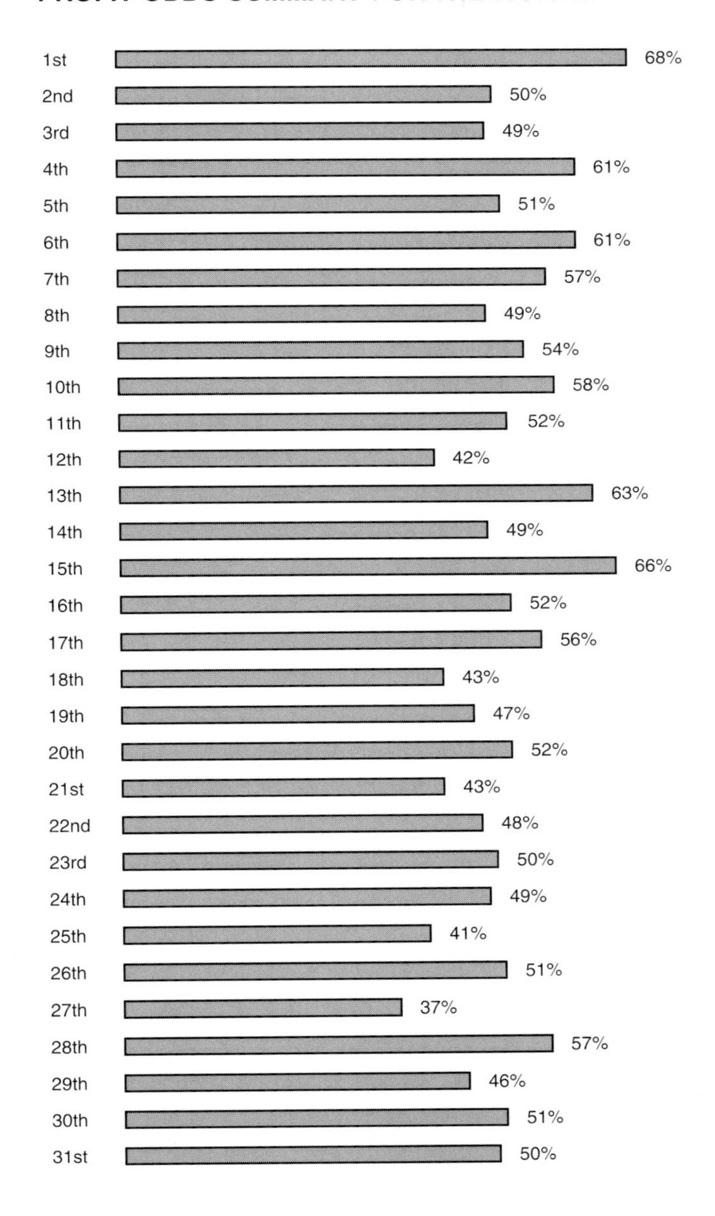

JULY 1 ODDS OF A PRICE RISE: 68%

Odds of different size price shift

	1935 to present
Large rise *(above +0.25%)*	45%
Small swing *(+0.25% to -0.25%)*	36%
Large fall *(below -0.25%)*	19%

Odds of rise based on yesterday

	1935 to present
Large rise yesterday *(above +0.25%)*	72%
Small swing yesterday *(+0.25% to -0.25%)*	59%
Large fall yesterday *(below -0.25%)*	75%

DIAGNOSTICS

Odds of price rise based on direction of 5-day and 20-day trend yesterday

	5-day trend	20-day trend
Yesterday rose more than +0.1%	76%	65%
Little change *(+0.1% to -0.1%)*	54%	71%
Yesterday fell more than -0.1%	71%	69%

Odds of rise based upon distance between trend and yesterday s closing price

	5-day trend	20-day trend
Yesterday more than +0.5% above trend	80%	63%
Yesterday near trend *(+0.5% to -0.5%)*	64%	*100%
Yesterday more than -0.5% below trend	60%	70%

Looking ahead: odds of rise in future

	Next 3 days	Next 5 days
Today rose over +0.25%	81%	81%
Today small swing *(+0.25% to -0.25%)*	59%	65%
Today fell below -0.25%	*33%	*44%

* *Per cent based on fewer than 10 observations*

JULY 2 ODDS OF A PRICE RISE: 50%

Odds of different size price shift

	1935 to present
Large rise *(above +0.25%)*	37%
Small swing *(+0.25% to -0.25%)*	41%
Large fall (*below -0.25%)*	22%

Odds of rise based on yesterday

	1935 to present
Large rise yesterday *(above +0.25%)*	68%
Small swing yesterday *(+0.25% to -0.25%)*	40%
Large fall yesterday (*below -0.25%)*	*22%

DIAGNOSTICS

Odds of price rise based on direction of 5-day and 20-day trend yesterday

	5-day trend	20-day trend
Yesterday rose more than +0.1%	62%	75%
Little change *(+0.1% to -0.1%)*	58%	40%
Yesterday fell more than -0.1%	23%	43%

Odds of rise based upon distance between trend and yesterday s closing price

	5-day trend	20-day trend
Yesterday more than +0.5% above trend	74%	52%
Yesterday near trend *(+0.5% to -0.5%)*	42%	*57%
Yesterday more than -0.5% below trend	*13%	44%

Looking ahead: odds of rise in future

	Next 3 days	Next 5 days
Today rose over +0.25%	65%	59%
Today small swing *(+0.25% to -0.25%)*	53%	63%
Today fell below -0.25%	60%	50%

JULY 3 ODDS OF A PRICE RISE: 49%

Odds of different size price shift

	1935 to present
Large rise *(above +0.25%)*	40%
Small swing *(+0.25% to -0.25%)*	33%
Large fall *(below -0.25%)*	27%

Odds of rise based on yesterday

	1935 to present
Large rise yesterday *(above +0.25%)*	56%
Small swing yesterday *(+0.25% to -0.25%)*	47%
Large fall yesterday *(below -0.25%)*	40%

DIAGNOSTICS

Odds of price rise based on direction of 5-day and 20-day trend yesterday

	5-day trend	20-day trend
Yesterday rose more than +0.1%	52%	45%
Little change *(+0.1% to -0.1%)*	*67%	65%
Yesterday fell more than -0.1%	36%	35%

Odds of rise based upon distance between trend and yesterday s closing price

	5-day trend	20-day trend
Yesterday more than +0.5% above trend	42%	60%
Yesterday near trend *(+0.5% to -0.5%)*	65%	*50%
Yesterday more than -0.5% below trend	*33%	37%

Looking ahead: odds of rise in future

	Next 3 days	Next 5 days
Today rose over +0.25%	78%	72%
Today small swing *(+0.25% to -0.25%)*	40%	60%
Today fell below -0.25%	42%	50%

* *Per cent based on fewer than 10 observations*

JULY 4 ODDS OF A PRICE RISE: 61%

Odds of different size price shift

	1935 to present
Large rise *(above +0.25%)*	50%
Small swing *(+0.25% to -0.25%)*	20%
Large fall (*below -0.25%)*	30%

Odds of rise based on yesterday

	1935 to present
Large rise yesterday *(above +0.25%)*	88%
Small swing yesterday *(+0.25% to -0.25%)*	40%
Large fall yesterday (*below -0.25%)*	54%

DIAGNOSTICS

Odds of price rise based on direction of 5-day and 20-day trend yesterday

	5-day trend	20-day trend
Yesterday rose more than +0.1%	57%	57%
Little change *(+0.1% to -0.1%)*	*67%	64%
Yesterday fell more than -0.1%	67%	63%

Odds of rise based upon distance between trend and yesterday s closing price

	5-day trend	20-day trend
Yesterday more than +0.5% above trend	71%	58%
Yesterday near trend *(+0.5% to -0.5%)*	55%	*57%
Yesterday more than -0.5% below trend	*63%	67%

Looking ahead: odds of rise in future

	Next 3 days	Next 5 days
Today rose over +0.25%	73%	64%
Today small swing *(+0.25% to -0.25%)*	*56%	*78%
Today fell below -0.25%	23%	38%

JULY 5 ODDS OF A PRICE RISE: 51%

Odds of different size price shift

	1935 to present
Large rise *(above +0.25%)*	36%
Small swing *(+0.25% to -0.25%)*	31%
Large fall (*below -0.25%)*	33%

Odds of rise based on yesterday

	1935 to present
Large rise yesterday *(above +0.25%)*	68%
Small swing yesterday *(+0.25% to -0.25%)*	*50%
Large fall yesterday (*below -0.25%)*	27%

DIAGNOSTICS

Odds of price rise based on direction of 5-day and 20-day trend yesterday

	5-day trend	20-day trend
Yesterday rose more than +0.1%	67%	50%
Little change *(+0.1% to -0.1%)*	*50%	67%
Yesterday fell more than -0.1%	31%	39%

Odds of rise based upon distance between trend and yesterday s closing price

	5-day trend	20-day trend
Yesterday more than +0.5% above trend	69%	75%
Yesterday near trend *(+0.5% to -0.5%)*	59%	45%
Yesterday more than -0.5% below trend	17%	33%

Looking ahead: odds of rise in future

	Next 3 days	Next 5 days
Today rose over +0.25%	56%	38%
Today small swing *(+0.25% to -0.25%)*	86%	93%
Today fell below -0.25%	67%	60%

* *Per cent based on fewer than 10 observations*

JULY 6 ODDS OF A PRICE RISE: 61%

Odds of different size price shift

	1935 to present
Large rise *(above +0.25%)*	39%
Small swing *(+0.25% to -0.25%)*	35%
Large fall *(below -0.25%)*	26%

Odds of rise based on yesterday

	1935 to present
Large rise yesterday *(above +0.25%)*	76%
Small swing yesterday *(+0.25% to -0.25%)*	44%
Large fall yesterday *(below -0.25%)*	62%

DIAGNOSTICS

Odds of price rise based on direction of 5-day and 20-day trend yesterday

	5-day trend	20-day trend
Yesterday rose more than +0.1%	64%	60%
Little change *(+0.1% to -0.1%)*	*63%	57%
Yesterday fell more than -0.1%	56%	65%

Odds of rise based upon distance between trend and yesterday s closing price

	5-day trend	20-day trend
Yesterday more than +0.5% above trend	76%	57%
Yesterday near trend *(+0.5% to -0.5%)*	47%	*50%
Yesterday more than -0.5% below trend	58%	68%

Looking ahead: odds of rise in future

	Next 3 days	Next 5 days
Today rose over +0.25%	72%	67%
Today small swing *(+0.25% to -0.25%)*	69%	75%
Today fell below -0.25%	33%	50%

JULY 7 ODDS OF A PRICE RISE: 57%

Odds of different size price shift

	1935 to present
Large rise *(above +0.25%)*	43%
Small swing *(+0.25% to -0.25%)*	36%
Large fall *(below -0.25%)*	21%

Odds of rise based on yesterday

	1935 to present
Large rise yesterday *(above +0.25%)*	65%
Small swing yesterday *(+0.25% to -0.25%)*	74%
Large fall yesterday *(below -0.25%)*	18%

DIAGNOSTICS

Odds of price rise based on direction of 5-day and 20-day trend yesterday

	5-day trend	20-day trend
Yesterday rose more than +0.1%	50%	44%
Little change *(+0.1% to -0.1%)*	*88%	56%
Yesterday fell more than -0.1%	54%	77%

Odds of rise based upon distance between trend and yesterday s closing price

	5-day trend	20-day trend
Yesterday more than +0.5% above trend	58%	52%
Yesterday near trend *(+0.5% to -0.5%)*	56%	*63%
Yesterday more than -0.5% below trend	60%	63%

Looking ahead: odds of rise in future

	Next 3 days	Next 5 days
Today rose over +0.25%	65%	70%
Today small swing *(+0.25% to -0.25%)*	65%	65%
Today fell below -0.25%	60%	70%

* *Per cent based on fewer than 10 observations*

JULY 8 ODDS OF A PRICE RISE: 49%

Odds of different size price shift

	1935 to present
Large rise *(above +0.25%)*	34%
Small swing *(+0.25% to -0.25%)*	43%
Large fall (*below -0.25%)*	23%

Odds of rise based on yesterday

	1935 to present
Large rise yesterday *(above +0.25%)*	53%
Small swing yesterday *(+0.25% to -0.25%)*	47%
Large fall yesterday (*below -0.25%)*	46%

DIAGNOSTICS

Odds of price rise based on direction of 5-day and 20-day trend yesterday

	5-day trend	20-day trend
Yesterday rose more than +0.1%	45%	40%
Little change *(+0.1% to -0.1%)*	*100%	50%
Yesterday fell more than -0.1%	38%	58%

Odds of rise based upon distance between trend and yesterday s closing price

	5-day trend	20-day trend
Yesterday more than +0.5% above trend	53%	45%
Yesterday near trend *(+0.5% to -0.5%)*	50%	67%
Yesterday more than -0.5% below trend	*38%	38%

Looking ahead: odds of rise in future

	Next 3 days	Next 5 days
Today rose over +0.25%	63%	56%
Today small swing *(+0.25% to -0.25%)*	55%	65%
Today fell below -0.25%	45%	55%

JULY 9 ODDS OF A PRICE RISE: 54%

Odds of different size price shift

	1935 to present
Large rise *(above +0.25%)*	35%
Small swing *(+0.25% to -0.25%)*	43%
Large fall (*below -0.25%)*	22%

Odds of rise based on yesterday

	1935 to present
Large rise yesterday *(above +0.25%)*	59%
Small swing yesterday *(+0.25% to -0.25%)*	50%
Large fall yesterday (*below -0.25%)*	55%

DIAGNOSTICS

Odds of price rise based on direction of 5-day and 20-day trend yesterday

	5-day trend	20-day trend
Yesterday rose more than +0.1%	61%	57%
Little change *(+0.1% to -0.1%)*	45%	47%
Yesterday fell more than -0.1%	50%	62%

Odds of rise based upon distance between trend and yesterday s closing price

	5-day trend	20-day trend
Yesterday more than +0.5% above trend	73%	55%
Yesterday near trend *(+0.5% to -0.5%)*	45%	*67%
Yesterday more than -0.5% below trend	45%	47%

Looking ahead: odds of rise in future

	Next 3 days	Next 5 days
Today rose over +0.25%	56%	50%
Today small swing *(+0.25% to -0.25%)*	65%	65%
Today fell below -0.25%	50%	50%

* *Per cent based on fewer than 10 observations*

JULY 10 ODDS OF A PRICE RISE: 58%

Odds of different size price shift

	1935 to present
Large rise *(above +0.25%)*	47%
Small swing *(+0.25% to -0.25%)*	29%
Large fall (*below -0.25%)*	24%

Odds of rise based on yesterday

	1935 to present
Large rise yesterday *(above +0.25%)*	65%
Small swing yesterda y*(+0.25% to -0.25%)*	61%
Large fall yesterday (*below -0.25%)*	40%

DIAGNOSTICS

Odds of price rise based on direction of 5-day and 20-day trend yesterday

	5-day trend	20-day trend
Yesterday rose more than +0.1%	63%	60%
Little change *(+0.1% to -0.1%)*	64%	65%
Yesterday fell more than -0.1%	47%	46%

Odds of rise based upon distance between trend and yesterday s closing price

	5-day trend	20-day trend
Yesterday more than +0.5% above trend	60%	52%
Yesterday near trend *(+0.5% to -0.5%)*	55%	*75%
Yesterday more than -0.5% below trend	60%	56%

Looking ahead: odds of rise in future

	Next 3 days	Next 5 days
Today rose over +0.25%	67%	67%
Today small swing *(+0.25% to -0.25%)*	54%	62%
Today fell below -0.25%	55%	45%

JULY 11 ODDS OF A PRICE RISE: 52%

Odds of different size price shift

	1935 to present
Large rise *(above +0.25%)*	41%
Small swing *(+0.25% to -0.25%)*	30%
Large fall (*below -0.25%)*	30%

Odds of rise based on yesterday

	1935 to present
Large rise yesterday *(above +0.25%)*	58%
Small swing yesterday *(+0.25% to -0.25%)*	62%
Large fall yesterday (*below -0.25%)*	33%

DIAGNOSTICS

Odds of price rise based on direction of 5-day and 20-day trend yesterday

	5-day trend	20-day trend
Yesterday rose more than +0.1%	56%	38%
Little change *(+0.1% to -0.1%)*	*75%	61%
Yesterday fell more than -0.1%	40%	54%

Odds of rise based upon distance between trend and yesterday s closing price

	5-day trend	20-day trend
Yesterday more than +0.5% above trend	67%	59%
Yesterday near trend *(+0.5% to -0.5%)*	45%	*33%
Yesterday more than -0.5% below trend	*44%	54%

Looking ahead: odds of rise in future

	Next 3 days	Next 5 days
Today rose over +0.25%	56%	50%
Today small swing *(+0.25% to -0.25%)*	69%	62%
Today fell below -0.25%	38%	46%

* *Per cent based on fewer than 10 observations*

JULY 12 ODDS OF A PRICE RISE: 42%

Odds of different size price shift

	1935 to present
Large rise *(above +0.25%)*	38%
Small swing *(+0.25% to -0.25%)*	22%
Large fall *(below -0.25%)*	40%

Odds of rise based on yesterday

	1935 to present
Large rise yesterday *(above +0.25%)*	53%
Small swing yesterday *(+0.25% to -0.25%)*	41%
Large fall yesterday *(below -0.25%)*	27%

DIAGNOSTICS

Odds of price rise based on direction of 5-day and 20-day trend yesterday

	5-day trend	20-day trend
Yesterday rose more than +0.1%	45%	33%
Little change *(+0.1% to -0.1%)*	35%	41%
Yesterday fell more than -0.1%	*50%	50%

Odds of rise based upon distance between trend and yesterday s closing price

	5-day trend	20-day trend
Yesterday more than +0.5% above trend	56%	30%
Yesterday near trend *(+0.5% to -0.5%)*	35%	*57%
Yesterday more than -0.5% below trend	*33%	53%

Looking ahead: odds of rise in future

	Next 3 days	Next 5 days
Today rose over +0.25%	71%	71%
Today small swing *(+0.25% to -0.25%)*	70%	40%
Today fell below -0.25%	56%	44%

JULY 13 ODDS OF A PRICE RISE: 63%

Odds of different size price shift

	1935 to present
Large rise *(above +0.25%)*	46%
Small swing *(+0.25% to -0.25%)*	30%
Large fall *(below -0.25%)*	24%

Odds of rise based on yesterday

	1935 to present
Large rise yesterday *(above +0.25%)*	75%
Small swing yesterday *(+0.25% to -0.25%)*	40%
Large fall yesterday *(below -0.25%)*	63%

DIAGNOSTICS

Odds of price rise based on direction of 5-day and 20-day trend yesterday

	5-day trend	20-day trend
Yesterday rose more than +0.1%	58%	62%
Little change *(+0.1% to -0.1%)*	73%	74%
Yesterday fell more than -0.1%	58%	50%

Odds of rise based upon distance between trend and yesterday s closing price

	5-day trend	20-day trend
Yesterday more than +0.5% above trend	77%	60%
Yesterday near trend *(+0.5% to -0.5%)*	60%	*100%
Yesterday more than -0.5% below trend	*50%	42%

Looking ahead: odds of rise in future

	Next 3 days	Next 5 days
Today rose over +0.25%	71%	57%
Today small swing *(+0.25% to -0.25%)*	43%	43%
Today fell below -0.25%	55%	64%

* *Per cent based on fewer than 10 observations*

JULY 14 ODDS OF A PRICE RISE: 49%

Odds of different size price shift

	1935 to present
Large rise *(above +0.25%)*	32%
Small swing *(+0.25% to -0.25%)*	36%
Large fall *(below -0.25%)*	32%

Odds of rise based on yesterday

	1935 to present
Large rise yesterday *(above +0.25%)*	62%
Small swing yesterday *(+0.25% to -0.25%)*	36%
Large fall yesterday *(below -0.25%)*	42%

DIAGNOSTICS

Odds of price rise based on direction of 5-day and 20-day trend yesterday

	5-day trend	20-day trend
Yesterday rose more than +0.1%	50%	50%
Little change *(+0.1% to -0.1%)*	64%	53%
Yesterday fell more than -0.1%	27%	40%

Odds of rise based upon distance between trend and yesterday s closing price

	5-day trend	20-day trend
Yesterday more than +0.5% above trend	67%	59%
Yesterday near trend *(+0.5% to -0.5%)*	42%	*33%
Yesterday more than -0.5% below trend	30%	36%

Looking ahead: odds of rise in future

	Next 3 days	Next 5 days
Today rose over +0.25%	87%	47%
Today small swing *(+0.25% to -0.25%)*	53%	53%
Today fell below -0.25%	33%	47%

JULY 15 ODDS OF A PRICE RISE: 66%

Odds of different size price shift

	1935 to present
Large rise *(above +0.25%)*	49%
Small swing *(+0.25% to -0.25%)*	23%
Large fall (*below -0.25%)*	28%

Odds of rise based on yesterday

	1935 to present
Large rise yesterday *(above +0.25%)*	93%
Small swing yesterday *(+0.25% to -0.25%)*	75%
Large fall yesterday (*below -0.25%)*	31%

DIAGNOSTICS

Odds of price rise based on direction of 5-day and 20-day trend yesterday

	5-day trend	20-day trend
Yesterday rose more than +0.1%	77%	73%
Little change *(+0.1% to -0.1%)*	70%	64%
Yesterday fell more than -0.1%	47%	60%

Odds of rise based upon distance between trend and yesterday s closing price

	5-day trend	20-day trend
Yesterday more than +0.5% above trend	87%	87%
Yesterday near trend *(+0.5% to -0.5%)*	63%	45%
Yesterday more than -0.5% below trend	46%	46%

Looking ahead: odds of rise in future

	Next 3 days	Next 5 days
Today rose over +0.25%	57%	43%
Today small swing *(+0.25% to -0.25%)*	45%	27%
Today fell below -0.25%	38%	62%

* *Per cent based on fewer than 10 observations*

JULY 16 ODDS OF A PRICE RISE: 52%

Odds of different size price shift

	1935 to present
Large rise *(above +0.25%)*	35%
Small swing *(+0.25% to -0.25%)*	46%
Large fall (*below -0.25%)*	20%

Odds of rise based on yesterday

	1935 to present
Large rise yesterday *(above +0.25%)*	54%
Small swing yesterday *(+0.25% to -0.25%)*	45%
Large fall yesterday (*below -0.25%)*	55%

DIAGNOSTICS

Odds of price rise based on direction of 5-day and 20-day trend yesterday

	5-day trend	20-day trend
Yesterday rose more than +0.1%	48%	50%
Little change *(+0.1% to -0.1%)*	50%	65%
Yesterday fell more than -0.1%	60%	30%

Odds of rise based upon distance between trend and yesterday s closing price

	5-day trend	20-day trend
Yesterday more than +0.5% above trend	53%	58%
Yesterday near trend *(+0.5% to -0.5%)*	44%	*43%
Yesterday more than -0.5% below trend	64%	47%

Looking ahead: odds of rise in future

	Next 3 days	Next 5 days
Today rose over +0.25%	31%	44%
Today small swing *(+0.25% to -0.25%)*	33%	24%
Today fell below -0.25%	*67%	*44%

JULY 17 ODDS OF A PRICE RISE: 56%

Odds of different size price shift

	1935 to present
Large rise *(above +0.25%)*	38%
Small swing *(+0.25% to -0.25%)*	31%
Large fall (*below -0.25%)*	31%

Odds of rise based on yesterday

	1935 to present
Large rise yesterday *(above +0.25%)*	53%
Small swing yesterday *(+0.25% to -0.25%)*	50%
Large fall yesterday (*below -0.25%)*	70%

DIAGNOSTICS

Odds of price rise based on direction of 5-day and 20-day trend yesterday

	5-day trend	20-day trend
Yesterday rose more than +0.1%	54%	47%
Little change *(+0.1% to -0.1%)*	*50%	63%
Yesterday fell more than -0.1%	62%	55%

Odds of rise based upon distance between trend and yesterday s closing price

	5-day trend	20-day trend
Yesterday more than +0.5% above trend	64%	63%
Yesterday near trend *(+0.5% to -0.5%)*	50%	*33%
Yesterday more than -0.5% below trend	55%	53%

Looking ahead: odds of rise in future

	Next 3 days	Next 5 days
Today rose over +0.25%	41%	35%
Today small swing *(+0.25% to -0.25%)*	57%	50%
Today fell below -0.25%	36%	36%

* *Per cent based on fewer than 10 observations*

JULY 18 ODDS OF A PRICE RISE: 43%

Odds of different size price shift

	1935 to present
Large rise *(above +0.25%)*	27%
Small swing *(+0.25% to -0.25%)*	30%
Large fall (*below -0.25%)*	43%

Odds of rise based on yesterday

	1935 to present
Large rise yesterday *(above +0.25%)*	47%
Small swing yesterday *(+0.25% to -0.25%)*	50%
Large fall yesterday (*below -0.25%)*	31%

DIAGNOSTICS

Odds of price rise based on direction of 5-day and 20-day trend yesterday

	5-day trend	20-day trend
Yesterday rose more than +0.1%	50%	38%
Little change *(+0.1% to -0.1%)*	40%	29%
Yesterday fell more than -0.1%	36%	73%

Odds of rise based upon distance between trend and yesterday s closing price

	5-day trend	20-day trend
Yesterday more than +0.5% above trend	53%	43%
Yesterday near trend *(+0.5% to -0.5%)*	38%	*29%
Yesterday more than -0.5% below trend	36%	50%

Looking ahead: odds of rise in future

	Next 3 days	Next 5 days
Today rose over +0.25%	75%	67%
Today small swing *(+0.25% to -0.25%)*	38%	23%
Today fell below -0.25%	37%	42%

JULY 19 ODDS OF A PRICE RISE: 47%

Odds of different size price shift

	1935 to present
Large rise *(above +0.25%)*	33%
Small swing *(+0.25% to -0.25%)*	31%
Large fall (*below -0.25%)*	36%

Odds of rise based on yesterday

	1935 to present
Large rise yesterday *(above +0.25%)*	77%
Small swing yesterday *(+0.25% to -0.25%)*	47%
Large fall yesterday (*below -0.25%)*	20%

DIAGNOSTICS

Odds of price rise based on direction of 5-day and 20-day trend yesterday

	5-day trend	20-day trend
Yesterday rose more than +0.1%	55%	64%
Little change *(+0.1% to -0.1%)*	*33%	29%
Yesterday fell more than -0.1%	43%	60%

Odds of rise based upon distance between trend and yesterday s closing price

	5-day trend	20-day trend
Yesterday more than +0.5% above trend	63%	52%
Yesterday near trend *(+0.5% to -0.5%)*	33%	10%
Yesterday more than -0.5% below trend	*50%	67%

Looking ahead: odds of rise in future

	Next 3 days	Next 5 days
Today rose over +0.25%	60%	47%
Today small swing *(+0.25% to -0.25%)*	50%	57%
Today fell below -0.25%	38%	56%

* *Per cent based on fewer than 10 observations*

JULY 20 ODDS OF A PRICE RISE: 52%

Odds of different size price shift

	1935 to present
Large rise *(above +0.25%)*	39%
Small swing *(+0.25% to -0.25%)*	35%
Large fall (*below -0.25%)*	26%

Odds of rise based on yesterday

	1935 to present
Large rise yesterday *(above +0.25%)*	65%
Small swing yesterday *(+0.25% to -0.25%)*	67%
Large fall yesterday (*below -0.25%)*	29%

DIAGNOSTICS

Odds of price rise based on direction of 5-day and 20-day trend yesterday

	5-day trend	20-day trend
Yesterday rose more than +0.1%	64%	63%
Little change *(+0.1% to -0.1%)*	*50%	45%
Yesterday fell more than -0.1%	38%	50%

Odds of rise based upon distance between trend and yesterday s closing price

	5-day trend	20-day trend
Yesterday more than +0.5% above trend	75%	57%
Yesterday near trend *(+0.5% to -0.5%)*	50%	42%
Yesterday more than -0.5% below trend	29%	54%

Looking ahead: odds of rise in future

	Next 3 days	Next 5 days
Today rose over +0.25%	39%	39%
Today small swing *(+0.25% to -0.25%)*	75%	63%
Today fell below -0.25%	33%	33%

JULY 21 ODDS OF A PRICE RISE: 43%

Odds of different size price shift

	1935 to present
Large rise *(above +0.25%)*	34%
Small swing *(+0.25% to -0.25%)*	23%
Large fall *(below -0.25%)*	43%

Odds of rise based on yesterday

	1935 to present
Large rise yesterday *(above +0.25%)*	59%
Small swing yesterday *(+0.25% to -0.25%)*	50%
Large fall yesterday *(below -0.25%)*	19%

DIAGNOSTICS

Odds of price rise based on direction of 5-day and 20-day trend yesterday

	5-day trend	20-day trend
Yesterday rose more than +0.1%	42%	47%
Little change *(+0.1% to -0.1%)*	*56%	31%
Yesterday fell more than -0.1%	37%	50%

Odds of rise based upon distance between trend and yesterday s closing price

	5-day trend	20-day trend
Yesterday more than +0.5% above trend	47%	46%
Yesterday near trend *(+0.5% to -0.5%)*	50%	*56%
Yesterday more than -0.5% below trend	31%	29%

Looking ahead: odds of rise in future

	Next 3 days	Next 5 days
Today rose over +0.25%	56%	56%
Today small swing *(+0.25% to -0.25%)*	64%	55%
Today fell below -0.25%	35%	40%

* *Per cent based on fewer than 10 observations*

JULY 22 ODDS OF A PRICE RISE: 48%

Odds of different size price shift

	1935 to present
Large rise *(above +0.25%)*	35%
Small swing *(+0.25% to -0.25%)*	35%
Large fall (*below -0.25%)*	30%

Odds of rise based on yesterday

	1935 to present
Large rise yesterday *(above +0.25%)*	46%
Small swing yesterday *(+0.25% to -0.25%)*	50%
Large fall yesterday (*below -0.25%)*	47%

DIAGNOSTICS

Odds of price rise based on direction of 5-day and 20-day trend yesterday

	5-day trend	20-day trend
Yesterday rose more than +0.1%	53%	55%
Little change *(+0.1% to -0.1%)*	*22%	21%
Yesterday fell more than -0.1%	55%	67%

Odds of rise based upon distance between trend and yesterday s closing price

	5-day trend	20-day trend
Yesterday more than +0.5% above trend	54%	50%
Yesterday near trend *(+0.5% to -0.5%)*	50%	36%
Yesterday more than -0.5% below trend	41%	53%

Looking ahead: odds of rise in future

	Next 3 days	Next 5 days
Today rose over +0.25%	56%	50%
Today small swing *(+0.25% to -0.25%)*	44%	31%
Today fell below -0.25%	21%	50%

JULY 23 ODDS OF A PRICE RISE: 50%

Odds of different size price shift

	1935 to present
Large rise *(above +0.25%)*	35%
Small swing *(+0.25% to -0.25%)*	24%
Large fall (*below -0.25%)*	41%

Odds of rise based on yesterday

	1935 to present
Large rise yesterday *(above +0.25%)*	65%
Small swing yesterday *(+0.25% to -0.25%)*	53%
Large fall yesterday (*below -0.25%)*	29%

DIAGNOSTICS

Odds of price rise based on direction of 5-day and 20-day trend yesterday

	5-day trend	20-day trend
Yesterday rose more than +0.1%	59%	48%
Little change *(+0.1% to -0.1%)*	*50%	54%
Yesterday fell more than -0.1%	43%	50%

Odds of rise based upon distance between trend and yesterday s closing price

	5-day trend	20-day trend
Yesterday more than +0.5% above trend	80%	50%
Yesterday near trend *(+0.5% to -0.5%)*	45%	60%
Yesterday more than -0.5% below trend	38%	44%

Looking ahead: odds of rise in future

	Next 3 days	Next 5 days
Today rose over +0.25%	50%	69%
Today small swing *(+0.25% to -0.25%)*	45%	55%
Today fell below -0.25%	47%	37%

* *Per cent based on fewer than 10 observations*

JULY 24 ODDS OF A PRICE RISE: 49%

Odds of different size price shift

	1935 to present
Large rise *(above +0.25%)*	36%
Small swing *(+0.25% to -0.25%)*	40%
Large fall (*below -0.25%)*	24%

Odds of rise based on yesterday

	1935 to present
Large rise yesterday *(above +0.25%)*	56%
Small swing yesterday *(+0.25% to -0.25%)*	*56%
Large fall yesterday (*below -0.25%)*	40%

DIAGNOSTICS

Odds of price rise based on direction of 5-day and 20-day trend yesterday

	5-day trend	20-day trend
Yesterday rose more than +0.1%	61%	47%
Little change *(+0.1% to -0.1%)*	*43%	69%
Yesterday fell more than -0.1%	40%	20%

Odds of rise based upon distance between trend and yesterday s closing price

	5-day trend	20-day trend
Yesterday more than +0.5% above trend	69%	52%
Yesterday near trend *(+0.5% to -0.5%)*	47%	*75%
Yesterday more than -0.5% below trend	33%	39%

Looking ahead: odds of rise in future

	Next 3 days	Next 5 days
Today rose over +0.25%	81%	81%
Today small swing *(+0.25% to -0.25%)*	28%	39%
Today fell below -0.25%	45%	45%

JULY 25 ODDS OF A PRICE RISE: 41%

Odds of different size price shift

	1935 to present
Large rise *(above +0.25%)*	27%
Small swing *(+0.25% to -0.25%)*	36%
Large fall (*below -0.25%)*	36%

Odds of rise based on yesterday

	1935 to present
Large rise yesterday *(above +0.25%)*	69%
Small swing yesterday *(+0.25% to -0.25%)*	26%
Large fall yesterday (*below -0.25%)*	33%

DIAGNOSTICS

Odds of price rise based on direction of 5-day and 20-day trend yesterday

	5-day trend	20-day trend
Yesterday rose more than +0.1%	38%	47%
Little change *(+0.1% to -0.1%)*	*63%	44%
Yesterday fell more than -0.1%	35%	27%

Odds of rise based upon distance between trend and yesterday s closing price

	5-day trend	20-day trend
Yesterday more than +0.5% above trend	46%	48%
Yesterday near trend *(+0.5% to -0.5%)*	36%	*14%
Yesterday more than -0.5% below trend	41%	43%

Looking ahead: odds of rise in future

	Next 3 days	Next 5 days
Today rose over +0.25%	42%	58%
Today small swing *(+0.25% to -0.25%)*	44%	44%
Today fell below -0.25%	56%	50%

* *Per cent based on fewer than 10 observations*

JULY 26 ODDS OF A PRICE RISE: 51%

Odds of different size price shift

	1935 to present
Large rise *(above +0.25%)*	40%
Small swing *(+0.25% to -0.25%)*	24%
Large fall (*below -0.25%)*	36%

Odds of rise based on yesterday

	1935 to present
Large rise yesterday *(above +0.25%)*	47%
Small swing yesterday *(+0.25% to -0.25%)*	69%
Large fall yesterday (*below -0.25%)*	36%

DIAGNOSTICS

Odds of price rise based on direction of 5-day and 20-day trend yesterday

	5-day trend	20-day trend
Yesterday rose more than +0.1%	59%	59%
Little change *(+0.1% to -0.1%)*	54%	50%
Yesterday fell more than -0.1%	40%	*38%

Odds of rise based upon distance between trend and yesterday s closing price

	5-day trend	20-day trend
Yesterday more than +0.5% above trend	67%	65%
Yesterday near trend *(+0.5% to -0.5%)*	48%	*43%
Yesterday more than -0.5% below trend	42%	39%

Looking ahead: odds of rise in future

	Next 3 days	Next 5 days
Today rose over +0.25%	61%	61%
Today small swing *(+0.25% to -0.25%)*	55%	45%
Today fell below -0.25%	31%	56%

JULY 27 ODDS OF A PRICE RISE: 37%

Odds of different size price shift

	1935 to present
Large rise *(above +0.25%)*	28%
Small swing *(+0.25% to -0.25%)*	24%
Large fall *(below -0.25%)*	48%

Odds of rise based on yesterday

	1935 to present
Large rise yesterday *(above +0.25%)*	50%
Small swing yesterday *(+0.25% to -0.25%)*	18%
Large fall yesterday *(below -0.25%)*	33%

DIAGNOSTICS

Odds of price rise based on direction of 5-day and 20-day trend yesterday

	5-day trend	20-day trend
Yesterday rose more than +0.1%	39%	35%
Little change *(+0.1% to -0.1%)*	40%	40%
Yesterday fell more than -0.1%	33%	*33%

Odds of rise based upon distance between trend and yesterday s closing price

	5-day trend	20-day trend
Yesterday more than +0.5% above trend	47%	42%
Yesterday near trend *(+0.5% to -0.5%)*	31%	*44%
Yesterday more than -0.5% below trend	31%	28%

Looking ahead: odds of rise in future

	Next 3 days	Next 5 days
Today rose over +0.25%	62%	69%
Today small swing *(+0.25% to -0.25%)*	73%	82%
Today fell below -0.25%	64%	68%

* *Per cent based on fewer than 10 observations*

JULY 28 ODDS OF A PRICE RISE: 57%

Odds of different size price shift

	1935 to present
Large rise *(above +0.25%)*	32%
Small swing *(+0.25% to -0.25%)*	49%
Large fall (*below -0.25%)*	19%

Odds of rise based on yesterday

	1935 to present
Large rise yesterday *(above +0.25%)*	64%
Small swing yesterday *(+0.25% to -0.25%)*	64%
Large fall yesterday (*below -0.25%)*	47%

DIAGNOSTICS

Odds of price rise based on direction of 5-day and 20-day trend yesterday

	5-day trend	20-day trend
Yesterday rose more than +0.1%	60%	56%
Little change *(+0.1% to -0.1%)*	67%	62%
Yesterday fell more than -0.1%	50%	*50%

Odds of rise based upon distance between trend and yesterday s closing price

	5-day trend	20-day trend
Yesterday more than +0.5% above trend	69%	59%
Yesterday near trend *(+0.5% to -0.5%)*	58%	*50%
Yesterday more than -0.5% below trend	47%	58%

Looking ahead: odds of rise in future

	Next 3 days	Next 5 days
Today rose over +0.25%	73%	67%
Today small swing *(+0.25% to -0.25%)*	78%	91%
Today fell below -0.25%	*44%	*44%

JULY 29 ODDS OF A PRICE RISE: 46%

Odds of different size price shift

	1935 to present
Large rise *(above +0.25%)*	30%
Small swing *(+0.25% to -0.25%)*	30%
Large fall (*below -0.25%)*	39%

Odds of rise based on yesterday

	1935 to present
Large rise yesterday *(above +0.25%)*	64%
Small swing yesterday *(+0.25% to -0.25%)*	52%
Large fall yesterday (*below -0.25%)*	9%

DIAGNOSTICS

Odds of price rise based on direction of 5-day and 20-day trend yesterday

	5-day trend	20-day trend
Yesterday rose more than +0.1%	77%	50%
Little change *(+0.1% to -0.1%)*	30%	42%
Yesterday fell more than -0.1%	35%	*50%

Odds of rise based upon distance between trend and yesterday s closing price

	5-day trend	20-day trend
Yesterday more than +0.5% above trend	55%	44%
Yesterday near trend *(+0.5% to -0.5%)*	57%	80%
Yesterday more than -0.5% below trend	21%	30%

Looking ahead: odds of rise in future

	Next 3 days	Next 5 days
Today rose over +0.25%	79%	79%
Today small swing *(+0.25% to -0.25%)*	64%	71%
Today fell below -0.25%	56%	61%

* *Per cent based on fewer than 10 observations*

JULY 30 ODDS OF A PRICE RISE: 51%

Odds of different size price shift

	1935 to present
Large rise *(above +0.25%)*	34%
Small swing *(+0.25% to -0.25%)*	30%
Large fall (*below -0.25%)*	36%

Odds of rise based on yesterday

	1935 to present
Large rise yesterday *(above +0.25%)*	69%
Small swing yesterday *(+0.25% to -0.25%)*	62%
Large fall yesterday (*below -0.25%)*	33%

DIAGNOSTICS

Odds of price rise based on direction of 5-day and 20-day trend yesterday

	5-day trend	20-day trend
Yesterday rose more than +0.1%	50%	57%
Little change *(+0.1% to -0.1%)*	55%	52%
Yesterday fell more than -0.1%	50%	42%

Odds of rise based upon distance between trend and yesterday s closing price

	5-day trend	20-day trend
Yesterday more than +0.5% above trend	64%	56%
Yesterday near trend *(+0.5% to -0.5%)*	53%	*67%
Yesterday more than -0.5% below trend	41%	40%

Looking ahead: odds of rise in future

	Next 3 days	Next 5 days
Today rose over +0.25%	69%	75%
Today small swing *(+0.25% to -0.25%)*	86%	86%
Today fell below -0.25%	47%	41%

JULY 31 ODDS OF A PRICE RISE: 50%

Odds of different size price shift

	1935 to present
Large rise *(above +0.25%)*	41%
Small swing *(+0.25% to -0.25%)*	30%
Large fall (*below -0.25%)*	28%

Odds of rise based on yesterday

	1935 to present
Large rise yesterday *(above +0.25%)*	53%
Small swing yesterday *(+0.25% to -0.25%)*	67%
Large fall yesterday (*below -0.25%)*	31%

DIAGNOSTICS

Odds of price rise based on direction of 5-day and 20-day trend yesterday

	5-day trend	20-day trend
Yesterday rose more than +0.1%	56%	40%
Little change *(+0.1% to -0.1%)*	*44%	71%
Yesterday fell more than -0.1%	47%	41%

Odds of rise based upon distance between trend and yesterday s closing price

	5-day trend	20-day trend
Yesterday more than +0.5% above trend	40%	58%
Yesterday near trend *(+0.5% to -0.5%)*	67%	*63%
Yesterday more than -0.5% below trend	38%	37%

Looking ahead: odds of rise in future

	Next 3 days	Next 5 days
Today rose over +0.25%	74%	79%
Today small swing *(+0.25% to -0.25%)*	71%	93%
Today fell below -0.25%	54%	46%

* *Per cent based on fewer than 10 observations*

AUGUST

PROFIT ODDS SUMMARY FOR THE MONTH

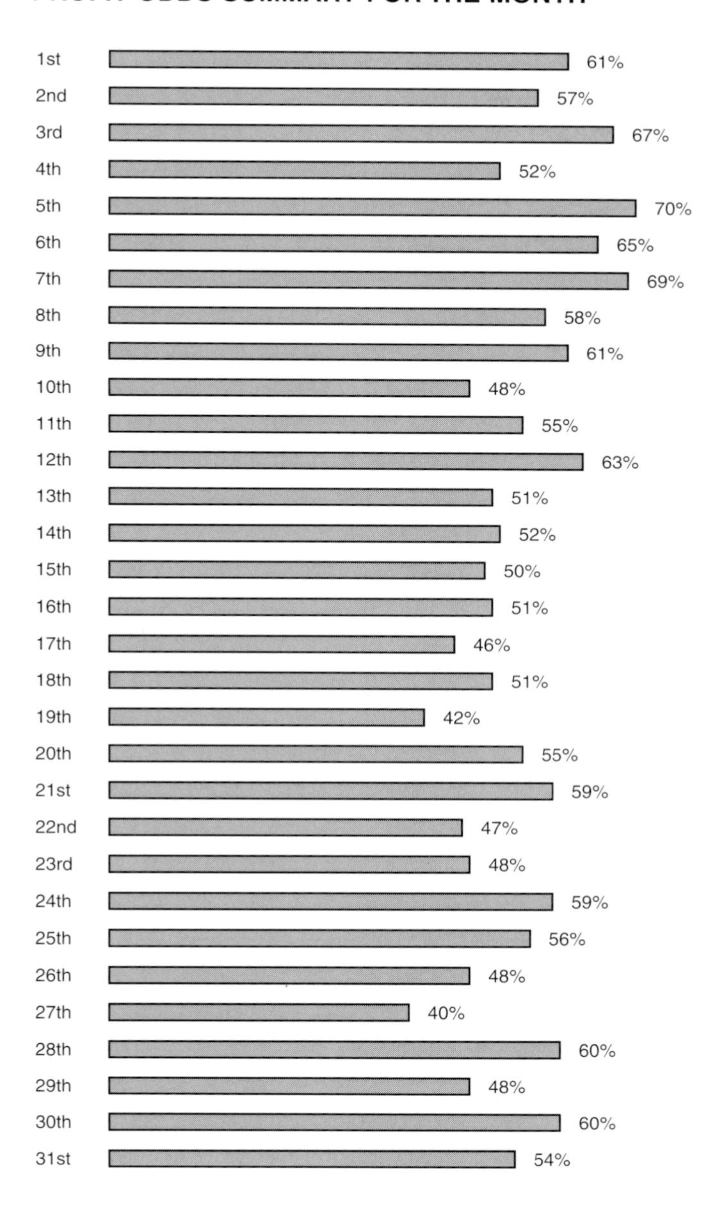

AUGUST 1 ODDS OF A PRICE RISE: 61%

Odds of different size price shift

	1935 to present
Large rise *(above +0.25%)*	49%
Small swing *(+0.25% to -0.25%)*	29%
Large fall (*below -0.25%)*	22%

Odds of rise based on yesterday

	1935 to present
Large rise yesterday *(above +0.25%)*	82%
Small swing yesterday *(+0.25% to -0.25%)*	64%
Large fall yesterday (*below -0.25%)*	31%

DIAGNOSTICS

Odds of price rise based on direction of 5-day and 20-day trend yesterday

	5-day trend	20-day trend
Yesterday rose more than +0.1%	73%	64%
Little change *(+0.1% to -0.1%)*	55%	70%
Yesterday fell more than -0.1%	53%	53%

Odds of rise based upon distance between trend and yesterday s closing price

	5-day trend	20-day trend
Yesterday more than +0.5% above trend	77%	67%
Yesterday near trend *(+0.5% to -0.5%)*	56%	*50%
Yesterday more than -0.5% below trend	50%	59%

Looking ahead: odds of rise in future

	Next 3 days	Next 5 days
Today rose over +0.25%	85%	80%
Today small swing *(+0.25% to -0.25%)*	67%	75%
Today fell below -0.25%	*89%	*67%

* *Per cent based on fewer than 10 observations*

AUGUST 2 ODDS OF A PRICE RISE: 57%

Odds of different size price shift

	1935 to present
Large rise *(above +0.25%)*	48%
Small swing *(+0.25% to -0.25%)*	26%
Large fall (*below -0.25%)*	26%

Odds of rise based on yesterday

	1935 to present
Large rise yesterday *(above +0.25%)*	70%
Small swing yesterday *(+0.25% to -0.25%)*	64%
Large fall yesterday (*below -0.25%)*	27%

DIAGNOSTICS

Odds of price rise based on direction of 5-day and 20-day trend yesterday

	5-day trend	20-day trend
Yesterday rose more than +0.1%	71%	53%
Little change *(+0.1% to -0.1%)*	60%	60%
Yesterday fell more than -0.1%	44%	58%

Odds of rise based upon distance between trend and yesterday s closing price

	5-day trend	20-day trend
Yesterday more than +0.5% above trend	69%	61%
Yesterday near trend *(+0.5% to -0.5%)*	72%	*67%
Yesterday more than -0.5% below trend	18%	50%

Looking ahead: odds of rise in future

	Next 3 days	Next 5 days
Today rose over +0.25%	85%	75%
Today small swing *(+0.25% to -0.25%)*	73%	55%
Today fell below -0.25%	55%	45%

AUGUST 3 ODDS OF A PRICE RISE: 67%

Odds of different size price shift

	1935 to present
Large rise *(above +0.25%)*	45%
Small swing *(+0.25% to -0.25%)*	33%
Large fall *(below -0.25%)*	21%

Odds of rise based on yesterday

	1935 to present
Large rise yesterday *(above +0.25%)*	79%
Small swing yesterday *(+0.25% to -0.25%)*	70%
Large fall yesterday *(below -0.25%)*	46%

DIAGNOSTICS

Odds of price rise based on direction of 5-day and 20-day trend yesterday

	5-day trend	20-day trend
Yesterday rose more than +0.1%	61%	65%
Little change *(+0.1% to -0.1%)*	*78%	69%
Yesterday fell more than -0.1%	67%	67%

Odds of rise based upon distance between trend and yesterday s closing price

	5-day trend	20-day trend
Yesterday more than +0.5% above trend	74%	71%
Yesterday near trend *(+0.5% to -0.5%)*	62%	*71%
Yesterday more than -0.5% below trend	60%	57%

Looking ahead: odds of rise in future

	Next 3 days	Next 5 days
Today rose over +0.25%	68%	68%
Today small swing *(+0.25% to -0.25%)*	64%	50%
Today fell below -0.25%	*11%	*22%

* *Per cent based on fewer than 10 observations*

AUGUST 4 ODDS OF A PRICE RISE: 52%

Odds of different size price shift

	1935 to present
Large rise *(above +0.25%)*	41%
Small swing *(+0.25% to -0.25%)*	36%
Large fall (*below -0.25%)*	23%

Odds of rise based on yesterday

	1935 to present
Large rise yesterday *(above +0.25%)*	65%
Small swing yesterday *(+0.25% to -0.25%)*	47%
Large fall yesterday (*below -0.25%)*	*38%

DIAGNOSTICS

Odds of price rise based on direction of 5-day and 20-day trend yesterday

	5-day trend	20-day trend
Yesterday rose more than +0.1%	57%	58%
Little change *(+0.1% to -0.1%)*	50%	60%
Yesterday fell more than -0.1%	*43%	30%

Odds of rise based upon distance between trend and yesterday s closing price

	5-day trend	20-day trend
Yesterday more than +0.5% above trend	61%	56%
Yesterday near trend *(+0.5% to -0.5%)*	58%	*80%
Yesterday more than -0.5% below trend	*14%	33%

Looking ahead: odds of rise in future

	Next 3 days	Next 5 days
Today rose over +0.25%	56%	72%
Today small swing *(+0.25% to -0.25%)*	63%	44%
Today fell below -0.25%	30%	50%

AUGUST 5 ODDS OF A PRICE RISE: 70%

Odds of different size price shift

	1935 to present
Large rise *(above +0.25%)*	52%
Small swing *(+0.25% to -0.25%)*	25%
Large fall (*below -0.25%)*	23%

Odds of rise based on yesterday

	1935 to present
Large rise yesterday *(above +0.25%)*	74%
Small swing yesterday *(+0.25% to -0.25%)*	71%
Large fall yesterday (*below -0.25%)*	64%

DIAGNOSTICS

Odds of price rise based on direction of 5-day and 20-day trend yesterday

	5-day trend	20-day trend
Yesterday rose more than +0.1%	78%	65%
Little change *(+0.1% to -0.1%)*	70%	87%
Yesterday fell more than -0.1%	55%	58%

Odds of rise based upon distance between trend and yesterday s closing price

	5-day trend	20-day trend
Yesterday more than +0.5% above trend	81%	70%
Yesterday near trend *(+0.5% to -0.5%)*	60%	*100%
Yesterday more than -0.5% below trend	*63%	69%

Looking ahead: odds of rise in future

	Next 3 days	Next 5 days
Today rose over +0.25%	61%	65%
Today small swing *(+0.25% to -0.25%)*	64%	55%
Today fell below -0.25%	60%	60%

* *Per cent based on fewer than 10 observations*

AUGUST 6 ODDS OF A PRICE RISE: 65%

Odds of different size price shift

	1935 to present
Large rise *(above +0.25%)*	51%
Small swing *(+0.25% to -0.25%)*	26%
Large fall *(below -0.25%)*	23%

Odds of rise based on yesterday

	1935 to present
Large rise yesterday *(above +0.25%)*	83%
Small swing yesterday *(+0.25% to -0.25%)*	45%
Large fall yesterday *(below -0.25%)*	*44%

DIAGNOSTICS

Odds of price rise based on direction of 5-day and 20-day trend yesterday

	5-day trend	20-day trend
Yesterday rose more than +0.1%	76%	68%
Little change *(+0.1% to -0.1%)*	*63%	70%
Yesterday fell more than -0.1%	40%	57%

Odds of rise based upon distance between trend and yesterday s closing price

	5-day trend	20-day trend
Yesterday more than +0.5% above trend	76%	74%
Yesterday near trend *(+0.5% to -0.5%)*	67%	*67%
Yesterday more than -0.5% below trend	40%	53%

Looking ahead: odds of rise in future

	Next 3 days	Next 5 days
Today rose over +0.25%	77%	77%
Today small swing *(+0.25% to -0.25%)*	55%	73%
Today fell below -0.25%	60%	60%

AUGUST 7 ODDS OF A PRICE RISE: 69%

Odds of different size price shift

	1935 to present
Large rise *(above +0.25%)*	48%
Small swing *(+0.25% to -0.25%)*	33%
Large fall (*below -0.25%)*	19%

Odds of rise based on yesterday

	1935 to present
Large rise yesterday *(above +0.25%)*	86%
Small swing yesterday *(+0.25% to -0.25%)*	58%
Large fall yesterday (*below -0.25%)*	*44%

DIAGNOSTICS

Odds of price rise based on direction of 5-day and 20-day trend yesterday

	5-day trend	20-day trend
Yesterday rose more than +0.1%	75%	60%
Little change *(+0.1% to -0.1%)*	*50%	100%
Yesterday fell more than -0.1%	58%	58%

Odds of rise based upon distance between trend and yesterday s closing price

	5-day trend	20-day trend
Yesterday more than +0.5% above trend	81%	67%
Yesterday near trend *(+0.5% to -0.5%)*	58%	*100%
Yesterday more than -0.5% below trend	*56%	62%

Looking ahead: odds of rise in future

	Next 3 days	Next 5 days
Today rose over +0.25%	65%	65%
Today small swing *(+0.25% to -0.25%)*	64%	79%
Today fell below -0.25%	*50%	*63%

* *Per cent based on fewer than 10 observations*

AUGUST 8 ODDS OF A PRICE RISE: 58%

Odds of different size price shift

	1935 to present
Large rise *(above +0.25%)*	36%
Small swing *(+0.25% to -0.25%)*	38%
Large fall (*below -0.25%)*	27%

Odds of rise based on yesterday

	1935 to present
Large rise yesterday *(above +0.25%)*	74%
Small swing yesterday *(+0.25% to -0.25%)*	50%
Large fall yesterday (*below -0.25%)*	*25%

DIAGNOSTICS

Odds of price rise based on direction of 5-day and 20-day trend yesterday

	5-day trend	20-day trend
Yesterday rose more than +0.1%	76%	63%
Little change *(+0.1% to -0.1%)*	*22%	60%
Yesterday fell more than -0.1%	45%	45%

Odds of rise based upon distance between trend and yesterday s closing price

	5-day trend	20-day trend
Yesterday more than +0.5% above trend	76%	67%
Yesterday near trend *(+0.5% to -0.5%)*	45%	*50%
Yesterday more than -0.5% below trend	*22%	43%

Looking ahead: odds of rise in future

	Next 3 days	Next 5 days
Today rose over +0.25%	88%	75%
Today small swing *(+0.25% to -0.25%)*	35%	53%
Today fell below -0.25%	50%	33%

AUGUST 9 ODDS OF A PRICE RISE: 61%

Odds of different size price shift

	1935 to present
Large rise *(above +0.25%)*	35%
Small swing *(+0.25% to -0.25%)*	39%
Large fall (*below -0.25%)*	26%

Odds of rise based on yesterday

	1935 to present
Large rise yesterday *(above +0.25%)*	83%
Small swing yesterday *(+0.25% to -0.25%)*	53%
Large fall yesterday (*below -0.25%)*	36%

DIAGNOSTICS

Odds of price rise based on direction of 5-day and 20-day trend yesterday

	5-day trend	20-day trend
Yesterday rose more than +0.1%	66%	64%
Little change *(+0.1% to -0.1%)*	*14%	54%
Yesterday fell more than -0.1%	80%	64%

Odds of rise based upon distance between trend and yesterday s closing price

	5-day trend	20-day trend
Yesterday more than +0.5% above trend	74%	63%
Yesterday near trend *(+0.5% to -0.5%)*	50%	*0%
Yesterday more than -0.5% below trend	*56%	60%

Looking ahead: odds of rise in future

	Next 3 days	Next 5 days
Today rose over +0.25%	56%	50%
Today small swing *(+0.25% to -0.25%)*	44%	56%
Today fell below -0.25%	67%	83%

* *Per cent based on fewer than 10 observations*

AUGUST 10 ODDS OF A PRICE RISE: 48%

Odds of different size price shift

	1935 to present
Large rise *(above +0.25%)*	37%
Small swing *(+0.25% to -0.25%)*	22%
Large fall *(below -0.25%)*	41%

Odds of rise based on yesterday

	1935 to present
Large rise yesterday *(above +0.25%)*	57%
Small swing yesterda y*(+0.25% to -0.25%)*	32%
Large fall yesterday *(below -0.25%)*	62%

DIAGNOSTICS

Odds of price rise based on direction of 5-day and 20-day trend yesterday

	5-day trend	20-day trend
Yesterday rose more than +0.1%	65%	35%
Little change *(+0.1% to -0.1%)*	*13%	64%
Yesterday fell more than -0.1%	40%	50%

Odds of rise based upon distance between trend and yesterday s closing price

	5-day trend	20-day trend
Yesterday more than +0.5% above trend	69%	50%
Yesterday near trend *(+0.5% to -0.5%)*	32%	*75%
Yesterday more than -0.5% below trend	45%	38%

Looking ahead: odds of rise in future

	Next 3 days	Next 5 days
Today rose over +0.25%	76%	88%
Today small swing *(+0.25% to -0.25%)*	20%	50%
Today fell below -0.25%	47%	58%

AUGUST 11 ODDS OF A PRICE RISE: 55%

Odds of different size price shift

	1935 to present
Large rise *(above +0.25%)*	43%
Small swing *(+0.25% to -0.25%)*	30%
Large fall (*below -0.25%)*	28%

Odds of rise based on yesterday

	1935 to present
Large rise yesterday *(above +0.25%)*	75%
Small swing yesterday *(+0.25% to -0.25%)*	27%
Large fall yesterday (*below -0.25%)*	55%

DIAGNOSTICS

Odds of price rise based on direction of 5-day and 20-day trend yesterday

	5-day trend	20-day trend
Yesterday rose more than +0.1%	57%	57%
Little change *(+0.1% to -0.1%)*	30%	57%
Yesterday fell more than -0.1%	69%	50%

Odds of rise based upon distance between trend and yesterday s closing price

	5-day trend	20-day trend
Yesterday more than +0.5% above trend	53%	52%
Yesterday near trend *(+0.5% to -0.5%)*	56%	*67%
Yesterday more than -0.5% below trend	57%	59%

Looking ahead: odds of rise in future

	Next 3 days	Next 5 days
Today rose over +0.25%	85%	65%
Today small swing *(+0.25% to -0.25%)*	29%	50%
Today fell below -0.25%	62%	62%

* *Per cent based on fewer than 10 observations*

AUGUST 12 ODDS OF A PRICE RISE: 63%

Odds of different size price shift

	1935 to present
Large rise *(above +0.25%)*	44%
Small swing *(+0.25% to -0.25%)*	35%
Large fall (*below -0.25%)*	21%

Odds of rise based on yesterday

	1935 to present
Large rise yesterday *(above +0.25%)*	74%
Small swing yesterday *(+0.25% to -0.25%)*	50%
Large fall yesterday (*below -0.25%)*	54%

DIAGNOSTICS

Odds of price rise based on direction of 5-day and 20-day trend yesterday

	5-day trend	20-day trend
Yesterday rose more than +0.1%	57%	63%
Little change *(+0.1% to -0.1%)*	73%	70%
Yesterday fell more than -0.1%	*67%	57%

Odds of rise based upon distance between trend and yesterday s closing price

	5-day trend	20-day trend
Yesterday more than +0.5% above trend	68%	64%
Yesterday near trend *(+0.5% to -0.5%)*	52%	*33%
Yesterday more than -0.5% below trend	*83%	65%

Looking ahead: odds of rise in future

	Next 3 days	Next 5 days
Today rose over +0.25%	62%	52%
Today small swing *(+0.25% to -0.25%)*	82%	71%
Today fell below -0.25%	20%	30%

AUGUST 13 ODDS OF A PRICE RISE: 51%

Odds of different size price shift

	1935 to present
Large rise *(above +0.25%)*	43%
Small swing *(+0.25% to -0.25%)*	32%
Large fall (*below -0.25%)*	26%

Odds of rise based on yesterday

	1935 to present
Large rise yesterday *(above +0.25%)*	65%
Small swing yesterday *(+0.25% to -0.25%)*	47%
Large fall yesterday (*below -0.25%)*	*22%

DIAGNOSTICS

Odds of price rise based on direction of 5-day and 20-day trend yesterday

	5-day trend	20-day trend
Yesterday rose more than +0.1%	58%	45%
Little change *(+0.1% to -0.1%)*	40%	57%
Yesterday fell more than -0.1%	45%	54%

Odds of rise based upon distance between trend and yesterday s closing price

	5-day trend	20-day trend
Yesterday more than +0.5% above trend	65%	52%
Yesterday near trend *(+0.5% to -0.5%)*	44%	*60%
Yesterday more than -0.5% below trend	*25%	46%

Looking ahead: odds of rise in future

	Next 3 days	Next 5 days
Today rose over +0.25%	65%	55%
Today small swing *(+0.25% to -0.25%)*	53%	60%
Today fell below -0.25%	50%	50%

* *Per cent based on fewer than 10 observations*

AUGUST 14 ODDS OF A PRICE RISE: 52%

Odds of different size price shift

	1935 to present
Large rise *(above +0.25%)*	48%
Small swing *(+0.25% to -0.25%)*	28%
Large fall *(below -0.25%)*	24%

Odds of rise based on yesterday

	1935 to present
Large rise yesterday *(above +0.25%)*	63%
Small swing yesterday *(+0.25% to -0.25%)*	44%
Large fall yesterday *(below -0.25%)*	45%

DIAGNOSTICS

Odds of price rise based on direction of 5-day and 20-day trend yesterday

	5-day trend	20-day trend
Yesterday rose more than +0.1%	52%	67%
Little change *(+0.1% to -0.1%)*	*67%	31%
Yesterday fell more than -0.1%	42%	58%

Odds of rise based upon distance between trend and yesterday s closing price

	5-day trend	20-day trend
Yesterday more than +0.5% above trend	50%	55%
Yesterday near trend *(+0.5% to -0.5%)*	57%	*25%
Yesterday more than -0.5% below trend	*43%	54%

Looking ahead: odds of rise in future

	Next 3 days	Next 5 days
Today rose over +0.25%	73%	68%
Today small swing *(+0.25% to -0.25%)*	38%	46%
Today fell below -0.25%	73%	45%

AUGUST 15 ODDS OF A PRICE RISE: 50%

Odds of different size price shift

	1935 to present
Large rise *(above +0.25%)*	34%
Small swing *(+0.25% to -0.25%)*	36%
Large fall (*below -0.25%)*	30%

Odds of rise based on yesterday

	1935 to present
Large rise yesterday *(above +0.25%)*	72%
Small swing yesterday *(+0.25% to -0.25%)*	29%
Large fall yesterday (*below -0.25%)*	42%

DIAGNOSTICS

Odds of price rise based on direction of 5-day and 20-day trend yesterday

	5-day trend	20-day trend
Yesterday rose more than +0.1%	48%	50%
Little change *(+0.1% to -0.1%)*	*57%	50%
Yesterday fell more than -0.1%	50%	50%

Odds of rise based upon distance between trend and yesterday s closing price

	5-day trend	20-day trend
Yesterday more than +0.5% above trend	54%	46%
Yesterday near trend *(+0.5% to -0.5%)*	48%	*60%
Yesterday more than -0.5% below trend	50%	54%

Looking ahead: odds of rise in future

	Next 3 days	Next 5 days
Today rose over +0.25%	67%	60%
Today small swing *(+0.25% to -0.25%)*	50%	69%
Today fell below -0.25%	46%	54%

* *Per cent based on fewer than 10 observations*

AUGUST 16 ODDS OF A PRICE RISE: 51%

Odds of different size price shift

	1935 to present
Large rise *(above +0.25%)*	33%
Small swing *(+0.25% to -0.25%)*	38%
Large fall (*below -0.25%)*	29%

Odds of rise based on yesterday

	1935 to present
Large rise yesterday *(above +0.25%)*	36%
Small swing yesterday *(+0.25% to -0.25%)*	63%
Large fall yesterday (*below -0.25%)*	50%

DIAGNOSTICS

Odds of price rise based on direction of 5-day and 20-day trend yesterday

	5-day trend	20-day trend
Yesterday rose more than +0.1%	45%	45%
Little change *(+0.1% to -0.1%)*	46%	67%
Yesterday fell more than -0.1%	67%	40%

Odds of rise based upon distance between trend and yesterday s closing price

	5-day trend	20-day trend
Yesterday more than +0.5% above trend	40%	48%
Yesterday near trend *(+0.5% to -0.5%)*	55%	*40%
Yesterday more than -0.5% below trend	*63%	62%

Looking ahead: odds of rise in future

	Next 3 days	Next 5 days
Today rose over +0.25%	60%	53%
Today small swing *(+0.25% to -0.25%)*	47%	65%
Today fell below -0.25%	31%	46%

AUGUST 17 ODDS OF A PRICE RISE: 46%

Odds of different size price shift

	1935 to present
Large rise *(above +0.25%)*	28%
Small swing *(+0.25% to -0.25%)*	33%
Large fall *(below -0.25%)*	39%

Odds of rise based on yesterday

	1935 to present
Large rise yesterday *(above +0.25%)*	60%
Small swing yesterday *(+0.25% to -0.25%)*	46%
Large fall yesterday *(below -0.25%)*	23%

DIAGNOSTICS

Odds of price rise based on direction of 5-day and 20-day trend yesterday

	5-day trend	20-day trend
Yesterday rose more than +0.1%	46%	57%
Little change *(+0.1% to -0.1%)*	*63%	36%
Yesterday fell more than -0.1%	36%	33%

Odds of rise based upon distance between trend and yesterday s closing price

	5-day trend	20-day trend
Yesterday more than +0.5% above trend	40%	50%
Yesterday near trend *(+0.5% to -0.5%)*	61%	*33%
Yesterday more than -0.5% below trend	*25%	45%

Looking ahead: odds of rise in future

	Next 3 days	Next 5 days
Today rose over +0.25%	62%	69%
Today small swing *(+0.25% to -0.25%)*	73%	67%
Today fell below -0.25%	28%	28%

* *Per cent based on fewer than 10 observations*

AUGUST 18 ODDS OF A PRICE RISE: 51%

Odds of different size price shift

	1935 to present
Large rise *(above +0.25%)*	32%
Small swing *(+0.25% to -0.25%)*	36%
Large fall (*below -0.25%)*	32%

Odds of rise based on yesterday

	1935 to present
Large rise yesterday *(above +0.25%)*	73%
Small swing yesterday *(+0.25% to -0.25%)*	53%
Large fall yesterday (*below -0.25%)*	29%

DIAGNOSTICS

Odds of price rise based on direction of 5-day and 20-day trend yesterday

	5-day trend	20-day trend
Yesterday rose more than +0.1%	56%	64%
Little change *(+0.1% to -0.1%)*	*33%	43%
Yesterday fell more than -0.1%	54%	36%

Odds of rise based upon distance between trend and yesterday s closing price

	5-day trend	20-day trend
Yesterday more than +0.5% above trend	71%	59%
Yesterday near trend *(+0.5% to -0.5%)*	50%	*56%
Yesterday more than -0.5% below trend	27%	27%

Looking ahead: odds of rise in future

	Next 3 days	Next 5 days
Today rose over +0.25%	67%	73%
Today small swing *(+0.25% to -0.25%)*	59%	71%
Today fell below -0.25%	33%	40%

AUGUST 19 ODDS OF A PRICE RISE: 42%

Odds of different size price shift

	1935 to present
Large rise *(above +0.25%)*	25%
Small swing *(+0.25% to -0.25%)*	40%
Large fall (*below -0.25%)*	35%

Odds of rise based on yesterday

	1935 to present
Large rise yesterday *(above +0.25%)*	43%
Small swing yesterday *(+0.25% to -0.25%)*	48%
Large fall yesterday (*below -0.25%)*	31%

DIAGNOSTICS

Odds of price rise based on direction of 5-day and 20-day trend yesterday

	5-day trend	20-day trend
Yesterday rose more than +0.1%	41%	41%
Little change *(+0.1% to -0.1%)*	50%	49%
Yesterday fell more than -0.1%	36%	36%

Odds of rise based upon distance between trend and yesterday s closing price

	5-day trend	20-day trend
Yesterday more than +0.5% above trend	47%	33%
Yesterday near trend *(+0.5% to -0.5%)*	44%	*67%
Yesterday more than -0.5% below trend	27%	50%

Looking ahead: odds of rise in future

	Next 3 days	Next 5 days
Today rose over +0.25%	67%	67%
Today small swing *(+0.25% to -0.25%)*	84%	89%
Today fell below -0.25%	47%	53%

* *Per cent based on fewer than 10 observations*

AUGUST 20 ODDS OF A PRICE RISE: 55%

Odds of different size price shift

	1935 to present
Large rise *(above +0.25%)*	47%
Small swing *(+0.25% to -0.25%)*	26%
Large fall (*below -0.25%)*	28%

Odds of rise based on yesterday

	1935 to present
Large rise yesterday *(above +0.25%)*	67%
Small swing yesterday *(+0.25% to -0.25%)*	56%
Large fall yesterday (*below -0.25%)*	47%

DIAGNOSTICS

Odds of price rise based on direction of 5-day and 20-day trend yesterday

	5-day trend	20-day trend
Yesterday rose more than +0.1%	64%	57%
Little change *(+0.1% to -0.1%)*	60%	71%
Yesterday fell more than -0.1%	40%	30%

Odds of rise based upon distance between trend and yesterday s closing price

	5-day trend	20-day trend
Yesterday more than +0.5% above trend	58%	65%
Yesterday near trend *(+0.5% to -0.5%)*	62%	*56%
Yesterday more than -0.5% below trend	43%	33%

Looking ahead: odds of rise in future

	Next 3 days	Next 5 days
Today rose over +0.25%	82%	77%
Today small swing *(+0.25% to -0.25%)*	75%	75%
Today fell below -0.25%	46%	38%

AUGUST 21 ODDS OF A PRICE RISE: 59%

Odds of different size price shift

	1935 to present
Large rise *(above +0.25%)*	48%
Small swing *(+0.25% to -0.25%)*	24%
Large fall (*below -0.25%)*	28%

Odds of rise based on yesterday

	1935 to present
Large rise yesterday *(above +0.25%)*	75%
Small swing yesterday *(+0.25% to -0.25%)*	58%
Large fall yesterday (*below -0.25%)*	36%

DIAGNOSTICS

Odds of price rise based on direction of 5-day and 20-day trend yesterday

	5-day trend	20-day trend
Yesterday rose more than +0.1%	65%	67%
Little change *(+0.1% to -0.1%)*	60%	53%
Yesterday fell more than -0.1%	50%	*56%

Odds of rise based upon distance between trend and yesterday s closing price

	5-day trend	20-day trend
Yesterday more than +0.5% above trend	63%	66%
Yesterday near trend *(+0.5% to -0.5%)*	65%	*75%
Yesterday more than -0.5% below trend	46%	38%

Looking ahead: odds of rise in future

	Next 3 days	Next 5 days
Today rose over +0.25%	55%	59%
Today small swing *(+0.25% to -0.25%)*	64%	73%
Today fell below -0.25%	23%	46%

* *Per cent based on fewer than 10 observations*

AUGUST 22 ODDS OF A PRICE RISE: 47%

Odds of different size price shift

	1935 to present
Large rise *(above +0.25%)*	40%
Small swing *(+0.25% to -0.25%)*	27%
Large fall *(below -0.25%)*	33%

Odds of rise based on yesterday

	1935 to present
Large rise yesterday *(above +0.25%)*	52%
Small swing yesterday *(+0.25% to -0.25%)*	*56%
Large fall yesterday *(below -0.25%)*	33%

DIAGNOSTICS

Odds of price rise based on direction of 5-day and 20-day trend yesterday

	5-day trend	20-day trend
Yesterday rose more than +0.1%	59%	63%
Little change *(+0.1% to -0.1%)*	53%	50%
Yesterday fell more than -0.1%	23%	9%

Odds of rise based upon distance between trend and yesterday s closing price

	5-day trend	20-day trend
Yesterday more than +0.5% above trend	46%	60%
Yesterday near trend *(+0.5% to -0.5%)*	64%	*33%
Yesterday more than -0.5% below trend	10%	17%

Looking ahead: odds of rise in future

	Next 3 days	Next 5 days
Today rose over +0.25%	56%	50%
Today small swing *(+0.25% to -0.25%)*	50%	67%
Today fell below -0.25%	47%	53%

AUGUST 23 ODDS OF A PRICE RISE: 48%

Odds of different size price shift

	1935 to present
Large rise *(above +0.25%)*	24%
Small swing *(+0.25% to -0.25%)*	46%
Large fall (*below -0.25%)*	30%

Odds of rise based on yesterday

	1935 to present
Large rise yesterday *(above +0.25%)*	42%
Small swing yesterday *(+0.25% to -0.25%)*	42%
Large fall yesterday (*below -0.25%)*	60%

DIAGNOSTICS

Odds of price rise based on direction of 5-day and 20-day trend yesterday

	5-day trend	20-day trend
Yesterday rose more than +0.1%	39%	55%
Little change *(+0.1% to -0.1%)*	*75%	46%
Yesterday fell more than -0.1%	45%	36%

Odds of rise based upon distance between trend and yesterday s closing price

	5-day trend	20-day trend
Yesterday more than +0.5% above trend	50%	46%
Yesterday near trend *(+0.5% to -0.5%)*	48%	*75%
Yesterday more than -0.5% below trend	45%	36%

Looking ahead: odds of rise in future

	Next 3 days	Next 5 days
Today rose over +0.25%	36%	45%
Today small swing *(+0.25% to -0.25%)*	57%	67%
Today fell below -0.25%	43%	57%

* *Per cent based on fewer than 10 observations*

AUGUST 24 ODDS OF A PRICE RISE: 59%

Odds of different size price shift

	1935 to present
Large rise *(above +0.25%)*	37%
Small swing *(+0.25% to -0.25%)*	41%
Large fall *(below -0.25%)*	22%

Odds of rise based on yesterday

	1935 to present
Large rise yesterday *(above +0.25%)*	*67%
Small swing yesterday *(+0.25% to -0.25%)*	64%
Large fall yesterday *(below -0.25%)*	47%

DIAGNOSTICS

Odds of price rise based on direction of 5-day and 20-day trend yesterday

	5-day trend	20-day trend
Yesterday rose more than +0.1%	71%	60%
Little change *(+0.1% to -0.1%)*	73%	53%
Yesterday fell more than -0.1%	39%	64%

Odds of rise based upon distance between trend and yesterday s closing price

	5-day trend	20-day trend
Yesterday more than +0.5% above trend	*56%	62%
Yesterday near trend *(+0.5% to -0.5%)*	70%	*67%
Yesterday more than -0.5% below trend	43%	50%

Looking ahead: odds of rise in future

	Next 3 days	Next 5 days
Today rose over +0.25%	53%	59%
Today small swing *(+0.25% to -0.25%)*	74%	58%
Today fell below -0.25%	30%	60%

AUGUST 25 ODDS OF A PRICE RISE: 56%

Odds of different size price shift

	1935 to present
Large rise *(above +0.25%)*	44%
Small swing *(+0.25% to -0.25%)*	30%
Large fall *(below -0.25%)*	26%

Odds of rise based on yesterday

	1935 to present
Large rise yesterday *(above +0.25%)*	75%
Small swing yesterday *(+0.25% to -0.25%)*	56%
Large fall yesterday *(below -0.25%)*	27%

DIAGNOSTICS

Odds of price rise based on direction of 5-day and 20-day trend yesterday

	5-day trend	20-day trend
Yesterday rose more than +0.1%	58%	47%
Little change *(+0.1% to -0.1%)*	*71%	67%
Yesterday fell more than -0.1%	47%	55%

Odds of rise based upon distance between trend and yesterday s closing price

	5-day trend	20-day trend
Yesterday more than +0.5% above trend	55%	58%
Yesterday near trend *(+0.5% to -0.5%)*	60%	*33%
Yesterday more than -0.5% below trend	50%	57%

Looking ahead: odds of rise in future

	Next 3 days	Next 5 days
Today rose over +0.25%	58%	42%
Today small swing *(+0.25% to -0.25%)*	54%	62%
Today fell below -0.25%	55%	73%

* *Per cent based on fewer than 10 observations*

AUGUST 26 ODDS OF A PRICE RISE: 48%

Odds of different size price shift

	1935 to present
Large rise *(above +0.25%)*	34%
Small swing *(+0.25% to -0.25%)*	41%
Large fall (*below -0.25%)*	25%

Odds of rise based on yesterday

	1935 to present
Large rise yesterday *(above +0.25%)*	55%
Small swing yesterday *(+0.25% to -0.25%)*	50%
Large fall yesterday (*below -0.25%)*	33%

DIAGNOSTICS

Odds of price rise based on direction of 5-day and 20-day trend yesterday

	5-day trend	20-day trend
Yesterday rose more than +0.1%	47%	45%
Little change *(+0.1% to -0.1%)*	55%	50%
Yesterday fell more than -0.1%	43%	50%

Odds of rise based upon distance between trend and yesterday s closing price

	5-day trend	20-day trend
Yesterday more than +0.5% above trend	59%	52%
Yesterday near trend *(+0.5% to -0.5%)*	35%	*38%
Yesterday more than -0.5% below trend	50%	45%

Looking ahead: odds of rise in future

	Next 3 days	Next 5 days
Today rose over +0.25%	67%	67%
Today small swing *(+0.25% to -0.25%)*	56%	50%
Today fell below -0.25%	36%	64%

AUGUST 27 ODDS OF A PRICE RISE: 40%

Odds of different size price shift

	1935 to present
Large rise *(above +0.25%)*	30%
Small swing *(+0.25% to -0.25%)*	44%
Large fall *(below -0.25%)*	26%

Odds of rise based on yesterday

	1935 to present
Large rise yesterday *(above +0.25%)*	46%
Small swing yesterday *(+0.25% to -0.25%)*	43%
Large fall yesterday *(below -0.25%)*	*22%

DIAGNOSTICS

Odds of price rise based on direction of 5-day and 20-day trend yesterday

	5-day trend	20-day trend
Yesterday rose more than +0.1%	29%	46%
Little change *(+0.1% to -0.1%)*	70%	*44%
Yesterday fell more than -0.1%	*33%	*13%

Odds of rise based upon distance between trend and yesterday s closing price

	5-day trend	20-day trend
Yesterday more than +0.5% above trend	33%	38%
Yesterday near trend *(+0.5% to -0.5%)*	35%	*75%
Yesterday more than -0.5% below trend	55%	30%

Looking ahead: odds of rise in future

	Next 3 days	Next 5 days
Today rose over +0.25%	69%	69%
Today small swing *(+0.25% to -0.25%)*	63%	74%
Today fell below -0.25%	45%	64%

* *Per cent based on fewer than 10 observations*

AUGUST 28 ODDS OF A PRICE RISE: 60%

Odds of different size price shift

	1935 to present
Large rise *(above +0.25%)*	29%
Small swing *(+0.25% to -0.25%)*	55%
Large fall (*below -0.25%)*	17%

Odds of rise based on yesterday

	1935 to present
Large rise yesterday *(above +0.25%)*	79%
Small swing yesterday *(+0.25% to -0.25%)*	50%
Large fall yesterday (*below -0.25%)*	*50%

DIAGNOSTICS

Odds of price rise based on direction of 5-day and 20-day trend yesterday

	5-day trend	20-day trend
Yesterday rose more than +0.1%	58%	60%
Little change *(+0.1% to -0.1%)*	50%	*71%
Yesterday fell more than -0.1%	69%	50%

Odds of rise based upon distance between trend and yesterday s closing price

	5-day trend	20-day trend
Yesterday more than +0.5% above trend	*86%	56%
Yesterday near trend *(+0.5% to -0.5%)*	56%	*100%
Yesterday more than -0.5% below trend	50%	54%

Looking ahead: odds of rise in future

	Next 3 days	Next 5 days
Today rose over +0.25%	58%	50%
Today small swing *(+0.25% to -0.25%)*	74%	74%
Today fell below -0.25%	*57%	*71%

AUGUST 29 ODDS OF A PRICE RISE: 48%

Odds of different size price shift

	1935 to present
Large rise *(above +0.25%)*	38%
Small swing *(+0.25% to -0.25%)*	35%
Large fall *(below -0.25%)*	28%

Odds of rise based on yesterday

	1935 to present
Large rise yesterday *(above +0.25%)*	57%
Small swing yesterday *(+0.25% to -0.25%)*	47%
Large fall yesterday *(below -0.25%)*	*29%

DIAGNOSTICS

Odds of price rise based on direction of 5-day and 20-day trend yesterday

	5-day trend	20-day trend
Yesterday rose more than +0.1%	47%	45%
Little change *(+0.1% to -0.1%)*	50%	50%
Yesterday fell more than -0.1%	45%	*50%

Odds of rise based upon distance between trend and yesterday s closing price

	5-day trend	20-day trend
Yesterday more than +0.5% above trend	*56%	42%
Yesterday near trend *(+0.5% to -0.5%)*	50%	*50%
Yesterday more than -0.5% below trend	*29%	58%

Looking ahead: odds of rise in future

	Next 3 days	Next 5 days
Today rose over +0.25%	60%	67%
Today small swing *(+0.25% to -0.25%)*	79%	79%
Today fell below -0.25%	36%	36%

* *Per cent based on fewer than 10 observations*

AUGUST 30 ODDS OF A PRICE RISE: 60%

Odds of different size price shift

	1935 to present
Large rise *(above +0.25%)*	38%
Small swing *(+0.25% to -0.25%)*	35%
Large fall (*below -0.25%)*	28%

Odds of rise based on yesterday

	1935 to present
Large rise yesterday *(above +0.25%)*	80%
Small swing yesterday *(+0.25% to -0.25%)*	57%
Large fall yesterday (*below -0.25%)*	36%

DIAGNOSTICS

Odds of price rise based on direction of 5-day and 20-day trend yesterday

	5-day trend	20-day trend
Yesterday rose more than +0.1%	54%	52%
Little change *(+0.1% to -0.1%)*	71%	90%
Yesterday fell more than -0.1%	50%	*44%

Odds of rise based upon distance between trend and yesterday s closing price

	5-day trend	20-day trend
Yesterday more than +0.5% above trend	64%	56%
Yesterday near trend *(+0.5% to -0.5%)*	67%	70%
Yesterday more than -0.5% below trend	*20%	58%

Looking ahead: odds of rise in future

	Next 3 days	Next 5 days
Today rose over +0.25%	47%	53%
Today small swing *(+0.25% to -0.25%)*	79%	79%
Today fell below -0.25%	18%	36%

AUGUST 31 ODDS OF A PRICE RISE: 54%

Odds of different size price shift

	1935 to present
Large rise *(above +0.25%)*	29%
Small swing *(+0.25% to -0.25%)*	44%
Large fall *(below -0.25%)*	27%

Odds of rise based on yesterday

	1935 to present
Large rise yesterday *(above +0.25%)*	47%
Small swing yesterday *(+0.25% to -0.25%)*	71%
Large fall yesterday *(below -0.25%)*	42%

DIAGNOSTICS

Odds of price rise based on direction of 5-day and 20-day trend yesterday

	5-day trend	20-day trend
Yesterday rose more than +0.1%	50%	59%
Little change *(+0.1% to -0.1%)*	55%	50%
Yesterday fell more than -0.1%	60%	*44%

Odds of rise based upon distance between trend and yesterday s closing price

	5-day trend	20-day trend
Yesterday more than +0.5% above trend	53%	63%
Yesterday near trend *(+0.5% to -0.5%)*	56%	*20%
Yesterday more than -0.5% below trend	*50%	50%

Looking ahead: odds of rise in future

	Next 3 days	Next 5 days
Today rose over +0.25%	67%	75%
Today small swing *(+0.25% to -0.25%)*	56%	56%
Today fell below -0.25%	64%	64%

* *Per cent based on fewer than 10 observations*

SEPTEMBER

PROFIT ODDS SUMMARY FOR THE MONTH

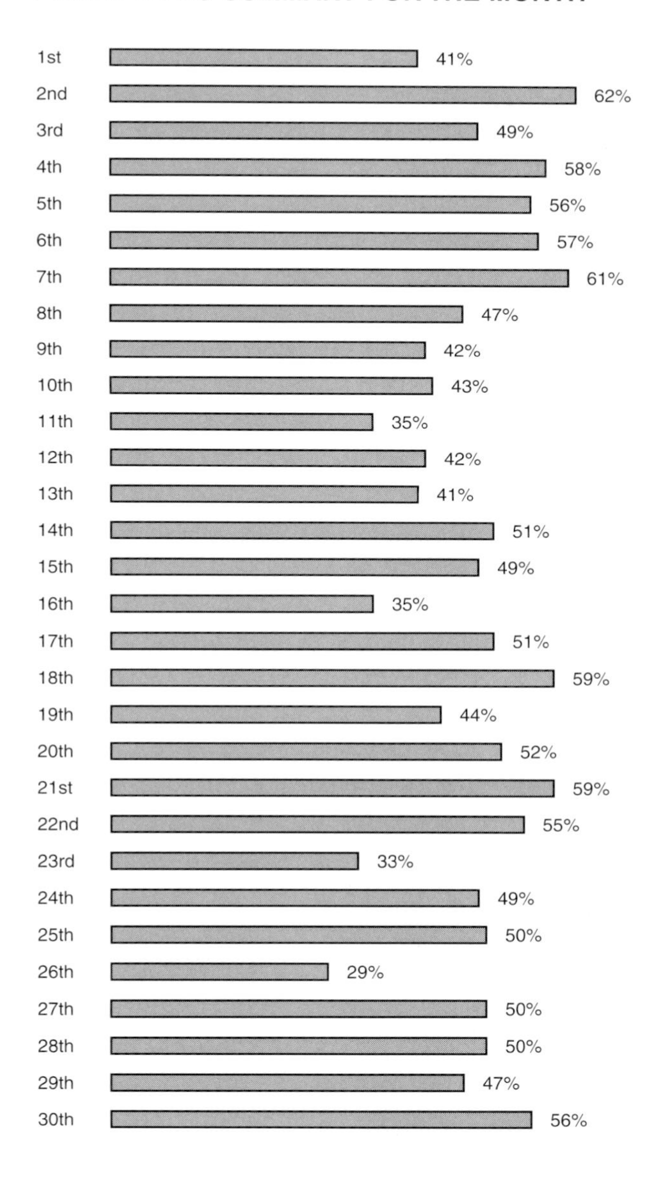

SEPTEMBER 1 ODDS OF A PRICE RISE: 41%

Odds of different size price shift

	1935 to present
Large rise *(above +0.25%)*	28%
Small swing *(+0.25% to -0.25%)*	35%
Large fall (*below -0.25%)*	37%

Odds of rise based on yesterday

	1935 to present
Large rise yesterday *(above +0.25%)*	64%
Small swing yesterday *(+0.25% to -0.25%)*	21%
Large fall yesterday (*below -0.25%)*	46%

DIAGNOSTICS

Odds of price rise based on direction of 5-day and 20-day trend yesterday

	5-day trend	20-day trend
Yesterday rose more than +0.1%	40%	57%
Little change *(+0.1% to -0.1%)*	*22%	21%
Yesterday fell more than -0.1%	53%	36%

Odds of rise based upon distance between trend and yesterday s closing price

	5-day trend	20-day trend
Yesterday more than +0.5% above trend	50%	45%
Yesterday near trend *(+0.5% to -0.5%)*	25%	*57%
Yesterday more than -0.5% below trend	50%	29%

Looking ahead: odds of rise in future

	Next 3 days	Next 5 days
Today rose over +0.25%	85%	69%
Today small swing *(+0.25% to -0.25%)*	88%	75%
Today fell below -0.25%	47%	59%

* *Per cent based on fewer than 10 observations*

SEPTEMBER 2 ODDS OF A PRICE RISE: 62%

Odds of different size price shift

	1935 to present
Large rise *(above +0.25%)*	47%
Small swing *(+0.25% to -0.25%)*	30%
Large fall (*below -0.25%)*	23%

Odds of rise based on yesterday

	1935 to present
Large rise yesterday *(above +0.25%)*	62%
Small swing yesterday *(+0.25% to -0.25%)*	61%
Large fall yesterday (*below -0.25%)*	63%

DIAGNOSTICS

Odds of price rise based on direction of 5-day and 20-day trend yesterday

	5-day trend	20-day trend
Yesterday rose more than +0.1%	60%	68%
Little change *(+0.1% to -0.1%)*	*44%	42%
Yesterday fell more than -0.1%	72%	70%

Odds of rise based upon distance between trend and yesterday s closing price

	5-day trend	20-day trend
Yesterday more than +0.5% above trend	57%	62%
Yesterday near trend *(+0.5% to -0.5%)*	62%	*57%
Yesterday more than -0.5% below trend	67%	64%

Looking ahead: odds of rise in future

	Next 3 days	Next 5 days
Today rose over +0.25%	91%	59%
Today small swing *(+0.25% to -0.25%)*	57%	57%
Today fell below -0.25%	73%	64%

SEPTEMBER 3 ODDS OF A PRICE RISE: 49%

Odds of different size price shift

	1935 to present
Large rise *(above +0.25%)*	32%
Small swing *(+0.25% to -0.25%)*	47%
Large fall (*below -0.25%)*	21%

Odds of rise based on yesterday

	1935 to present
Large rise yesterday *(above +0.25%)*	55%
Small swing yesterday *(+0.25% to -0.25%)*	43%
Large fall yesterday (*below -0.25%)*	45%

DIAGNOSTICS

Odds of price rise based on direction of 5-day and 20-day trend yesterday

	5-day trend	20-day trend
Yesterday rose more than +0.1%	48%	46%
Little change *(+0.1% to -0.1%)*	62%	*67%
Yesterday fell more than -0.1%	36%	40%

Odds of rise based upon distance between trend and yesterday s closing price

	5-day trend	20-day trend
Yesterday more than +0.5% above trend	60%	48%
Yesterday near trend *(+0.5% to -0.5%)*	44%	58%
Yesterday more than -0.5% below trend	*43%	40%

Looking ahead: odds of rise in future

	Next 3 days	Next 5 days
Today rose over +0.25%	67%	47%
Today small swing *(+0.25% to -0.25%)*	41%	36%
Today fell below -0.25%	60%	60%

* *Per cent based on fewer than 10 observations*

SEPTEMBER 4 ODDS OF A PRICE RISE: 58%

Odds of different size price shift

	1935 to present
Large rise *(above +0.25%)*	53%
Small swing *(+0.25% to -0.25%)*	18%
Large fall (*below -0.25%)*	29%

Odds of rise based on yesterday

	1935 to present
Large rise yesterday *(above +0.25%)*	93%
Small swing yesterday *(+0.25% to -0.25%)*	43%
Large fall yesterday (*below -0.25%)*	40%

DIAGNOSTICS

Odds of price rise based on direction of 5-day and 20-day trend yesterday

	5-day trend	20-day trend
Yesterday rose more than +0.1%	72%	61%
Little change *(+0.1% to -0.1%)*	30%	57%
Yesterday fell more than -0.1%	50%	*50%

Odds of rise based upon distance between trend and yesterday s closing price

	5-day trend	20-day trend
Yesterday more than +0.5% above trend	73%	67%
Yesterday near trend *(+0.5% to -0.5%)*	57%	60%
Yesterday more than -0.5% below trend	*33%	36%

Looking ahead: odds of rise in future

	Next 3 days	Next 5 days
Today rose over +0.25%	54%	58%
Today small swing *(+0.25% to -0.25%)*	*75%	*75%
Today fell below -0.25%	54%	54%

SEPTEMBER 5 ODDS OF A PRICE RISE: 56%

Odds of different size price shift

	1935 to present
Large rise *(above +0.25%)*	38%
Small swing *(+0.25% to -0.25%)*	40%
Large fall *(below -0.25%)*	22%

Odds of rise based on yesterday

	1935 to present
Large rise yesterday *(above +0.25%)*	63%
Small swing yesterday *(+0.25% to -0.25%)*	*63%
Large fall yesterday *(below -0.25%)*	38%

DIAGNOSTICS

Odds of price rise based on direction of 5-day and 20-day trend yesterday

	5-day trend	20-day trend
Yesterday rose more than +0.1%	54%	62%
Little change *(+0.1% to -0.1%)*	*71%	50%
Yesterday fell more than -0.1%	50%	50%

Odds of rise based upon distance between trend and yesterday s closing price

	5-day trend	20-day trend
Yesterday more than +0.5% above trend	65%	62%
Yesterday near trend *(+0.5% to -0.5%)*	47%	*44%
Yesterday more than -0.5% below trend	55%	53%

Looking ahead: odds of rise in future

	Next 3 days	Next 5 days
Today rose over +0.25%	59%	47%
Today small swing *(+0.25% to -0.25%)*	61%	50%
Today fell below -0.25%	30%	30%

* *Per cent based on fewer than 10 observations*

SEPTEMBER 6 ODDS OF A PRICE RISE: 57%

Odds of different size price shift

	1935 to present
Large rise *(above +0.25%)*	41%
Small swing *(+0.25% to -0.25%)*	35%
Large fall (*below -0.25%)*	24%

Odds of rise based on yesterday

	1935 to present
Large rise yesterday *(above +0.25%)*	59%
Small swing yesterday *(+0.25% to -0.25%)*	56%
Large fall yesterday (*below -0.25%)*	55%

DIAGNOSTICS

Odds of price rise based on direction of 5-day and 20-day trend yesterday

	5-day trend	20-day trend
Yesterday rose more than +0.1%	50%	67%
Little change *(+0.1% to -0.1%)*	80%	58%
Yesterday fell more than -0.1%	50%	38%

Odds of rise based upon distance between trend and yesterday s closing price

	5-day trend	20-day trend
Yesterday more than +0.5% above trend	60%	63%
Yesterday near trend *(+0.5% to -0.5%)*	53%	*43%
Yesterday more than -0.5% below trend	58%	53%

Looking ahead: odds of rise in future

	Next 3 days	Next 5 days
Today rose over +0.25%	42%	37%
Today small swing *(+0.25% to -0.25%)*	44%	38%
Today fell below -0.25%	36%	36%

SEPTEMBER 7 ODDS OF A PRICE RISE: 61%

Odds of different size price shift

	1935 to present
Large rise *(above +0.25%)*	43%
Small swing *(+0.25% to -0.25%)*	39%
Large fall (*below -0.25%)*	17%

Odds of rise based on yesterday

	1935 to present
Large rise yesterday *(above +0.25%)*	67%
Small swing yesterday *(+0.25% to -0.25%)*	50%
Large fall yesterday (*below -0.25%)*	67%

DIAGNOSTICS

Odds of price rise based on direction of 5-day and 20-day trend yesterday

	5-day trend	20-day trend
Yesterday rose more than +0.1%	63%	61%
Little change *(+0.1% to -0.1%)*	67%	56%
Yesterday fell more than -0.1%	53%	67%

Odds of rise based upon distance between trend and yesterday s closing price

	5-day trend	20-day trend
Yesterday more than +0.5% above trend	67%	75%
Yesterday near trend *(+0.5% to -0.5%)*	60%	36%
Yesterday more than -0.5% below trend	55%	60%

Looking ahead: odds of rise in future

	Next 3 days	Next 5 days
Today rose over +0.25%	30%	40%
Today small swing *(+0.25% to -0.25%)*	50%	44%
Today fell below -0.25%	*25%	*25%

* *Per cent based on fewer than 10 observations*

SEPTEMBER 8 ODDS OF A PRICE RISE: 47%

Odds of different size price shift

	1935 to present
Large rise *(above +0.25%)*	19%
Small swing *(+0.25% to -0.25%)*	47%
Large fall (*below -0.25%)*	34%

Odds of rise based on yesterday

	1935 to present
Large rise yesterday *(above +0.25%)*	47%
Small swing yesterday *(+0.25% to -0.25%)*	55%
Large fall yesterday (*below -0.25%)*	*25%

DIAGNOSTICS

Odds of price rise based on direction of 5-day and 20-day trend yesterday

	5-day trend	20-day trend
Yesterday rose more than +0.1%	52%	48%
Little change *(+0.1% to -0.1%)*	*50%	53%
Yesterday fell more than -0.1%	30%	*33%

Odds of rise based upon distance between trend and yesterday s closing price

	5-day trend	20-day trend
Yesterday more than +0.5% above trend	45%	46%
Yesterday near trend *(+0.5% to -0.5%)*	55%	*57%
Yesterday more than -0.5% below trend	*20%	43%

Looking ahead: odds of rise in future

	Next 3 days	Next 5 days
Today rose over +0.25%	*67%	*56%
Today small swing *(+0.25% to -0.25%)*	45%	41%
Today fell below -0.25%	25%	25%

SEPTEMBER 9 ODDS OF A PRICE RISE: 42%

Odds of different size price shift

	1935 to present
Large rise *(above +0.25%)*	29%
Small swing *(+0.25% to -0.25%)*	25%
Large fall (*below -0.25%)*	46%

Odds of rise based on yesterday

	1935 to present
Large rise yesterday *(above +0.25%)*	40%
Small swing yesterday *(+0.25% to -0.25%)*	48%
Large fall yesterday (*below -0.25%)*	33%

DIAGNOSTICS

Odds of price rise based on direction of 5-day and 20-day trend yesterday

	5-day trend	20-day trend
Yesterday rose more than +0.1%	38%	39%
Little change *(+0.1% to -0.1%)*	50%	40%
Yesterday fell more than -0.1%	*38%	50%

Odds of rise based upon distance between trend and yesterday s closing price

	5-day trend	20-day trend
Yesterday more than +0.5% above trend	46%	38%
Yesterday near trend *(+0.5% to -0.5%)*	44%	60%
Yesterday more than -0.5% below trend	30%	33%

Looking ahead: odds of rise in future

	Next 3 days	Next 5 days
Today rose over +0.25%	36%	36%
Today small swing *(+0.25% to -0.25%)*	50%	58%
Today fell below -0.25%	23%	36%

* *Per cent based on fewer than 10 observations*

SEPTEMBER 10 ODDS OF A PRICE RISE: 43%

Odds of different size price shift

	1935 to present
Large rise *(above +0.25%)*	21%
Small swing *(+0.25% to -0.25%)*	43%
Large fall (*below -0.25%)*	36%

Odds of rise based on yesterday

	1935 to present
Large rise yesterday *(above +0.25%)*	47%
Small swing yesterda y*(+0.25% to -0.25%)*	54%
Large fall yesterday (*below -0.25%)*	29%

DIAGNOSTICS

Odds of price rise based on direction of 5-day and 20-day trend yesterday

	5-day trend	20-day trend
Yesterday rose more than +0.1%	53%	33%
Little change *(+0.1% to -0.1%)*	35%	56%
Yesterday fell more than -0.1%	36%	40%

Odds of rise based upon distance between trend and yesterday s closing price

	5-day trend	20-day trend
Yesterday more than +0.5% above trend	47%	38%
Yesterday near trend *(+0.5% to -0.5%)*	35%	*50%
Yesterday more than -0.5% below trend	50%	46%

Looking ahead: odds of rise in future

	Next 3 days	Next 5 days
Today rose over +0.25%	70%	80%
Today small swing *(+0.25% to -0.25%)*	35%	50%
Today fell below -0.25%	35%	29%

SEPTEMBER 11 ODDS OF A PRICE RISE: 35%

Odds of different size price shift

	1935 to present
Large rise *(above +0.25%)*	26%
Small swing *(+0.25% to -0.25%)*	28%
Large fall *(below -0.25%)*	46%

Odds of rise based on yesterday

	1935 to present
Large rise yesterday *(above +0.25%)*	46%
Small swing yesterday *(+0.25% to -0.25%)*	40%
Large fall yesterday *(below -0.25%)*	22%

DIAGNOSTICS

Odds of price rise based on direction of 5-day and 20-day trend yesterday

	5-day trend	20-day trend
Yesterday rose more than +0.1%	33%	13%
Little change *(+0.1% to -0.1%)*	45%	65%
Yesterday fell more than -0.1%	29%	23%

Odds of rise based upon distance between trend and yesterday s closing price

	5-day trend	20-day trend
Yesterday more than +0.5% above trend	50%	29%
Yesterday near trend *(+0.5% to -0.5%)*	35%	60%
Yesterday more than -0.5% below trend	23%	25%

Looking ahead: odds of rise in future

	Next 3 days	Next 5 days
Today rose over +0.25%	50%	67%
Today small swing *(+0.25% to -0.25%)*	54%	54%
Today fell below -0.25%	43%	48%

* *Per cent based on fewer than 10 observations*

SEPTEMBER 12 ODDS OF A PRICE RISE: 42%

Odds of different size price shift

	1935 to present
Large rise *(above +0.25%)*	33%
Small swing *(+0.25% to -0.25%)*	31%
Large fall *(below -0.25%)*	36%

Odds of rise based on yesterday

	1935 to present
Large rise yesterday *(above +0.25%)*	*67%
Small swing yesterday *(+0.25% to -0.25%)*	45%
Large fall yesterday *(below -0.25%)*	32%

DIAGNOSTICS

Odds of price rise based on direction of 5-day and 20-day trend yesterday

	5-day trend	20-day trend
Yesterday rose more than +0.1%	62%	33%
Little change *(+0.1% to -0.1%)*	29%	56%
Yesterday fell more than -0.1%	39%	36%

Odds of rise based upon distance between trend and yesterday s closing price

	5-day trend	20-day trend
Yesterday more than +0.5% above trend	*71%	37%
Yesterday near trend *(+0.5% to -0.5%)*	30%	*56%
Yesterday more than -0.5% below trend	44%	41%

Looking ahead: odds of rise in future

	Next 3 days	Next 5 days
Today rose over +0.25%	53%	47%
Today small swing *(+0.25% to -0.25%)*	64%	71%
Today fell below -0.25%	31%	31%

SEPTEMBER 13 ODDS OF A PRICE RISE: 41%

Odds of different size price shift

	1935 to present
Large rise *(above +0.25%)*	33%
Small swing *(+0.25% to -0.25%)*	26%
Large fall *(below -0.25%)*	41%

Odds of rise based on yesterday

	1935 to present
Large rise yesterday *(above +0.25%)*	69%
Small swing yesterday *(+0.25% to -0.25%)*	22%
Large fall yesterday *(below -0.25%)*	40%

DIAGNOSTICS

Odds of price rise based on direction of 5-day and 20-day trend yesterday

	5-day trend	20-day trend
Yesterday rose more than +0.1%	58%	38%
Little change *(+0.1% to -0.1%)*	38%	33%
Yesterday fell more than -0.1%	33%	53%

Odds of rise based upon distance between trend and yesterday s closing price

	5-day trend	20-day trend
Yesterday more than +0.5% above trend	*67%	47%
Yesterday near trend *(+0.5% to -0.5%)*	42%	42%
Yesterday more than -0.5% below trend	31%	35%

Looking ahead: odds of rise in future

	Next 3 days	Next 5 days
Today rose over +0.25%	47%	33%
Today small swing *(+0.25% to -0.25%)*	50%	58%
Today fell below -0.25%	32%	32%

* *Per cent based on fewer than 10 observations*

SEPTEMBER 14 ODDS OF A PRICE RISE: 51%

Odds of different size price shift

	1935 to present
Large rise *(above +0.25%)*	40%
Small swing *(+0.25% to -0.25%)*	31%
Large fall (*below -0.25%)*	29%

Odds of rise based on yesterday

	1935 to present
Large rise yesterday *(above +0.25%)*	67%
Small swing yesterday *(+0.25% to -0.25%)*	42%
Large fall yesterday (*below -0.25%)*	44%

DIAGNOSTICS

Odds of price rise based on direction of 5-day and 20-day trend yesterday

	5-day trend	20-day trend
Yesterday rose more than +0.1%	53%	54%
Little change *(+0.1% to -0.1%)*	*56%	53%
Yesterday fell more than -0.1%	48%	46%

Odds of rise based upon distance between trend and yesterday s closing price

	5-day trend	20-day trend
Yesterday more than +0.5% above trend	*75%	63%
Yesterday near trend *(+0.5% to -0.5%)*	45%	*56%
Yesterday more than -0.5% below trend	47%	35%

Looking ahead: odds of rise in future

	Next 3 days	Next 5 days
Today rose over +0.25%	56%	56%
Today small swing *(+0.25% to -0.25%)*	43%	57%
Today fell below -0.25%	38%	46%

SEPTEMBER 15 ODDS OF A PRICE RISE: 49%

Odds of different size price shift

	1935 to present
Large rise *(above +0.25%)*	34%
Small swing *(+0.25% to -0.25%)*	32%
Large fall *(below -0.25%)*	34%

Odds of rise based on yesterday

	1935 to present
Large rise yesterday *(above +0.25%)*	50%
Small swing yesterday *(+0.25% to -0.25%)*	33%
Large fall yesterday *(below -0.25%)*	64%

DIAGNOSTICS

Odds of price rise based on direction of 5-day and 20-day trend yesterday

	5-day trend	20-day trend
Yesterday rose more than +0.1%	29%	50%
Little change *(+0.1% to -0.1%)*	50%	39%
Yesterday fell more than -0.1%	61%	62%

Odds of rise based upon distance between trend and yesterday s closing price

	5-day trend	20-day trend
Yesterday more than +0.5% above trend	45%	45%
Yesterday near trend *(+0.5% to -0.5%)*	50%	*50%
Yesterday more than -0.5% below trend	50%	53%

Looking ahead: odds of rise in future

	Next 3 days	Next 5 days
Today rose over +0.25%	69%	63%
Today small swing *(+0.25% to -0.25%)*	40%	47%
Today fell below -0.25%	50%	63%

* *Per cent based on fewer than 10 observations*

SEPTEMBER 16 ODDS OF A PRICE RISE: 35%

Odds of different size price shift

	1935 to present
Large rise *(above +0.25%)*	25%
Small swing *(+0.25% to -0.25%)*	25%
Large fall (*below -0.25%)*	50%

Odds of rise based on yesterday

	1935 to present
Large rise yesterday *(above +0.25%)*	53%
Small swing yesterday *(+0.25% to -0.25%)*	29%
Large fall yesterday (*below -0.25%)*	25%

DIAGNOSTICS

Odds of price rise based on direction of 5-day and 20-day trend yesterday

	5-day trend	20-day trend
Yesterday rose more than +0.1%	46%	40%
Little change *(+0.1% to -0.1%)*	42%	40%
Yesterday fell more than -0.1%	26%	23%

Odds of rise based upon distance between trend and yesterday s closing price

	5-day trend	20-day trend
Yesterday more than +0.5% above trend	50%	38%
Yesterday near trend *(+0.5% to -0.5%)*	36%	45%
Yesterday more than -0.5% below trend	23%	25%

Looking ahead: odds of rise in future

	Next 3 days	Next 5 days
Today rose over +0.25%	67%	58%
Today small swing *(+0.25% to -0.25%)*	58%	67%
Today fell below -0.25%	50%	46%

SEPTEMBER 17 ODDS OF A PRICE RISE: 51%

Odds of different size price shift

	1935 to present
Large rise *(above +0.25%)*	36%
Small swing *(+0.25% to -0.25%)*	40%
Large fall (*below -0.25%)*	23%

Odds of rise based on yesterday

	1935 to present
Large rise yesterday *(above +0.25%)*	73%
Small swing yesterday *(+0.25% to -0.25%)*	50%
Large fall yesterday (*below -0.25%)*	35%

DIAGNOSTICS

Odds of price rise based on direction of 5-day and 20-day trend yesterday

	5-day trend	20-day trend
Yesterday rose more than +0.1%	67%	56%
Little change *(+0.1% to -0.1%)*	67%	53%
Yesterday fell more than -0.1%	35%	43%

Odds of rise based upon distance between trend and yesterday s closing price

	5-day trend	20-day trend
Yesterday more than +0.5% above trend	64%	56%
Yesterday near trend *(+0.5% to -0.5%)*	58%	57%
Yesterday more than -0.5% below trend	35%	40%

Looking ahead: odds of rise in future

	Next 3 days	Next 5 days
Today rose over +0.25%	76%	71%
Today small swing *(+0.25% to -0.25%)*	74%	68%
Today fell below -0.25%	45%	45%

* *Per cent based on fewer than 10 observations*

SEPTEMBER 18 ODDS OF A PRICE RISE: 59%

Odds of different size price shift

	1935 to present
Large rise *(above +0.25%)*	43%
Small swing *(+0.25% to -0.25%)*	33%
Large fall (*below -0.25%)*	24%

Odds of rise based on yesterday

	1935 to present
Large rise yesterday *(above +0.25%)*	79%
Small swing yesterday *(+0.25% to -0.25%)*	47%
Large fall yesterday (*below -0.25%)*	40%

DIAGNOSTICS

Odds of price rise based on direction of 5-day and 20-day trend yesterday

	5-day trend	20-day trend
Yesterday rose more than +0.1%	72%	59%
Little change *(+0.1% to -0.1%)*	60%	65%
Yesterday fell more than -0.1%	44%	*44%

Odds of rise based upon distance between trend and yesterday s closing price

	5-day trend	20-day trend
Yesterday more than +0.5% above trend	93%	70%
Yesterday near trend *(+0.5% to -0.5%)*	42%	*50%
Yesterday more than -0.5% below trend	46%	47%

Looking ahead: odds of rise in future

	Next 3 days	Next 5 days
Today rose over +0.25%	45%	50%
Today small swing *(+0.25% to -0.25%)*	67%	67%
Today fell below -0.25%	27%	9%

SEPTEMBER 19 ODDS OF A PRICE RISE: 44%

Odds of different size price shift

	1935 to present
Large rise *(above +0.25%)*	38%
Small swing *(+0.25% to -0.25%)*	18%
Large fall (*below -0.25%)*	44%

Odds of rise based on yesterday

	1935 to present
Large rise yesterday *(above +0.25%)*	47%
Small swing yesterday *(+0.25% to -0.25%)*	47%
Large fall yesterday (*below -0.25%)*	40%

DIAGNOSTICS

Odds of price rise based on direction of 5-day and 20-day trend yesterday

	5-day trend	20-day trend
Yesterday rose more than +0.1%	57%	75%
Little change *(+0.1% to -0.1%)*	*57%	38%
Yesterday fell more than -0.1%	24%	25%

Odds of rise based upon distance between trend and yesterday s closing price

	5-day trend	20-day trend
Yesterday more than +0.5% above trend	67%	60%
Yesterday near trend *(+0.5% to -0.5%)*	38%	*50%
Yesterday more than -0.5% below trend	*33%	26%

Looking ahead: odds of rise in future

	Next 3 days	Next 5 days
Today rose over +0.25%	29%	41%
Today small swing *(+0.25% to -0.25%)*	*38%	*25%
Today fell below -0.25%	50%	40%

* *Per cent based on fewer than 10 observations*

SEPTEMBER 20 ODDS OF A PRICE RISE: 52%

Odds of different size price shift

	1935 to present
Large rise *(above +0.25%)*	35%
Small swing *(+0.25% to -0.25%)*	37%
Large fall *(below -0.25%)*	28%

Odds of rise based on yesterday

	1935 to present
Large rise yesterday *(above +0.25%)*	69%
Small swing yesterday *(+0.25% to -0.25%)*	55%
Large fall yesterday *(below -0.25%)*	37%

DIAGNOSTICS

Odds of price rise based on direction of 5-day and 20-day trend yesterday

	5-day trend	20-day trend
Yesterday rose more than +0.1%	60%	58%
Little change *(+0.1% to -0.1%)*	*56%	52%
Yesterday fell more than -0.1%	45%	46%

Odds of rise based upon distance between trend and yesterday s closing price

	5-day trend	20-day trend
Yesterday more than +0.5% above trend	*75%	60%
Yesterday near trend *(+0.5% to -0.5%)*	52%	*63%
Yesterday more than -0.5% below trend	40%	43%

Looking ahead: odds of rise in future

	Next 3 days	Next 5 days
Today rose over +0.25%	31%	44%
Today small swing *(+0.25% to -0.25%)*	35%	41%
Today fell below -0.25%	54%	54%

SEPTEMBER 21 ODDS OF A PRICE RISE: 59%

Odds of different size price shift

	1935 to present
Large rise *(above +0.25%)*	37%
Small swing *(+0.25% to -0.25%)*	39%
Large fall (*below -0.25%)*	24%

Odds of rise based on yesterday

	1935 to present
Large rise yesterday *(above +0.25%)*	65%
Small swing yesterday *(+0.25% to -0.25%)*	50%
Large fall yesterday (*below -0.25%)*	60%

DIAGNOSTICS

Odds of price rise based on direction of 5-day and 20-day trend yesterday

	5-day trend	20-day trend
Yesterday rose more than +0.1%	67%	50%
Little change *(+0.1% to -0.1%)*	42%	58%
Yesterday fell more than -0.1%	63%	69%

Odds of rise based upon distance between trend and yesterday s closing price

	5-day trend	20-day trend
Yesterday more than +0.5% above trend	54%	47%
Yesterday near trend *(+0.5% to -0.5%)*	61%	*67%
Yesterday more than -0.5% below trend	60%	67%

Looking ahead: odds of rise in future

	Next 3 days	Next 5 days
Today rose over +0.25%	59%	53%
Today small swing *(+0.25% to -0.25%)*	50%	50%
Today fell below -0.25%	27%	55%

* *Per cent based on fewer than 10 observations*

SEPTEMBER 22 ODDS OF A PRICE RISE: 55%

Odds of different size price shift

	1935 to present
Large rise *(above +0.25%)*	36%
Small swing *(+0.25% to -0.25%)*	30%
Large fall (*below -0.25%)*	34%

Odds of rise based on yesterday

	1935 to present
Large rise yesterday *(above +0.25%)*	72%
Small swing yesterday *(+0.25% to -0.25%)*	57%
Large fall yesterday (*below -0.25%)*	33%

DIAGNOSTICS

Odds of price rise based on direction of 5-day and 20-day trend yesterday

	5-day trend	20-day trend
Yesterday rose more than +0.1%	56%	56%
Little change *(+0.1% to -0.1%)*	55%	47%
Yesterday fell more than -0.1%	56%	67%

Odds of rise based upon distance between trend and yesterday s closing price

	5-day trend	20-day trend
Yesterday more than +0.5% above trend	60%	45%
Yesterday near trend *(+0.5% to -0.5%)*	55%	55%
Yesterday more than -0.5% below trend	50%	71%

Looking ahead: odds of rise in future

	Next 3 days	Next 5 days
Today rose over +0.25%	29%	35%
Today small swing *(+0.25% to -0.25%)*	43%	43%
Today fell below -0.25%	44%	44%

SEPTEMBER 23 ODDS OF A PRICE RISE: 33%

Odds of different size price shift

	1935 to present
Large rise *(above +0.25%)*	25%
Small swing *(+0.25% to -0.25%)*	29%
Large fall (*below -0.25%)*	46%

Odds of rise based on yesterday

	1935 to present
Large rise yesterday *(above +0.25%)*	32%
Small swing yesterday *(+0.25% to -0.25%)*	29%
Large fall yesterday (*below -0.25%)*	40%

DIAGNOSTICS

Odds of price rise based on direction of 5-day and 20-day trend yesterday

	5-day trend	20-day trend
Yesterday rose more than +0.1%	33%	33%
Little change *(+0.1% to -0.1%)*	20%	20%
Yesterday fell more than -0.1%	47%	54%

Odds of rise based upon distance between trend and yesterday s closing price

	5-day trend	20-day trend
Yesterday more than +0.5% above trend	35%	27%
Yesterday near trend *(+0.5% to -0.5%)*	25%	*38%
Yesterday more than -0.5% below trend	45%	39%

Looking ahead: odds of rise in future

	Next 3 days	Next 5 days
Today rose over +0.25%	58%	50%
Today small swing *(+0.25% to -0.25%)*	71%	57%
Today fell below -0.25%	45%	45%

* *Per cent based on fewer than 10 observations*

SEPTEMBER 24 ODDS OF A PRICE RISE: 49%

Odds of different size price shift

	1935 to present
Large rise *(above +0.25%)*	34%
Small swing *(+0.25% to -0.25%)*	30%
Large fall (*below -0.25%)*	36%

Odds of rise based on yesterday

	1935 to present
Large rise yesterday *(above +0.25%)*	50%
Small swing yesterday *(+0.25% to -0.25%)*	63%
Large fall yesterday (*below -0.25%)*	37%

DIAGNOSTICS

Odds of price rise based on direction of 5-day and 20-day trend yesterday

	5-day trend	20-day trend
Yesterday rose more than +0.1%	50%	67%
Little change *(+0.1% to -0.1%)*	73%	50%
Yesterday fell more than -0.1%	29%	20%

Odds of rise based upon distance between trend and yesterday s closing price

	5-day trend	20-day trend
Yesterday more than +0.5% above trend	42%	62%
Yesterday near trend *(+0.5% to -0.5%)*	62%	*56%
Yesterday more than -0.5% below trend	*22%	29%

Looking ahead: odds of rise in future

	Next 3 days	Next 5 days
Today rose over +0.25%	75%	50%
Today small swing *(+0.25% to -0.25%)*	50%	71%
Today fell below -0.25%	35%	41%

SEPTEMBER 25 ODDS OF A PRICE RISE: 50%

Odds of different size price shift

	1935 to present
Large rise *(above +0.25%)*	35%
Small swing *(+0.25% to -0.25%)*	30%
Large fall *(below -0.25%)*	35%

Odds of rise based on yesterday

	1935 to present
Large rise yesterday *(above +0.25%)*	77%
Small swing yesterday *(+0.25% to -0.25%)*	58%
Large fall yesterday *(below -0.25%)*	29%

DIAGNOSTICS

Odds of price rise based on direction of 5-day and 20-day trend yesterday

	5-day trend	20-day trend
Yesterday rose more than +0.1%	53%	60%
Little change *(+0.1% to -0.1%)*	46%	50%
Yesterday fell more than -0.1%	50%	36%

Odds of rise based upon distance between trend and yesterday s closing price

	5-day trend	20-day trend
Yesterday more than +0.5% above trend	50%	63%
Yesterday near trend *(+0.5% to -0.5%)*	58%	*56%
Yesterday more than -0.5% below trend	41%	33%

Looking ahead: odds of rise in future

	Next 3 days	Next 5 days
Today rose over +0.25%	50%	63%
Today small swing *(+0.25% to -0.25%)*	50%	71%
Today fell below -0.25%	38%	38%

* *Per cent based on fewer than 10 observations*

SEPTEMBER 26 ODDS OF A PRICE RISE: 29%

Odds of different size price shift

	1935 to present
Large rise *(above +0.25%)*	22%
Small swing *(+0.25% to -0.25%)*	36%
Large fall *(below -0.25%)*	42%

Odds of rise based on yesterday

	1935 to present
Large rise yesterday *(above +0.25%)*	36%
Small swing yesterday *(+0.25% to -0.25%)*	29%
Large fall yesterday *(below -0.25%)*	24%

DIAGNOSTICS

Odds of price rise based on direction of 5-day and 20-day trend yesterday

	5-day trend	20-day trend
Yesterday rose more than +0.1%	*38%	44%
Little change *(+0.1% to -0.1%)*	24%	29%
Yesterday fell more than -0.1%	30%	13%

Odds of rise based upon distance between trend and yesterday s closing price

	5-day trend	20-day trend
Yesterday more than +0.5% above trend	*38%	35%
Yesterday near trend *(+0.5% to -0.5%)*	20%	*29%
Yesterday more than -0.5% below trend	35%	24%

Looking ahead: odds of rise in future

	Next 3 days	Next 5 days
Today rose over +0.25%	60%	70%
Today small swing *(+0.25% to -0.25%)*	69%	69%
Today fell below -0.25%	42%	32%

SEPTEMBER 27 ODDS OF A PRICE RISE: 50%

Odds of different size price shift

	1935 to present
Large rise *(above +0.25%)*	30%
Small swing *(+0.25% to -0.25%)*	41%
Large fall *(below -0.25%)*	28%

Odds of rise based on yesterday

	1935 to present
Large rise yesterday *(above +0.25%)*	70%
Small swing yesterday *(+0.25% to -0.25%)*	42%
Large fall yesterday *(below -0.25%)*	47%

DIAGNOSTICS

Odds of price rise based on direction of 5-day and 20-day trend yesterday

	5-day trend	20-day trend
Yesterday rose more than +0.1%	47%	55%
Little change *(+0.1% to -0.1%)*	46%	35%
Yesterday fell more than -0.1%	56%	61%

Odds of rise based upon distance between trend and yesterday s closing price

	5-day trend	20-day trend
Yesterday more than +0.5% above trend	50%	62%
Yesterday near trend *(+0.5% to -0.5%)*	50%	27%
Yesterday more than -0.5% below trend	50%	55%

Looking ahead: odds of rise in future

	Next 3 days	Next 5 days
Today rose over +0.25%	71%	79%
Today small swing *(+0.25% to -0.25%)*	53%	42%
Today fell below -0.25%	54%	69%

* *Per cent based on fewer than 10 observations*

SEPTEMBER 28 ODDS OF A PRICE RISE: 50%

Odds of different size price shift

	1935 to present
Large rise *(above +0.25%)*	22%
Small swing *(+0.25% to -0.25%)*	46%
Large fall (*below -0.25%)*	33%

Odds of rise based on yesterday

	1935 to present
Large rise yesterday *(above +0.25%)*	44%
Small swing yesterday *(+0.25% to -0.25%)*	69%
Large fall yesterday (*below -0.25%)*	36%

DIAGNOSTICS

Odds of price rise based on direction of 5-day and 20-day trend yesterday

	5-day trend	20-day trend
Yesterday rose more than +0.1%	58%	57%
Little change *(+0.1% to -0.1%)*	67%	41%
Yesterday fell more than -0.1%	27%	53%

Odds of rise based upon distance between trend and yesterday s closing price

	5-day trend	20-day trend
Yesterday more than +0.5% above trend	45%	63%
Yesterday near trend *(+0.5% to -0.5%)*	64%	50%
Yesterday more than -0.5% below trend	31%	40%

Looking ahead: odds of rise in future

	Next 3 days	Next 5 days
Today rose over +0.25%	20%	50%
Today small swing *(+0.25% to -0.25%)*	57%	57%
Today fell below -0.25%	67%	73%

SEPTEMBER 29 ODDS OF A PRICE RISE: 47%

Odds of different size price shift

	1935 to present
Large rise *(above +0.25%)*	26%
Small swing *(+0.25% to -0.25%)*	40%
Large fall *(below -0.25%)*	34%

Odds of rise based on yesterday

	1935 to present
Large rise yesterday *(above +0.25%)*	54%
Small swing yesterday *(+0.25% to -0.25%)*	50%
Large fall yesterday *(below -0.25%)*	39%

DIAGNOSTICS

Odds of price rise based on direction of 5-day and 20-day trend yesterday

	5-day trend	20-day trend
Yesterday rose more than +0.1%	41%	38%
Little change *(+0.1% to -0.1%)*	43%	53%
Yesterday fell more than -0.1%	56%	50%

Odds of rise based upon distance between trend and yesterday s closing price

	5-day trend	20-day trend
Yesterday more than +0.5% above trend	33%	44%
Yesterday near trend *(+0.5% to -0.5%)*	42%	*25%
Yesterday more than -0.5% below trend	63%	57%

Looking ahead: odds of rise in future

	Next 3 days	Next 5 days
Today rose over +0.25%	83%	83%
Today small swing *(+0.25% to -0.25%)*	63%	68%
Today fell below -0.25%	56%	50%

* *Per cent based on fewer than 10 observations*

SEPTEMBER 30 ODDS OF A PRICE RISE: 56%

Odds of different size price shift

	1935 to present
Large rise *(above +0.25%)*	40%
Small swing *(+0.25% to -0.25%)*	27%
Large fall (*below -0.25%)*	33%

Odds of rise based on yesterday

	1935 to present
Large rise yesterday *(above +0.25%)*	73%
Small swing yesterday *(+0.25% to -0.25%)*	57%
Large fall yesterday (*below -0.25%)*	44%

DIAGNOSTICS

Odds of price rise based on direction of 5-day and 20-day trend yesterday

	5-day trend	20-day trend
Yesterday rose more than +0.1%	59%	69%
Little change *(+0.1% to -0.1%)*	67%	50%
Yesterday fell more than -0.1%	47%	54%

Odds of rise based upon distance between trend and yesterday s closing price

	5-day trend	20-day trend
Yesterday more than +0.5% above trend	70%	69%
Yesterday near trend *(+0.5% to -0.5%)*	52%	50%
Yesterday more than -0.5% below trend	54%	50%

Looking ahead: odds of rise in future

	Next 3 days	Next 5 days
Today rose over +0.25%	74%	74%
Today small swing *(+0.25% to -0.25%)*	92%	85%
Today fell below -0.25%	50%	44%

OCTOBER

PROFIT ODDS SUMMARY FOR THE MONTH

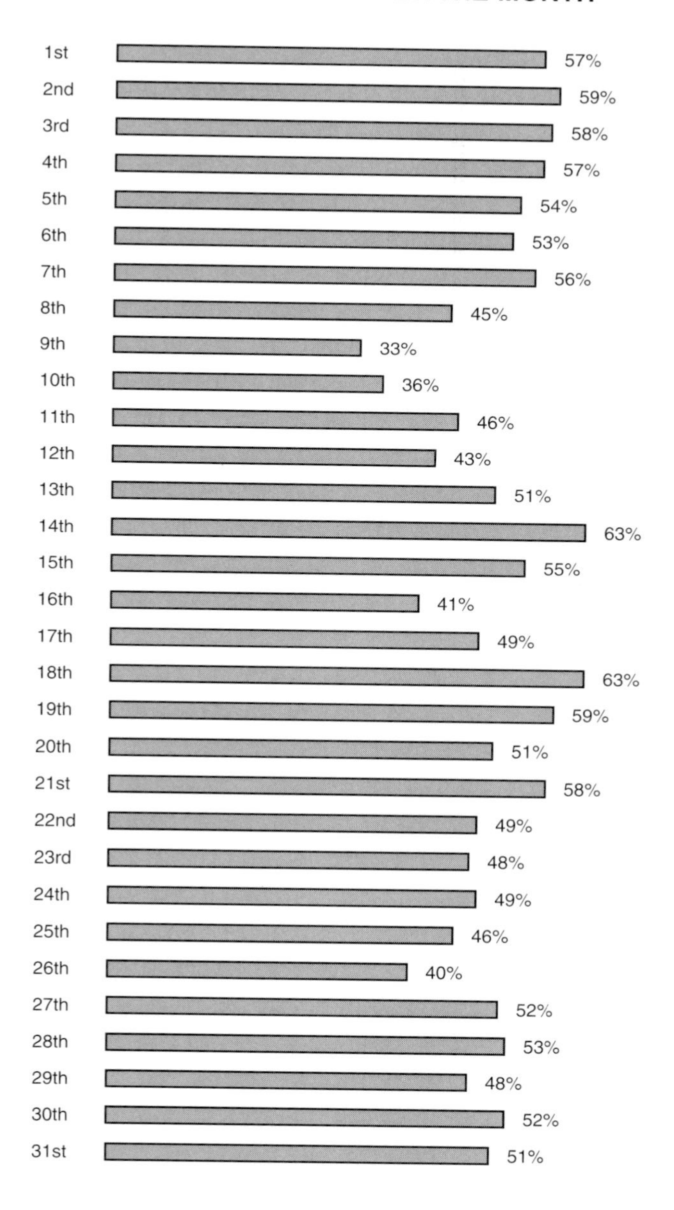

OCTOBER 1 ODDS OF A PRICE RISE: 57%

Odds of different size price shift

	1935 to present
Large rise *(above +0.25%)*	49%
Small swing *(+0.25% to -0.25%)*	23%
Large fall (*below -0.25%)*	28%

Odds of rise based on yesterday

	1935 to present
Large rise yesterday *(above +0.25%)*	80%
Small swing yesterday *(+0.25% to -0.25%)*	58%
Large fall yesterday (*below -0.25%)*	31%

DIAGNOSTICS

Odds of price rise based on direction of 5-day and 20-day trend yesterday

	5-day trend	20-day trend
Yesterday rose more than +0.1%	60%	63%
Little change *(+0.1% to -0.1%)*	64%	53%
Yesterday fell more than -0.1%	50%	57%

Odds of rise based upon distance between trend and yesterday s closing price

	5-day trend	20-day trend
Yesterday more than +0.5% above trend	79%	63%
Yesterday near trend *(+0.5% to -0.5%)*	50%	62%
Yesterday more than -0.5% below trend	45%	50%

Looking ahead: odds of rise in future

	Next 3 days	Next 5 days
Today rose over +0.25%	61%	61%
Today small swing *(+0.25% to -0.25%)*	73%	73%
Today fell below -0.25%	46%	69%

* *Per cent based on fewer than 10 observations*

OCTOBER 2 ODDS OF A PRICE RISE: 59%

Odds of different size price shift

	1935 to present
Large rise *(above +0.25%)*	54%
Small swing *(+0.25% to -0.25%)*	24%
Large fall (*below -0.25%)*	22%

Odds of rise based on yesterday

	1935 to present
Large rise yesterday *(above +0.25%)*	71%
Small swing yesterday *(+0.25% to -0.25%)*	55%
Large fall yesterday (*below -0.25%)*	36%

DIAGNOSTICS

Odds of price rise based on direction of 5-day and 20-day trend yesterday

	5-day trend	20-day trend
Yesterday rose more than +0.1%	72%	63%
Little change *(+0.1% to -0.1%)*	62%	50%
Yesterday fell more than -0.1%	40%	64%

Odds of rise based upon distance between trend and yesterday s closing price

	5-day trend	20-day trend
Yesterday more than +0.5% above trend	76%	61%
Yesterday near trend *(+0.5% to -0.5%)*	67%	60%
Yesterday more than -0.5% below trend	18%	56%

Looking ahead: odds of rise in future

	Next 3 days	Next 5 days
Today rose over +0.25%	80%	68%
Today small swing *(+0.25% to -0.25%)*	36%	18%
Today fell below -0.25%	80%	70%

OCTOBER 3 ODDS OF A PRICE RISE: 58%

Odds of different size price shift

	1935 to present
Large rise *(above +0.25%)*	44%
Small swing *(+0.25% to -0.25%)*	24%
Large fall *(below -0.25%)*	31%

Odds of rise based on yesterday

	1935 to present
Large rise yesterday *(above +0.25%)*	73%
Small swing yesterday *(+0.25% to -0.25%)*	27%
Large fall yesterday *(below -0.25%)*	58%

DIAGNOSTICS

Odds of price rise based on direction of 5-day and 20-day trend yesterday

	5-day trend	20-day trend
Yesterday rose more than +0.1%	65%	67%
Little change *(+0.1% to -0.1%)*	64%	60%
Yesterday fell more than -0.1%	47%	46%

Odds of rise based upon distance between trend and yesterday s closing price

	5-day trend	20-day trend
Yesterday more than +0.5% above trend	61%	57%
Yesterday near trend *(+0.5% to -0.5%)*	53%	75%
Yesterday more than -0.5% below trend	60%	47%

Looking ahead: odds of rise in future

	Next 3 days	Next 5 days
Today rose over +0.25%	55%	55%
Today small swing *(+0.25% to -0.25%)*	55%	55%
Today fell below -0.25%	50%	36%

* *Per cent based on fewer than 10 observations*

OCTOBER 4 ODDS OF A PRICE RISE: 57%

Odds of different size price shift

	1935 to present
Large rise *(above +0.25%)*	46%
Small swing *(+0.25% to -0.25%)*	28%
Large fall (*below -0.25%)*	26%

Odds of rise based on yesterday

	1935 to present
Large rise yesterday *(above +0.25%)*	56%
Small swing yesterday *(+0.25% to -0.25%)*	54%
Large fall yesterday (*below -0.25%)*	60%

DIAGNOSTICS

Odds of price rise based on direction of 5-day and 20-day trend yesterday

	5-day trend	20-day trend
Yesterday rose more than +0.1%	50%	45%
Little change *(+0.1% to -0.1%)*	50%	58%
Yesterday fell more than -0.1%	69%	63%

Odds of rise based upon distance between trend and yesterday s closing price

	5-day trend	20-day trend
Yesterday more than +0.5% above trend	63%	44%
Yesterday near trend *(+0.5% to -0.5%)*	33%	50%
Yesterday more than -0.5% below trend	83%	70%

Looking ahead: odds of rise in future

	Next 3 days	Next 5 days
Today rose over +0.25%	57%	62%
Today small swing *(+0.25% to -0.25%)*	31%	38%
Today fell below -0.25%	50%	42%

OCTOBER 5 ODDS OF A PRICE RISE: 54%

Odds of different size price shift

	1935 to present
Large rise *(above +0.25%)*	41%
Small swing *(+0.25% to -0.25%)*	30%
Large fall *(below -0.25%)*	28%

Odds of rise based on yesterday

	1935 to present
Large rise yesterday *(above +0.25%)*	76%
Small swing yesterday *(+0.25% to -0.25%)*	23%
Large fall yesterday *(below -0.25%)*	50%

DIAGNOSTICS

Odds of price rise based on direction of 5-day and 20-day trend yesterday

	5-day trend	20-day trend
Yesterday rose more than +0.1%	70%	56%
Little change *(+0.1% to -0.1%)*	54%	50%
Yesterday fell more than -0.1%	31%	57%

Odds of rise based upon distance between trend and yesterday s closing price

	5-day trend	20-day trend
Yesterday more than +0.5% above trend	67%	60%
Yesterday near trend *(+0.5% to -0.5%)*	50%	*56%
Yesterday more than -0.5% below trend	*29%	47%

Looking ahead: odds of rise in future

	Next 3 days	Next 5 days
Today rose over +0.25%	63%	58%
Today small swing *(+0.25% to -0.25%)*	36%	36%
Today fell below -0.25%	38%	46%

* *Per cent based on fewer than 10 observations*

OCTOBER 6 ODDS OF A PRICE RISE: 53%

Odds of different size price shift

	1935 to present
Large rise *(above +0.25%)*	45%
Small swing *(+0.25% to -0.25%)*	28%
Large fall (*below -0.25%)*	28%

Odds of rise based on yesterday

	1935 to present
Large rise yesterday *(above +0.25%)*	70%
Small swing yesterday *(+0.25% to -0.25%)*	33%
Large fall yesterday (*below -0.25%)*	47%

DIAGNOSTICS

Odds of price rise based on direction of 5-day and 20-day trend yesterday

	5-day trend	20-day trend
Yesterday rose more than +0.1%	54%	54%
Little change *(+0.1% to -0.1%)*	60%	44%
Yesterday fell more than -0.1%	46%	63%

Odds of rise based upon distance between trend and yesterday s closing price

	5-day trend	20-day trend
Yesterday more than +0.5% above trend	60%	55%
Yesterday near trend *(+0.5% to -0.5%)*	56%	45%
Yesterday more than -0.5% below trend	*33%	56%

Looking ahead: odds of rise in future

	Next 3 days	Next 5 days
Today rose over +0.25%	62%	52%
Today small swing *(+0.25% to -0.25%)*	31%	62%
Today fell below -0.25%	38%	46%

OCTOBER 7 ODDS OF A PRICE RISE: 56%

Odds of different size price shift

	1935 to present
Large rise *(above +0.25%)*	40%
Small swing *(+0.25% to -0.25%)*	29%
Large fall *(below -0.25%)*	31%

Odds of rise based on yesterday

	1935 to present
Large rise yesterday *(above +0.25%)*	65%
Small swing yesterday *(+0.25% to -0.25%)*	45%
Large fall yesterday *(below -0.25%)*	45%

DIAGNOSTICS

Odds of price rise based on direction of 5-day and 20-day trend yesterday

	5-day trend	20-day trend
Yesterday rose more than +0.1%	59%	62%
Little change *(+0.1% to -0.1%)*	*67%	45%
Yesterday fell more than -0.1%	42%	67%

Odds of rise based upon distance between trend and yesterday s closing price

	5-day trend	20-day trend
Yesterday more than +0.5% above trend	68%	61%
Yesterday near trend *(+0.5% to -0.5%)*	50%	*25%
Yesterday more than -0.5% below trend	40%	65%

Looking ahead: odds of rise in future

	Next 3 days	Next 5 days
Today rose over +0.25%	63%	58%
Today small swing *(+0.25% to -0.25%)*	43%	43%
Today fell below -0.25%	33%	47%

* *Per cent based on fewer than 10 observations*

OCTOBER 8 ODDS OF A PRICE RISE: 45%

Odds of different size price shift

	1935 to present
Large rise *(above +0.25%)*	30%
Small swing *(+0.25% to -0.25%)*	38%
Large fall (*below -0.25%)*	32%

Odds of rise based on yesterday

	1935 to present
Large rise yesterday *(above +0.25%)*	58%
Small swing yesterday *(+0.25% to -0.25%)*	47%
Large fall yesterday (*below -0.25%)*	23%

DIAGNOSTICS

Odds of price rise based on direction of 5-day and 20-day trend yesterday

	5-day trend	20-day trend
Yesterday rose more than +0.1%	48%	55%
Little change *(+0.1% to -0.1%)*	*38%	38%
Yesterday fell more than -0.1%	40%	36%

Odds of rise based upon distance between trend and yesterday s closing price

	5-day trend	20-day trend
Yesterday more than +0.5% above trend	60%	54%
Yesterday near trend *(+0.5% to -0.5%)*	26%	*38%
Yesterday more than -0.5% below trend	*50%	31%

Looking ahead: odds of rise in future

	Next 3 days	Next 5 days
Today rose over +0.25%	57%	71%
Today small swing *(+0.25% to -0.25%)*	39%	56%
Today fell below -0.25%	47%	60%

OCTOBER 9 ODDS OF A PRICE RISE: 33%

Odds of different size price shift

	1935 to present
Large rise *(above +0.25%)*	24%
Small swing *(+0.25% to -0.25%)*	30%
Large fall *(below -0.25%)*	46%

Odds of rise based on yesterday

	1935 to present
Large rise yesterday *(above +0.25%)*	47%
Small swing yesterday *(+0.25% to -0.25%)*	27%
Large fall yesterday *(below -0.25%)*	25%

DIAGNOSTICS

Odds of price rise based on direction of 5-day and 20-day trend yesterday

	5-day trend	20-day trend
Yesterday rose more than +0.1%	44%	35%
Little change *(+0.1% to -0.1%)*	10%	8%
Yesterday fell more than -0.1%	27%	50%

Odds of rise based upon distance between trend and yesterday s closing price

	5-day trend	20-day trend
Yesterday more than +0.5% above trend	39%	32%
Yesterday near trend *(+0.5% to -0.5%)*	29%	33%
Yesterday more than -0.5% below trend	*22%	33%

Looking ahead: odds of rise in future

	Next 3 days	Next 5 days
Today rose over +0.25%	64%	64%
Today small swing *(+0.25% to -0.25%)*	43%	50%
Today fell below -0.25%	48%	57%

* *Per cent based on fewer than 10 observations*

OCTOBER 10 ODDS OF A PRICE RISE: 36%

Odds of different size price shift

	1935 to present
Large rise *(above +0.25%)*	27%
Small swing *(+0.25% to -0.25%)*	31%
Large fall (*below -0.25%)*	42%

Odds of rise based on yesterday

	1935 to present
Large rise yesterday *(above +0.25%)*	82%
Small swing yesterda y*(+0.25% to -0.25%)*	18%
Large fall yesterday (*below -0.25%)*	22%

DIAGNOSTICS

Odds of price rise based on direction of 5-day and 20-day trend yesterday

	5-day trend	20-day trend
Yesterday rose more than +0.1%	43%	47%
Little change *(+0.1% to -0.1%)*	*38%	25%
Yesterday fell more than -0.1%	25%	36%

Odds of rise based upon distance between trend and yesterday s closing price

	5-day trend	20-day trend
Yesterday more than +0.5% above trend	46%	47%
Yesterday near trend *(+0.5% to -0.5%)*	35%	*22%
Yesterday more than -0.5% below trend	27%	29%

Looking ahead: odds of rise in future

	Next 3 days	Next 5 days
Today rose over +0.25%	58%	58%
Today small swing *(+0.25% to -0.25%)*	71%	64%
Today fell below -0.25%	53%	47%

OCTOBER 11 ODDS OF A PRICE RISE: 46%

Odds of different size price shift

	1935 to present
Large rise *(above +0.25%)*	35%
Small swing *(+0.25% to -0.25%)*	28%
Large fall *(below -0.25%)*	37%

Odds of rise based on yesterday

	1935 to present
Large rise yesterday *(above +0.25%)*	55%
Small swing yesterday *(+0.25% to -0.25%)*	56%
Large fall yesterday *(below -0.25%)*	29%

DIAGNOSTICS

Odds of price rise based on direction of 5-day and 20-day trend yesterday

	5-day trend	20-day trend
Yesterday rose more than +0.1%	59%	58%
Little change *(+0.1% to -0.1%)*	*38%	56%
Yesterday fell more than -0.1%	31%	25%

Odds of rise based upon distance between trend and yesterday s closing price

	5-day trend	20-day trend
Yesterday more than +0.5% above trend	50%	59%
Yesterday near trend *(+0.5% to -0.5%)*	63%	*50%
Yesterday more than -0.5% below trend	25%	25%

Looking ahead: odds of rise in future

	Next 3 days	Next 5 days
Today rose over +0.25%	56%	63%
Today small swing *(+0.25% to -0.25%)*	54%	69%
Today fell below -0.25%	47%	41%

* *Per cent based on fewer than 10 observations*

OCTOBER 12 ODDS OF A PRICE RISE: 43%

Odds of different size price shift

	1935 to present
Large rise *(above +0.25%)*	26%
Small swing *(+0.25% to -0.25%)*	39%
Large fall (*below -0.25%)*	35%

Odds of rise based on yesterday

	1935 to present
Large rise yesterday *(above +0.25%)*	71%
Small swing yesterday *(+0.25% to -0.25%)*	39%
Large fall yesterday (*below -0.25%)*	21%

DIAGNOSTICS

Odds of price rise based on direction of 5-day and 20-day trend yesterday

	5-day trend	20-day trend
Yesterday rose more than +0.1%	43%	44%
Little change *(+0.1% to -0.1%)*	*38%	31%
Yesterday fell more than -0.1%	47%	57%

Odds of rise based upon distance between trend and yesterday s closing price

	5-day trend	20-day trend
Yesterday more than +0.5% above trend	58%	41%
Yesterday near trend *(+0.5% to -0.5%)*	42%	*50%
Yesterday more than -0.5% below trend	33%	46%

Looking ahead: odds of rise in future

	Next 3 days	Next 5 days
Today rose over +0.25%	58%	58%
Today small swing *(+0.25% to -0.25%)*	56%	67%
Today fell below -0.25%	38%	25%

OCTOBER 13 ODDS OF A PRICE RISE: 51%

Odds of different size price shift

	1935 to present
Large rise *(above +0.25%)*	47%
Small swing *(+0.25% to -0.25%)*	19%
Large fall (*below -0.25%)*	34%

Odds of rise based on yesterday

	1935 to present
Large rise yesterday *(above +0.25%)*	62%
Small swing yesterday *(+0.25% to -0.25%)*	47%
Large fall yesterday (*below -0.25%)*	47%

DIAGNOSTICS

Odds of price rise based on direction of 5-day and 20-day trend yesterday

	5-day trend	20-day trend
Yesterday rose more than +0.1%	50%	44%
Little change *(+0.1% to -0.1%)*	*44%	56%
Yesterday fell more than -0.1%	55%	53%

Odds of rise based upon distance between trend and yesterday s closing price

	5-day trend	20-day trend
Yesterday more than +0.5% above trend	67%	48%
Yesterday near trend *(+0.5% to -0.5%)*	40%	*43%
Yesterday more than -0.5% below trend	47%	60%

Looking ahead: odds of rise in future

	Next 3 days	Next 5 days
Today rose over +0.25%	59%	55%
Today small swing *(+0.25% to -0.25%)*	*44%	*44%
Today fell below -0.25%	38%	56%

* *Per cent based on fewer than 10 observations*

OCTOBER 14 ODDS OF A PRICE RISE: 63%

Odds of different size price shift

	1935 to present
Large rise *(above +0.25%)*	35%
Small swing *(+0.25% to -0.25%)*	33%
Large fall (*below -0.25%)*	31%

Odds of rise based on yesterday

	1935 to present
Large rise yesterday *(above +0.25%)*	67%
Small swing yesterday *(+0.25% to -0.25%)*	*67%
Large fall yesterday (*below -0.25%)*	56%

DIAGNOSTICS

Odds of price rise based on direction of 5-day and 20-day trend yesterday

	5-day trend	20-day trend
Yesterday rose more than +0.1%	61%	78%
Little change *(+0.1% to -0.1%)*	58%	47%
Yesterday fell more than -0.1%	67%	64%

Odds of rise based upon distance between trend and yesterday s closing price

	5-day trend	20-day trend
Yesterday more than +0.5% above trend	71%	68%
Yesterday near trend *(+0.5% to -0.5%)*	60%	*20%
Yesterday more than -0.5% below trend	56%	67%

Looking ahead: odds of rise in future

	Next 3 days	Next 5 days
Today rose over +0.25%	59%	65%
Today small swing *(+0.25% to -0.25%)*	88%	69%
Today fell below -0.25%	33%	47%

OCTOBER 15 ODDS OF A PRICE RISE: 55%

Odds of different size price shift

	1935 to present
Large rise *(above +0.25%)*	36%
Small swing *(+0.25% to -0.25%)*	36%
Large fall (*below -0.25%)*	28%

Odds of rise based on yesterday

	1935 to present
Large rise yesterday *(above +0.25%)*	65%
Small swing yesterday *(+0.25% to -0.25%)*	72%
Large fall yesterday (*below -0.25%)*	17%

DIAGNOSTICS

Odds of price rise based on direction of 5-day and 20-day trend yesterday

	5-day trend	20-day trend
Yesterday rose more than +0.1%	39%	40%
Little change *(+0.1% to -0.1%)*	82%	61%
Yesterday fell more than -0.1%	56%	*78%

Odds of rise based upon distance between trend and yesterday s closing price

	5-day trend	20-day trend
Yesterday more than +0.5% above trend	44%	46%
Yesterday near trend *(+0.5% to -0.5%)*	70%	60%
Yesterday more than -0.5% below trend	45%	69%

Looking ahead: odds of rise in future

	Next 3 days	Next 5 days
Today rose over +0.25%	59%	59%
Today small swing *(+0.25% to -0.25%)*	71%	65%
Today fell below -0.25%	38%	62%

* *Per cent based on fewer than 10 observations*

OCTOBER 16 ODDS OF A PRICE RISE: 41%

Odds of different size price shift

	1935 to present
Large rise *(above +0.25%)*	30%
Small swing *(+0.25% to -0.25%)*	35%
Large fall (*below -0.25%)*	35%

Odds of rise based on yesterday

	1935 to present
Large rise yesterday *(above +0.25%)*	50%
Small swing yesterday *(+0.25% to -0.25%)*	40%
Large fall yesterday (*below -0.25%)*	33%

DIAGNOSTICS

Odds of price rise based on direction of 5-day and 20-day trend yesterday

	5-day trend	20-day trend
Yesterday rose more than +0.1%	60%	50%
Little change *(+0.1% to -0.1%)*	38%	39%
Yesterday fell more than -0.1%	28%	33%

Odds of rise based upon distance between trend and yesterday s closing price

	5-day trend	20-day trend
Yesterday more than +0.5% above trend	43%	46%
Yesterday near trend *(+0.5% to -0.5%)*	45%	*50%
Yesterday more than -0.5% below trend	30%	29%

Looking ahead: odds of rise in future

	Next 3 days	Next 5 days
Today rose over +0.25%	71%	79%
Today small swing *(+0.25% to -0.25%)*	56%	56%
Today fell below -0.25%	69%	69%

OCTOBER 17 ODDS OF A PRICE RISE: 49%

Odds of different size price shift

	1935 to present
Large rise *(above +0.25%)*	38%
Small swing *(+0.25% to -0.25%)*	31%
Large fall (*below -0.25%)*	31%

Odds of rise based on yesterday

	1935 to present
Large rise yesterday *(above +0.25%)*	45%
Small swing yesterday *(+0.25% to -0.25%)*	63%
Large fall yesterday (*below -0.25%)*	39%

DIAGNOSTICS

Odds of price rise based on direction of 5-day and 20-day trend yesterday

	5-day trend	20-day trend
Yesterday rose more than +0.1%	71%	64%
Little change *(+0.1% to -0.1%)*	44%	41%
Yesterday fell more than -0.1%	33%	50%

Odds of rise based upon distance between trend and yesterday s closing price

	5-day trend	20-day trend
Yesterday more than +0.5% above trend	*67%	63%
Yesterday near trend *(+0.5% to -0.5%)*	55%	20%
Yesterday more than -0.5% below trend	31%	50%

Looking ahead: odds of rise in future

	Next 3 days	Next 5 days
Today rose over +0.25%	47%	41%
Today small swing *(+0.25% to -0.25%)*	64%	64%
Today fell below -0.25%	71%	64%

* *Per cent based on fewer than 10 observations*

OCTOBER 18 ODDS OF A PRICE RISE: 63%

Odds of different size price shift

	1935 to present
Large rise *(above +0.25%)*	39%
Small swing *(+0.25% to -0.25%)*	35%
Large fall (*below -0.25%)*	26%

Odds of rise based on yesterday

	1935 to present
Large rise yesterday *(above +0.25%)*	63%
Small swing yesterday *(+0.25% to -0.25%)*	77%
Large fall yesterday (*below -0.25%)*	50%

DIAGNOSTICS

Odds of price rise based on direction of 5-day and 20-day trend yesterday

	5-day trend	20-day trend
Yesterday rose more than +0.1%	79%	50%
Little change *(+0.1% to -0.1%)*	*63%	63%
Yesterday fell more than -0.1%	47%	77%

Odds of rise based upon distance between trend and yesterday s closing price

	5-day trend	20-day trend
Yesterday more than +0.5% above trend	88%	61%
Yesterday near trend *(+0.5% to -0.5%)*	47%	75%
Yesterday more than -0.5% below trend	54%	56%

Looking ahead: odds of rise in future

	Next 3 days	Next 5 days
Today rose over +0.25%	61%	61%
Today small swing *(+0.25% to -0.25%)*	69%	50%
Today fell below -0.25%	58%	58%

OCTOBER 19 ODDS OF A PRICE RISE: 59%

Odds of different size price shift

	1935 to present
Large rise *(above +0.25%)*	48%
Small swing *(+0.25% to -0.25%)*	30%
Large fall (*below -0.25%)*	22%

Odds of rise based on yesterday

	1935 to present
Large rise yesterday *(above +0.25%)*	69%
Small swing yesterday *(+0.25% to -0.25%)*	59%
Large fall yesterday (*below -0.25%)*	46%

DIAGNOSTICS

Odds of price rise based on direction of 5-day and 20-day trend yesterday

	5-day trend	20-day trend
Yesterday rose more than +0.1%	53%	79%
Little change *(+0.1% to -0.1%)*	*67%	45%
Yesterday fell more than -0.1%	60%	60%

Odds of rise based upon distance between trend and yesterday s closing price

	5-day trend	20-day trend
Yesterday more than +0.5% above trend	57%	61%
Yesterday near trend *(+0.5% to -0.5%)*	70%	55%
Yesterday more than -0.5% below trend	42%	59%

Looking ahead: odds of rise in future

	Next 3 days	Next 5 days
Today rose over +0.25%	45%	50%
Today small swing *(+0.25% to -0.25%)*	79%	50%
Today fell below -0.25%	50%	50%

* *Per cent based on fewer than 10 observations*

OCTOBER 20 ODDS OF A PRICE RISE: 51%

Odds of different size price shift

	1935 to present
Large rise *(above +0.25%)*	34%
Small swing *(+0.25% to -0.25%)*	36%
Large fall *(below -0.25%)*	30%

Odds of rise based on yesterday

	1935 to present
Large rise yesterday *(above +0.25%)*	55%
Small swing yesterday *(+0.25% to -0.25%)*	43%
Large fall yesterday *(below -0.25%)*	54%

DIAGNOSTICS

Odds of price rise based on direction of 5-day and 20-day trend yesterday

	5-day trend	20-day trend
Yesterday rose more than +0.1%	41%	50%
Little change *(+0.1% to -0.1%)*	40%	45%
Yesterday fell more than -0.1%	73%	62%

Odds of rise based upon distance between trend and yesterday s closing price

	5-day trend	20-day trend
Yesterday more than +0.5% above trend	41%	39%
Yesterday near trend *(+0.5% to -0.5%)*	52%	*57%
Yesterday more than -0.5% below trend	*67%	65%

Looking ahead: odds of rise in future

	Next 3 days	Next 5 days
Today rose over +0.25%	56%	63%
Today small swing *(+0.25% to -0.25%)*	53%	65%
Today fell below -0.25%	29%	21%

OCTOBER 21 ODDS OF A PRICE RISE: 58%

Odds of different size price shift

	1935 to present
Large rise *(above +0.25%)*	50%
Small swing *(+0.25% to -0.25%)*	23%
Large fall (*below -0.25%)*	27%

Odds of rise based on yesterday

	1935 to present
Large rise yesterday *(above +0.25%)*	61%
Small swing yesterday *(+0.25% to -0.25%)*	67%
Large fall yesterday (*below -0.25%)*	47%

DIAGNOSTICS

Odds of price rise based on direction of 5-day and 20-day trend yesterday

	5-day trend	20-day trend
Yesterday rose more than +0.1%	57%	63%
Little change *(+0.1% to -0.1%)*	*56%	43%
Yesterday fell more than -0.1%	63%	67%

Odds of rise based upon distance between trend and yesterday s closing price

	5-day trend	20-day trend
Yesterday more than +0.5% above trend	56%	60%
Yesterday near trend *(+0.5% to -0.5%)*	52%	*71%
Yesterday more than -0.5% below trend	73%	50%

Looking ahead: odds of rise in future

	Next 3 days	Next 5 days
Today rose over +0.25%	54%	54%
Today small swing *(+0.25% to -0.25%)*	36%	45%
Today fell below -0.25%	31%	54%

* *Per cent based on fewer than 10 observations*

OCTOBER 22 ODDS OF A PRICE RISE: 49%

Odds of different size price shift

	1935 to present
Large rise *(above +0.25%)*	43%
Small swing *(+0.25% to -0.25%)*	19%
Large fall (*below -0.25%)*	38%

Odds of rise based on yesterday

	1935 to present
Large rise yesterday *(above +0.25%)*	58%
Small swing yesterday *(+0.25% to -0.25%)*	45%
Large fall yesterday (*below -0.25%)*	30%

DIAGNOSTICS

Odds of price rise based on direction of 5-day and 20-day trend yesterday

	5-day trend	20-day trend
Yesterday rose more than +0.1%	57%	40%
Little change *(+0.1% to -0.1%)*	23%	63%
Yesterday fell more than -0.1%	64%	*38%

Odds of rise based upon distance between trend and yesterday s closing price

	5-day trend	20-day trend
Yesterday more than +0.5% above trend	63%	52%
Yesterday near trend *(+0.5% to -0.5%)*	43%	*75%
Yesterday more than -0.5% below trend	*20%	36%

Looking ahead: odds of rise in future

	Next 3 days	Next 5 days
Today rose over +0.25%	70%	55%
Today small swing *(+0.25% to -0.25%)*	*11%	*44%
Today fell below -0.25%	33%	39%

OCTOBER 23 ODDS OF A PRICE RISE: 48%

Odds of different size price shift

	1935 to present
Large rise *(above +0.25%)*	33%
Small swing *(+0.25% to -0.25%)*	26%
Large fall (*below -0.25%)*	41%

Odds of rise based on yesterday

	1935 to present
Large rise yesterday *(above +0.25%)*	65%
Small swing yesterday *(+0.25% to -0.25%)*	45%
Large fall yesterday (*below -0.25%)*	27%

DIAGNOSTICS

Odds of price rise based on direction of 5-day and 20-day trend yesterday

	5-day trend	20-day trend
Yesterday rose more than +0.1%	65%	47%
Little change *(+0.1% to -0.1%)*	31%	58%
Yesterday fell more than -0.1%	46%	*25%

Odds of rise based upon distance between trend and yesterday s closing price

	5-day trend	20-day trend
Yesterday more than +0.5% above trend	59%	60%
Yesterday near trend *(+0.5% to -0.5%)*	45%	*29%
Yesterday more than -0.5% below trend	*29%	36%

Looking ahead: odds of rise in future

	Next 3 days	Next 5 days
Today rose over +0.25%	67%	67%
Today small swing *(+0.25% to -0.25%)*	50%	50%
Today fell below -0.25%	47%	53%

* *Per cent based on fewer than 10 observations*

OCTOBER 24 ODDS OF A PRICE RISE: 49%

Odds of different size price shift

	1935 to present
Large rise *(above +0.25%)*	33%
Small swing *(+0.25% to -0.25%)*	31%
Large fall (*below -0.25%)*	36%

Odds of rise based on yesterday

	1935 to present
Large rise yesterday *(above +0.25%)*	71%
Small swing yesterday *(+0.25% to -0.25%)*	45%
Large fall yesterday (*below -0.25%)*	29%

DIAGNOSTICS

Odds of price rise based on direction of 5-day and 20-day trend yesterday

	5-day trend	20-day trend
Yesterday rose more than +0.1%	61%	64%
Little change *(+0.1% to -0.1%)*	50%	45%
Yesterday fell more than -0.1%	33%	36%

Odds of rise based upon distance between trend and yesterday s closing price

	5-day trend	20-day trend
Yesterday more than +0.5% above trend	60%	59%
Yesterday near trend *(+0.5% to -0.5%)*	50%	*67%
Yesterday more than -0.5% below trend	38%	29%

Looking ahead: odds of rise in future

	Next 3 days	Next 5 days
Today rose over +0.25%	73%	67%
Today small swing *(+0.25% to -0.25%)*	36%	43%
Today fell below -0.25%	56%	44%

OCTOBER 25 ODDS OF A PRICE RISE: 46%

Odds of different size price shift

	1935 to present
Large rise *(above +0.25%)*	37%
Small swing *(+0.25% to -0.25%)*	20%
Large fall *(below -0.25%)*	43%

Odds of rise based on yesterday

	1935 to present
Large rise yesterday *(above +0.25%)*	71%
Small swing yesterday *(+0.25% to -0.25%)*	33%
Large fall yesterday *(below -0.25%)*	29%

DIAGNOSTICS

Odds of price rise based on direction of 5-day and 20-day trend yesterday

	5-day trend	20-day trend
Yesterday rose more than +0.1%	43%	53%
Little change *(+0.1% to -0.1%)*	*50%	38%
Yesterday fell more than -0.1%	47%	43%

Odds of rise based upon distance between trend and yesterday s closing price

	5-day trend	20-day trend
Yesterday more than +05% above trend	56%	46%
Yesterday near trend *(+0.5% to -0.5%)*	41%	*67%
Yesterday more than -0.5% below trend	38%	38%

Looking ahead: odds of rise in future

	Next 3 days	Next 5 days
Today rose over +0.25%	59%	65%
Today small swing *(+0.25% to -0.25%)*	*56%	*44%
Today fell below -0.25%	35%	45%

* *Per cent based on fewer than 10 observations*

OCTOBER 26 ODDS OF A PRICE RISE: 40%

Odds of different size price shift

	1935 to present
Large rise *(above +0.25%)*	22%
Small swing *(+0.25% to -0.25%)*	40%
Large fall (*below -0.25%)*	38%

Odds of rise based on yesterday

	1935 to present
Large rise yesterday *(above +0.25%)*	43%
Small swing yesterday *(+0.25% to -0.25%)*	45%
Large fall yesterday (*below -0.25%)*	35%

DIAGNOSTICS

Odds of price rise based on direction of 5-day and 20-day trend yesterday

	5-day trend	20-day trend
Yesterday rose more than +0.1%	35%	33%
Little change *(+0.1% to -0.1%)*	50%	40%
Yesterday fell more than -0.1%	36%	50%

Odds of rise based upon distance between trend and yesterday s closing price

	5-day trend	20-day trend
Yesterday more than +0.5% above trend	38%	38%
Yesterday near trend *(+0.5% to -0.5%)*	47%	*50%
Yesterday more than -0.5% below trend	33%	38%

Looking ahead: odds of rise in future

	Next 3 days	Next 5 days
Today rose over +0.25%	70%	60%
Today small swing *(+0.25% to -0.25%)*	67%	67%
Today fell below -0.25%	35%	47%

OCTOBER 27 ODDS OF A PRICE RISE: 52%

Odds of different size price shift

	1935 to present
Large rise *(above +0.25%)*	37%
Small swing *(+0.25% to -0.25%)*	28%
Large fall (*below -0.25%)*	35%

Odds of rise based on yesterday

	1935 to present
Large rise yesterday *(above +0.25%)*	55%
Small swing yesterday *(+0.25% to -0.25%)*	72%
Large fall yesterday (*below -0.25%)*	29%

DIAGNOSTICS

Odds of price rise based on direction of 5-day and 20-day trend yesterday

	5-day trend	20-day trend
Yesterday rose more than +0.1%	53%	53%
Little change *(+0.1% to -0.1%)*	50%	50%
Yesterday fell more than -0.1%	53%	53%

Odds of rise based upon distance between trend and yesterday s closing price

	5-day trend	20-day trend
Yesterday more than +0.5% above trend	67%	57%
Yesterday near trend *(+0.5% to -0.5%)*	37%	*43%
Yesterday more than -0.5% below trend	60%	50%

Looking ahead: odds of rise in future

	Next 3 days	Next 5 days
Today rose over +0.25%	65%	53%
Today small swing *(+0.25% to -0.25%)*	62%	46%
Today fell below -0.25%	63%	69%

* *Per cent based on fewer than 10 observations*

OCTOBER 28 ODDS OF A PRICE RISE: 53%

Odds of different size price shift

	1935 to present
Large rise *(above +0.25%)*	40%
Small swing *(+0.25% to -0.25%)*	32%
Large fall *(below -0.25%)*	28%

Odds of rise based on yesterday

	1935 to present
Large rise yesterday *(above +0.25%)*	52%
Small swing yesterday *(+0.25% to -0.25%)*	38%
Large fall yesterday *(below -0.25%)*	69%

DIAGNOSTICS

Odds of price rise based on direction of 5-day and 20-day trend yesterday

	5-day trend	20-day trend
Yesterday rose more than +0.1%	56%	62%
Little change *(+0.1% to -0.1%)*	36%	50%
Yesterday fell more than -0.1%	65%	42%

Odds of rise based upon distance between trend and yesterday s closing price

	5-day trend	20-day trend
Yesterday more than +0.5% above trend	46%	60%
Yesterday near trend *(+0.5% to -0.5%)*	52%	58%
Yesterday more than -0.5% below trend	64%	40%

Looking ahead: odds of rise in future

	Next 3 days	Next 5 days
Today rose over +0.25%	58%	53%
Today small swing *(+0.25% to -0.25%)*	53%	40%
Today fell below -0.25%	62%	46%

OCTOBER 29 ODDS OF A PRICE RISE: 48%

Odds of different size price shift

	1935 to present
Large rise *(above +0.25%)*	37%
Small swing *(+0.25% to -0.25%)*	39%
Large fall (*below -0.25%)*	24%

Odds of rise based on yesterday

	1935 to present
Large rise yesterday *(above +0.25%)*	56%
Small swing yesterday *(+0.25% to -0.25%)*	47%
Large fall yesterday (*below -0.25%)*	38%

DIAGNOSTICS

Odds of price rise based on direction of 5-day and 20-day trend yesterday

	5-day trend	20-day trend
Yesterday rose more than +0.1%	31%	52%
Little change *(+0.1% to -0.1%)*	55%	42%
Yesterday fell more than -0.1%	58%	45%

Odds of rise based upon distance between trend and yesterday s closing price

	5-day trend	20-day trend
Yesterday more than +0.5% above trend	40%	45%
Yesterday near trend *(+0.5% to -0.5%)*	48%	45%
Yesterday more than -0.5% below trend	60%	53%

Looking ahead: odds of rise in future

	Next 3 days	Next 5 days
Today rose over +0.25%	71%	71%
Today small swing *(+0.25% to -0.25%)*	50%	50%
Today fell below -0.25%	18%	27%

* *Per cent based on fewer than 10 observations*

OCTOBER 30 ODDS OF A PRICE RISE: 52%

Odds of different size price shift

	1935 to present
Large rise *(above +0.25%)*	39%
Small swing *(+0.25% to -0.25%)*	22%
Large fall (*below -0.25%)*	39%

Odds of rise based on yesterday

	1935 to present
Large rise yesterday *(above +0.25%)*	75%
Small swing yesterday *(+0.25% to -0.25%)*	46%
Large fall yesterday (*below -0.25%)*	35%

DIAGNOSTICS

Odds of price rise based on direction of 5-day and 20-day trend yesterday

	5-day trend	20-day trend
Yesterday rose more than +0.1%	56%	61%
Little change *(+0.1% to -0.1%)*	70%	44%
Yesterday fell more than -0.1%	39%	50%

Odds of rise based upon distance between trend and yesterday s closing price

	5-day trend	20-day trend
Yesterday more than +0.5% above trend	69%	62%
Yesterday near trend *(+0.5% to -0.5%)*	60%	*38%
Yesterday more than -0.5% below trend	27%	47%

Looking ahead: odds of rise in future

	Next 3 days	Next 5 days
Today rose over +0.25%	78%	83%
Today small swing *(+0.25% to -0.25%)*	60%	60%
Today fell below -0.25%	39%	33%

OCTOBER 31 ODDS OF A PRICE RISE: 51%

Odds of different size price shift

	1935 to present
Large rise *(above +0.25%)*	38%
Small swing *(+0.25% to -0.25%)*	24%
Large fall (*below -0.25%)*	38%

Odds of rise based on yesterday

	1935 to present
Large rise yesterday *(above +0.25%)*	77%
Small swing yesterday *(+0.25% to -0.25%)*	62%
Large fall yesterday (*below -0.25%)*	26%

DIAGNOSTICS

Odds of price rise based on direction of 5-day and 20-day trend yesterday

	5-day trend	20-day trend
Yesterday rose more than +0.1%	60%	60%
Little change *(+0.1% to -0.1%)*	*44%	53%
Yesterday fell more than -0.1%	44%	36%

Odds of rise based upon distance between trend and yesterday s closing price

	5-day trend	20-day trend
Yesterday more than +0.5% above trend	58%	55%
Yesterday near trend *(+0.5% to -0.5%)*	67%	*33%
Yesterday more than -0.5% below trend	33%	53%

Looking ahead: odds of rise in future

	Next 3 days	Next 5 days
Today rose over +0.25%	65%	65%
Today small swing *(+0.25% to -0.25%)*	55%	36%
Today fell below -0.25%	29%	29%

* *Per cent based on fewer than 10 observations*

NOVEMBER

PROFIT ODDS SUMMARY FOR THE MONTH

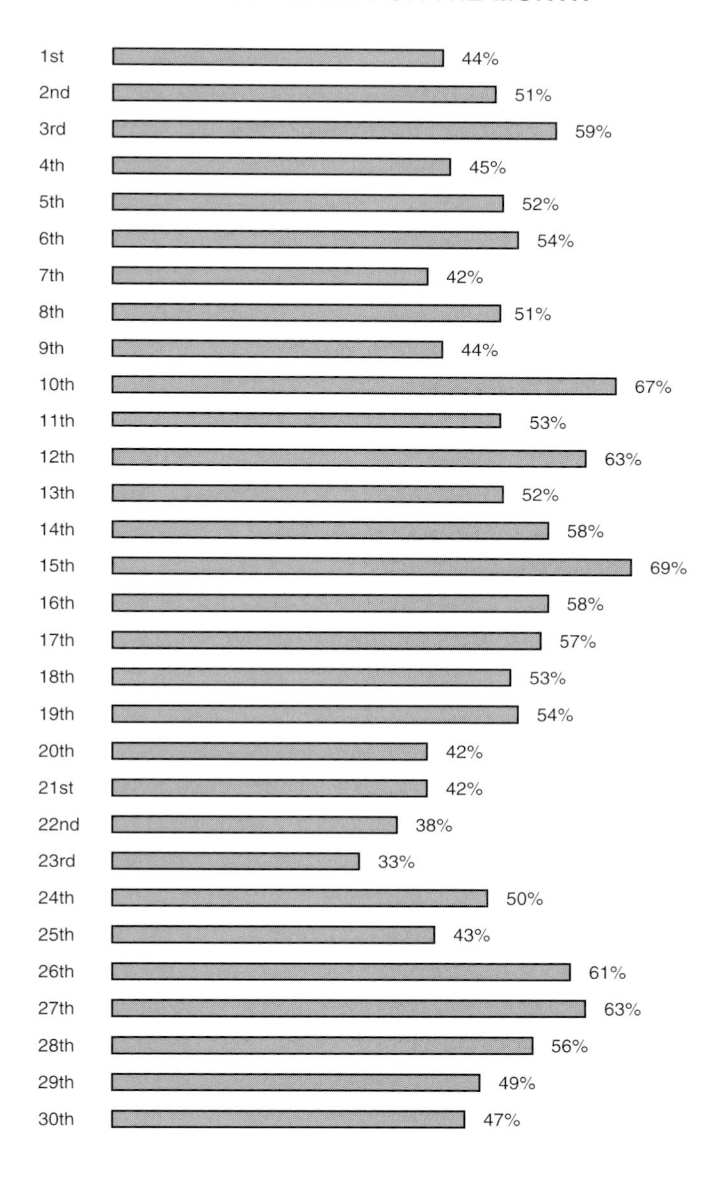

NOVEMBER 1 ODDS OF A PRICE RISE: 44%

Odds of different size price shift

	1935 to present
Large rise *(above +0.25%)*	31%
Small swing *(+0.25% to -0.25%)*	31%
Large fall (*below -0.25%)*	38%

Odds of rise based on yesterday

	1935 to present
Large rise yesterday *(above +0.25%)*	67%
Small swing yesterday *(+0.25% to -0.25%)*	44%
Large fall yesterday (*below -0.25%)*	21%

DIAGNOSTICS

Odds of price rise based on direction of 5-day and 20-day trend yesterday

	5-day trend	20-day trend
Yesterday rose more than +0.1%	69%	69%
Little change *(+0.1% to -0.1%)*	31%	35%
Yesterday fell more than -0.1%	31%	25%

Odds of rise based upon distance between trend and yesterday s closing price

	5-day trend	20-day trend
Yesterday more than +0.5% above trend	71%	59%
Yesterday near trend *(+0.5% to -0.5%)*	40%	*43%
Yesterday more than -0.5% below trend	18%	25%

Looking ahead: odds of rise in future

	Next 3 days	Next 5 days
Today rose over +0.25%	71%	71%
Today small swing *(+0.25% to -0.25%)*	57%	43%
Today fell below -0.25%	41%	35%

* *Per cent based on fewer than 10 observations*

NOVEMBER 2 ODDS OF A PRICE RISE: 51%

Odds of different size price shift

	1935 to present
Large rise *(above +0.25%)*	29%
Small swing *(+0.25% to -0.25%)*	33%
Large fall (*below -0.25%)*	38%

Odds of rise based on yesterday

	1935 to present
Large rise yesterday *(above +0.25%)*	72%
Small swing yesterday *(+0.25% to -0.25%)*	46%
Large fall yesterday (*below -0.25%)*	29%

DIAGNOSTICS

Odds of price rise based on direction of 5-day and 20-day trend yesterday

	5-day trend	20-day trend
Yesterday rose more than +0.1%	68%	74%
Little change *(+0.1% to -0.1%)*	30%	54%
Yesterday fell more than -0.1%	44%	15%

Odds of rise based upon distance between trend and yesterday s closing price

	5-day trend	20-day trend
Yesterday more than +0.5% above trend	65%	71%
Yesterday near trend *(+0.5% to -0.5%)*	60%	*75%
Yesterday more than -0.5% below trend	23%	18%

Looking ahead: odds of rise in future

	Next 3 days	Next 5 days
Today rose over +0.25%	69%	46%
Today small swing *(+0.25% to -0.25%)*	53%	60%
Today fell below -0.25%	29%	41%

NOVEMBER 3 ODDS OF A PRICE RISE: 59%

Odds of different size price shift

	1935 to present
Large rise *(above +0.25%)*	43%
Small swing *(+0.25% to -0.25%)*	33%
Large fall (*below -0.25%)*	24%

Odds of rise based on yesterday

	1935 to present
Large rise yesterday *(above +0.25%)*	80%
Small swing yesterday *(+0.25% to -0.25%)*	62%
Large fall yesterday (*below -0.25%)*	39%

DIAGNOSTICS

Odds of price rise based on direction of 5-day and 20-day trend yesterday

	5-day trend	20-day trend
Yesterday rose more than +0.1%	71%	67%
Little change *(+0.1% to -0.1%)*	33%	54%
Yesterday fell more than -0.1%	62%	53%

Odds of rise based upon distance between trend and yesterday s closing price

	5-day trend	20-day trend
Yesterday more than +0.5% above trend	70%	62%
Yesterday near trend *(+0.5% to -0.5%)*	62%	*60%
Yesterday more than -0.5% below trend	38%	53%

Looking ahead: odds of rise in future

	Next 3 days	Next 5 days
Today rose over +0.25%	65%	70%
Today small swing *(+0.25% to -0.25%)*	40%	33%
Today fell below -0.25%	36%	45%

* *Per cent based on fewer than 10 observations*

NOVEMBER 4 ODDS OF A PRICE RISE: 45%

Odds of different size price shift

	1935 to present
Large rise *(above +0.25%)*	32%
Small swing *(+0.25% to -0.25%)*	38%
Large fall (*below -0.25%)*	30%

Odds of rise based on yesterday

	1935 to present
Large rise yesterday *(above +0.25%)*	65%
Small swing yesterday *(+0.25% to -0.25%)*	46%
Large fall yesterday (*below -0.25%)*	14%

DIAGNOSTICS

Odds of price rise based on direction of 5-day and 20-day trend yesterday

	5-day trend	20-day trend
Yesterday rose more than +0.1%	67%	59%
Little change *(+0.1% to -0.1%)*	30%	*44%
Yesterday fell more than -0.1%	25%	25%

Odds of rise based upon distance between trend and yesterday s closing price

	5-day trend	20-day trend
Yesterday more than +0.5% above trend	75%	61%
Yesterday near trend *(+0.5% to -0.5%)*	39%	*33%
Yesterday more than -0.5% below trend	15%	19%

Looking ahead: odds of rise in future

	Next 3 days	Next 5 days
Today rose over +0.25%	60%	67%
Today small swing *(+0.25% to -0.25%)*	33%	33%
Today fell below -0.25%	43%	64%

NOVEMBER 5 ODDS OF A PRICE RISE: 52%

Odds of different size price shift

	1935 to present
Large rise *(above +0.25%)*	43%
Small swing *(+0.25% to -0.25%)*	28%
Large fall *(below -0.25%)*	28%

Odds of rise based on yesterday

	1935 to present
Large rise yesterday *(above +0.25%)*	63%
Small swing yesterday *(+0.25% to -0.25%)*	40%
Large fall yesterday *(below -0.25%)*	53%

DIAGNOSTICS

Odds of price rise based on direction of 5-day and 20-day trend yesterday

	5-day trend	20-day trend
Yesterday rose more than +0.1%	67%	55%
Little change *(+0.1% to -0.1%)*	*25%	50%
Yesterday fell more than -0.1%	43%	50%

Odds of rise based upon distance between trend and yesterday s closing price

	5-day trend	20-day trend
Yesterday more than +0.5% above trend	67%	58%
Yesterday near trend *(+0.5% to -0.5%)*	33%	*25%
Yesterday more than -0.5% below trend	54%	50%

Looking ahead: odds of rise in future

	Next 3 days	Next 5 days
Today rose over +0.25%	65%	70%
Today small swing *(+0.25% to -0.25%)*	38%	54%
Today fell below -0.25%	46%	38%

* *Per cent based on fewer than 10 observations*

NOVEMBER 6 ODDS OF A PRICE RISE: 54%

Odds of different size price shift

	1935 to present
Large rise *(above +0.25%)*	48%
Small swing *(+0.25% to -0.25%)*	24%
Large fall (*below -0.25%)*	28%

Odds of rise based on yesterday

	1935 to present
Large rise yesterday *(above +0.25%)*	67%
Small swing yesterday *(+0.25% to -0.25%)*	50%
Large fall yesterday (*below -0.25%)*	36%

DIAGNOSTICS

Odds of price rise based on direction of 5-day and 20-day trend yesterday

	5-day trend	20-day trend
Yesterday rose more than +0.1%	57%	53%
Little change *(+0.1% to -0.1%)*	*43%	58%
Yesterday fell more than -0.1%	56%	53%

Odds of rise based upon distance between trend and yesterday s closing price

	5-day trend	20-day trend
Yesterday more than +0.5% above trend	59%	56%
Yesterday near trend *(+0.5% to -0.5%)*	42%	*40%
Yesterday more than -0.5% below trend	70%	56%

Looking ahead: odds of rise in future

	Next 3 days	Next 5 days
Today rose over +0.25%	50%	64%
Today small swing *(+0.25% to -0.25%)*	55%	73%
Today fell below -0.25%	69%	54%

NOVEMBER 7 ODDS OF A PRICE RISE: 42%

Odds of different size price shift

	1935 to present
Large rise *(above +0.25%)*	22%
Small swing *(+0.25% to -0.25%)*	38%
Large fall *(below -0.25%)*	40%

Odds of rise based on yesterday

	1935 to present
Large rise yesterday *(above +0.25%)*	48%
Small swing yesterday *(+0.25% to -0.25%)*	42%
Large fall yesterday *(below -0.25%)*	33%

DIAGNOSTICS

Odds of price rise based on direction of 5-day and 20-day trend yesterday

	5-day trend	20-day trend
Yesterday rose more than +0.1%	50%	47%
Little change *(+0.1% to -0.1%)*	*29%	47%
Yesterday fell more than -0.1%	39%	27%

Odds of rise based upon distance between trend and yesterday s closing price

	5-day trend	20-day trend
Yesterday more than +0.5% above trend	62%	50%
Yesterday near trend *(+0.5% to -0.5%)*	36%	*43%
Yesterday more than -0.5% below trend	*29%	31%

Looking ahead: odds of rise in future

	Next 3 days	Next 5 days
Today rose over +0.25%	70%	60%
Today small swing *(+0.25% to -0.25%)*	71%	71%
Today fell below -0.25%	61%	61%

* *Per cent based on fewer than 10 observations*

NOVEMBER 8 ODDS OF A PRICE RISE: 51%

Odds of different size price shift

	1935 to present
Large rise *(above +0.25%)*	36%
Small swing *(+0.25% to -0.25%)*	29%
Large fall (*below -0.25%)*	36%

Odds of rise based on yesterday

	1935 to present
Large rise yesterday *(above +0.25%)*	*63%
Small swing yesterday *(+0.25% to -0.25%)*	67%
Large fall yesterday (*below -0.25%)*	32%

DIAGNOSTICS

Odds of price rise based on direction of 5-day and 20-day trend yesterday

	5-day trend	20-day trend
Yesterday rose more than +0.1%	56%	35%
Little change *(+0.1% to -0.1%)*	*56%	69%
Yesterday fell more than -0.1%	45%	50%

Odds of rise based upon distance between trend and yesterday s closing price

	5-day trend	20-day trend
Yesterday more than +0.5% above trend	50%	50%
Yesterday near trend *(+0.5% to -0.5%)*	59%	*57%
Yesterday more than -0.5% below trend	44%	50%

Looking ahead: odds of rise in future

	Next 3 days	Next 5 days
Today rose over +0.25%	56%	63%
Today small swing *(+0.25% to -0.25%)*	77%	85%
Today fell below -0.25%	56%	63%

NOVEMBER 9 ODDS OF A PRICE RISE: 44%

Odds of different size price shift

	1935 to present
Large rise *(above +0.25%)*	31%
Small swing *(+0.25% to -0.25%)*	24%
Large fall (*below -0.25%)*	44%

Odds of rise based on yesterday

	1935 to present
Large rise yesterday *(above +0.25%)*	50%
Small swing yesterday *(+0.25% to -0.25%)*	36%
Large fall yesterday (*below -0.25%)*	47%

DIAGNOSTICS

Odds of price rise based on direction of 5-day and 20-day trend yesterday

	5-day trend	20-day trend
Yesterday rose more than +0.1%	33%	28%
Little change *(+0.1% to -0.1%)*	62%	79%
Yesterday fell more than -0.1%	41%	31%

Odds of rise based upon distance between trend and yesterday s closing price

	5-day trend	20-day trend
Yesterday more than +0.5% above trend	*25%	41%
Yesterday near trend *(+0.5% to -0.5%)*	45%	*71%
Yesterday more than -0.5% below trend	53%	38%

Looking ahead: odds of rise in future

	Next 3 days	Next 5 days
Today rose over +0.25%	43%	57%
Today small swing *(+0.25% to -0.25%)*	82%	55%
Today fell below -0.25%	60%	65%

* *Per cent based on fewer than 10 observations*

NOVEMBER 10 ODDS OF A PRICE RISE: 67%

Odds of different size price shift

	1935 to present
Large rise *(above +0.25%)*	50%
Small swing *(+0.25% to -0.25%)*	33%
Large fall (*below -0.25%)*	17%

Odds of rise based on yesterday

	1935 to present
Large rise yesterday *(above +0.25%)*	80%
Small swing yesterda y*(+0.25% to -0.25%)*	50%
Large fall yesterday (*below -0.25%)*	67%

DIAGNOSTICS

Odds of price rise based on direction of 5-day and 20-day trend yesterday

	5-day trend	20-day trend
Yesterday rose more than +0.1%	56%	62%
Little change *(+0.1% to -0.1%)*	*78%	71%
Yesterday fell more than -0.1%	74%	73%

Odds of rise based upon distance between trend and yesterday s closing price

	5-day trend	20-day trend
Yesterday more than +0.5% above trend	55%	58%
Yesterday near trend *(+0.5% to -0.5%)*	71%	*75%
Yesterday more than -0.5% below trend	72%	78%

Looking ahead: odds of rise in future

	Next 3 days	Next 5 days
Today rose over +0.25%	65%	70%
Today small swing *(+0.25% to -0.25%)*	53%	67%
Today fell below -0.25%	*75%	*63%

NOVEMBER 11 ODDS OF A PRICE RISE: 53%

Odds of different size price shift

	1935 to present
Large rise *(above +0.25%)*	40%
Small swing *(+0.25% to -0.25%)*	36%
Large fall (*below -0.25%)*	23%

Odds of rise based on yesterday

	1935 to present
Large rise yesterday *(above +0.25%)*	59%
Small swing yesterday *(+0.25% to -0.25%)*	41%
Large fall yesterday (*below -0.25%)*	*63%

DIAGNOSTICS

Odds of price rise based on direction of 5-day and 20-day trend yesterday

	5-day trend	20-day trend
Yesterday rose more than +0.1%	60%	52%
Little change *(+0.1% to -0.1%)*	*44%	50%
Yesterday fell more than -0.1%	50%	58%

Odds of rise based upon distance between trend and yesterday s closing price

	5-day trend	20-day trend
Yesterday more than +0.5% above trend	62%	52%
Yesterday near trend *(+0.5% to -0.5%)*	45%	*20%
Yesterday more than -0.5% below trend	58%	63%

Looking ahead: odds of rise in future

	Next 3 days	Next 5 days
Today rose over +0.25%	68%	42%
Today small swing *(+0.25% to -0.25%)*	65%	76%
Today fell below -0.25%	55%	73%

* *Per cent based on fewer than 10 observations*

NOVEMBER 12 ODDS OF A PRICE RISE: 63%

Odds of different size price shift

	1935 to present
Large rise *(above +0.25%)*	48%
Small swing *(+0.25% to -0.25%)*	28%
Large fall (*below -0.25%)*	24%

Odds of rise based on yesterday

	1935 to present
Large rise yesterday *(above +0.25%)*	67%
Small swing yesterday *(+0.25% to -0.25%)*	65%
Large fall yesterday (*below -0.25%)*	55%

DIAGNOSTICS

Odds of price rise based on direction of 5-day and 20-day trend yesterday

	5-day trend	20-day trend
Yesterday rose more than +0.1%	82%	77%
Little change *(+0.1% to -0.1%)*	80%	54%
Yesterday fell more than -0.1%	21%	45%

Odds of rise based upon distance between trend and yesterday s closing price

	5-day trend	20-day trend
Yesterday more than +0.5% above trend	92%	77%
Yesterday near trend *(+0.5% to -0.5%)*	56%	*75%
Yesterday more than -0.5% below trend	*33%	38%

Looking ahead: odds of rise in future

	Next 3 days	Next 5 days
Today rose over +0.25%	55%	55%
Today small swing *(+0.25% to -0.25%)*	62%	69%
Today fell below -0.25%	55%	55%

NOVEMBER 13 ODDS OF A PRICE RISE: 52%

Odds of different size price shift

	1935 to present
Large rise *(above +0.25%)*	30%
Small swing *(+0.25% to -0.25%)*	37%
Large fall (*below -0.25%)*	33%

Odds of rise based on yesterday

	1935 to present
Large rise yesterday *(above +0.25%)*	44%
Small swing yesterday *(+0.25% to -0.25%)*	82%
Large fall yesterday (*below -0.25%)*	40%

DIAGNOSTICS

Odds of price rise based on direction of 5-day and 20-day trend yesterday

	5-day trend	20-day trend
Yesterday rose more than +0.1%	37%	59%
Little change *(+0.1% to -0.1%)*	75%	62%
Yesterday fell more than -0.1%	45%	27%

Odds of rise based upon distance between trend and yesterday s closing price

	5-day trend	20-day trend
Yesterday more than +0.5% above trend	33%	56%
Yesterday near trend *(+0.5% to -0.5%)*	81%	*71%
Yesterday more than -0.5% below trend	*14%	33%

Looking ahead: odds of rise in future

	Next 3 days	Next 5 days
Today rose over +0.25%	64%	50%
Today small swing *(+0.25% to -0.25%)*	59%	71%
Today fell below -0.25%	40%	33%

* *Per cent based on fewer than 10 observations*

NOVEMBER 14 ODDS OF A PRICE RISE: 58%

Odds of different size price shift

	1935 to present
Large rise *(above +0.25%)*	51%
Small swing *(+0.25% to -0.25%)*	20%
Large fall (*below -0.25%)*	29%

Odds of rise based on yesterday

	1935 to present
Large rise yesterday *(above +0.25%)*	67%
Small swing yesterday *(+0.25% to -0.25%)*	53%
Large fall yesterday (*below -0.25%)*	50%

DIAGNOSTICS

Odds of price rise based on direction of 5-day and 20-day trend yesterday

	5-day trend	20-day trend
Yesterday rose more than +0.1%	61%	58%
Little change *(+0.1% to -0.1%)*	69%	63%
Yesterday fell more than -0.1%	43%	50%

Odds of rise based upon distance between trend and yesterday s closing price

	5-day trend	20-day trend
Yesterday more than +0.5% above trend	59%	57%
Yesterday near trend *(+0.5% to -0.5%)*	67%	*88%
Yesterday more than -0.5% below trend	40%	44%

Looking ahead: odds of rise in future

	Next 3 days	Next 5 days
Today rose over +0.25%	83%	74%
Today small swing *(+0.25% to -0.25%)*	*44%	*33%
Today fell below -0.25%	69%	54%

NOVEMBER 15 ODDS OF A PRICE RISE: 69%

Odds of different size price shift

	1935 to present
Large rise *(above +0.25%)*	51%
Small swing *(+0.25% to -0.25%)*	22%
Large fall (*below -0.25%)*	27%

Odds of rise based on yesterday

	1935 to present
Large rise yesterday *(above +0.25%)*	90%
Small swing yesterday *(+0.25% to -0.25%)*	64%
Large fall yesterday (*below -0.25%)*	43%

DIAGNOSTICS

Odds of price rise based on direction of 5-day and 20-day trend yesterday

	5-day trend	20-day trend
Yesterday rose more than +0.1%	65%	76%
Little change *(+0.1% to -0.1%)*	82%	60%
Yesterday fell more than -0.1%	64%	69%

Odds of rise based upon distance between trend and yesterday s closing price

	5-day trend	20-day trend
Yesterday more than +0.5% above trend	75%	74%
Yesterday near trend *(+0.5% to -0.5%)*	68%	80%
Yesterday more than -0.5% below trend	60%	56%

Looking ahead: odds of rise in future

	Next 3 days	Next 5 days
Today rose over +0.25%	70%	65%
Today small swing *(+0.25% to -0.25%)*	50%	20%
Today fell below -0.25%	42%	25%

* *Per cent based on fewer than 10 observations*

NOVEMBER 16 ODDS OF A PRICE RISE: 58%

Odds of different size price shift

	1935 to present
Large rise *(above +0.25%)*	44%
Small swing *(+0.25% to -0.25%)*	22%
Large fall (*below -0.25%)*	33%

Odds of rise based on yesterday

	1935 to present
Large rise yesterday *(above +0.25%)*	76%
Small swing yesterday *(+0.25% to -0.25%)*	43%
Large fall yesterday (*below -0.25%)*	50%

DIAGNOSTICS

Odds of price rise based on direction of 5-day and 20-day trend yesterday

	5-day trend	20-day trend
Yesterday rose more than +0.1%	47%	47%
Little change *(+0.1% to -0.1%)*	54%	77%
Yesterday fell more than -0.1%	77%	53%

Odds of rise based upon distance between trend and yesterday s closing price

	5-day trend	20-day trend
Yesterday more than +0.5% above trend	50%	50%
Yesterday near trend *(+0.5% to -0.5%)*	62%	*71%
Yesterday more than -0.5% below trend	*63%	63%

Looking ahead: odds of rise in future

	Next 3 days	Next 5 days
Today rose over +0.25%	50%	45%
Today small swing *(+0.25% to -0.25%)*	70%	40%
Today fell below -0.25%	53%	53%

NOVEMBER 17 ODDS OF A PRICE RISE: 57%

Odds of different size price shift

	1935 to present
Large rise *(above +0.25%)*	33%
Small swing *(+0.25% to -0.25%)*	39%
Large fall *(below -0.25%)*	28%

Odds of rise based on yesterday

	1935 to present
Large rise yesterday *(above +0.25%)*	68%
Small swing yesterday *(+0.25% to -0.25%)*	55%
Large fall yesterday *(below -0.25%)*	44%

DIAGNOSTICS

Odds of price rise based on direction of 5-day and 20-day trend yesterday

	5-day trend	20-day trend
Yesterday rose more than +0.1%	54%	35%
Little change *(+0.1% to -0.1%)*	55%	71%
Yesterday fell more than -0.1%	64%	*78%

Odds of rise based upon distance between trend and yesterday s closing price

	5-day trend	20-day trend
Yesterday more than +0.5% above trend	60%	52%
Yesterday near trend *(+0.5% to -0.5%)*	53%	*67%
Yesterday more than -0.5% below trend	*56%	62%

Looking ahead: odds of rise in future

	Next 3 days	Next 5 days
Today rose over +0.25%	47%	47%
Today small swing *(+0.25% to -0.25%)*	72%	67%
Today fell below -0.25%	15%	38%

* *Per cent based on fewer than 10 observations*

NOVEMBER 18 ODDS OF A PRICE RISE: 53%

Odds of different size price shift

	1935 to present
Large rise *(above +0.25%)*	30%
Small swing *(+0.25% to -0.25%)*	34%
Large fall (*below -0.25%)*	36%

Odds of rise based on yesterday

	1935 to present
Large rise yesterday *(above +0.25%)*	72%
Small swing yesterday *(+0.25% to -0.25%)*	47%
Large fall yesterday (*below -0.25%)*	36%

DIAGNOSTICS

Odds of price rise based on direction of 5-day and 20-day trend yesterday

	5-day trend	20-day trend
Yesterday rose more than +0.1%	63%	48%
Little change *(+0.1% to -0.1%)*	*44%	71%
Yesterday fell more than -0.1%	36%	*33%

Odds of rise based upon distance between trend and yesterday s closing price

	5-day trend	20-day trend
Yesterday more than +0.5% above trend	73%	59%
Yesterday near trend *(+0.5% to -0.5%)*	53%	*29%
Yesterday more than -0.5% below trend	10%	55%

Looking ahead: odds of rise in future

	Next 3 days	Next 5 days
Today rose over +0.25%	64%	43%
Today small swing *(+0.25% to -0.25%)*	50%	50%
Today fell below -0.25%	35%	47%

NOVEMBER 19 ODDS OF A PRICE RISE: 54%

Odds of different size price shift

	1935 to present
Large rise *(above +0.25%)*	30%
Small swing *(+0.25% to -0.25%)*	35%
Large fall *(below -0.25%)*	35%

Odds of rise based on yesterday

	1935 to present
Large rise yesterday *(above +0.25%)*	61%
Small swing yesterday *(+0.25% to -0.25%)*	67%
Large fall yesterday *(below -0.25%)*	38%

DIAGNOSTICS

Odds of price rise based on direction of 5-day and 20-day trend yesterday

	5-day trend	20-day trend
Yesterday rose more than +0.1%	52%	53%
Little change *(+0.1% to -0.1%)*	*75%	73%
Yesterday fell more than -0.1%	47%	36%

Odds of rise based upon distance between trend and yesterday s closing price

	5-day trend	20-day trend
Yesterday more than +0.5% above trend	47%	58%
Yesterday near trend *(+0.5% to -0.5%)*	63%	*67%
Yesterday more than -0.5% below trend	50%	38%

Looking ahead: odds of rise in future

	Next 3 days	Next 5 days
Today rose over +0.25%	86%	86%
Today small swing *(+0.25% to -0.25%)*	38%	38%
Today fell below -0.25%	25%	50%

* *Per cent based on fewer than 10 observations*

NOVEMBER 20 ODDS OF A PRICE RISE: 42%

Odds of different size price shift

	1935 to present
Large rise *(above +0.25%)*	33%
Small swing *(+0.25% to -0.25%)*	27%
Large fall (*below -0.25%)*	40%

Odds of rise based on yesterday

	1935 to present
Large rise yesterday *(above +0.25%)*	57%
Small swing yesterday *(+0.25% to -0.25%)*	50%
Large fall yesterday (*below -0.25%)*	15%

DIAGNOSTICS

Odds of price rise based on direction of 5-day and 20-day trend yesterday

	5-day trend	20-day trend
Yesterday rose more than +0.1%	46%	45%
Little change *(+0.1% to -0.1%)*	*29%	50%
Yesterday fell more than -0.1%	43%	27%

Odds of rise based upon distance between trend and yesterday s closing price

	5-day trend	20-day trend
Yesterday more than +0.5% above trend	53%	48%
Yesterday near trend *(+0.5% to -0.5%)*	33%	*50%
Yesterday more than -0.5% below trend	*44%	25%

Looking ahead: odds of rise in future

	Next 3 days	Next 5 days
Today rose over +0.25%	53%	60%
Today small swing *(+0.25% to -0.25%)*	42%	50%
Today fell below -0.25%	50%	50%

NOVEMBER 21 ODDS OF A PRICE RISE: 42%

Odds of different size price shift

	1935 to present
Large rise *(above +0.25%)*	27%
Small swing *(+0.25% to -0.25%)*	40%
Large fall (*below -0.25%)*	33%

Odds of rise based on yesterday

	1935 to present
Large rise yesterday *(above +0.25%)*	57%
Small swing yesterday *(+0.25% to -0.25%)*	21%
Large fall yesterday (*below -0.25%)*	47%

DIAGNOSTICS

Odds of price rise based on direction of 5-day and 20-day trend yesterday

	5-day trend	20-day trend
Yesterday rose more than +0.1%	48%	48%
Little change *(+0.1% to -0.1%)*	*33%	25%
Yesterday fell more than -0.1%	36%	50%

Odds of rise based upon distance between trend and yesterday s closing price

	5-day trend	20-day trend
Yesterday more than +0.5% above trend	57%	46%
Yesterday near trend *(+0.5% to -0.5%)*	35%	*25%
Yesterday more than -0.5% below trend	36%	45%

Looking ahead: odds of rise in future

	Next 3 days	Next 5 days
Today rose over +0.25%	58%	67%
Today small swing *(+0.25% to -0.25%)*	44%	50%
Today fell below -0.25%	27%	20%

* *Per cent based on fewer than 10 observations*

NOVEMBER 22 ODDS OF A PRICE RISE: 38%

Odds of different size price shift

	1935 to present
Large rise *(above +0.25%)*	27%
Small swing *(+0.25% to -0.25%)*	40%
Large fall (*below -0.25%)*	33%

Odds of rise based on yesterday

	1935 to present
Large rise yesterday *(above +0.25%)*	70%
Small swing yesterday *(+0.25% to -0.25%)*	33%
Large fall yesterday (*below -0.25%)*	24%

DIAGNOSTICS

Odds of price rise based on direction of 5-day and 20-day trend yesterday

	5-day trend	20-day trend
Yesterday rose more than +0.1%	65%	43%
Little change *(+0.1% to -0.1%)*	10%	42%
Yesterday fell more than -0.1%	20%	25%

Odds of rise based upon distance between trend and yesterday s closing price

	5-day trend	20-day trend
Yesterday more than +0.5% above trend	*89%	45%
Yesterday near trend *(+0.5% to -0.5%)*	30%	42%
Yesterday more than -0.5% below trend	15%	18%

Looking ahead: odds of rise in future

	Next 3 days	Next 5 days
Today rose over +0.25%	67%	58%
Today small swing *(+0.25% to -0.25%)*	50%	61%
Today fell below -0.25%	47%	40%

NOVEMBER 23 ODDS OF A PRICE RISE: 33%

Odds of different size price shift

	1935 to present
Large rise *(above +0.25%)*	31%
Small swing *(+0.25% to -0.25%)*	31%
Large fall *(below -0.25%)*	38%

Odds of rise based on yesterday

	1935 to present
Large rise yesterday *(above +0.25%)*	33%
Small swing yesterday *(+0.25% to -0.25%)*	41%
Large fall yesterday *(below -0.25%)*	25%

DIAGNOSTICS

Odds of price rise based on direction of 5-day and 20-day trend yesterday

	5-day trend	20-day trend
Yesterday rose more than +0.1%	33%	33%
Little change *(+0.1% to -0.1%)*	29%	41%
Yesterday fell more than -0.1%	38%	23%

Odds of rise based upon distance between trend and yesterday s closing price

	5-day trend	20-day trend
Yesterday more than +0.5% above trend	18%	40%
Yesterday near trend *(+0.5% to -0.5%)*	43%	29%
Yesterday more than -0.5% below trend	31%	27%

Looking ahead: odds of rise in future

	Next 3 days	Next 5 days
Today rose over +0.25%	50%	43%
Today small swing *(+0.25% to -0.25%)*	57%	71%
Today fell below -0.25%	59%	53%

* *Per cent based on fewer than 10 observations*

NOVEMBER 24 ODDS OF A PRICE RISE: 50%

Odds of different size price shift

	1935 to present
Large rise *(above +0.25%)*	26%
Small swing *(+0.25% to -0.25%)*	50%
Large fall (*below -0.25%)*	24%

Odds of rise based on yesterday

	1935 to present
Large rise yesterday *(above +0.25%)*	53%
Small swing yesterday *(+0.25% to -0.25%)*	43%
Large fall yesterday (*below -0.25%)*	53%

DIAGNOSTICS

Odds of price rise based on direction of 5-day and 20-day trend yesterday

	5-day trend	20-day trend
Yesterday rose more than +0.1%	48%	63%
Little change *(+0.1% to -0.1%)*	64%	35%
Yesterday fell more than -0.1%	43%	*57%

Odds of rise based upon distance between trend and yesterday s closing price

	5-day trend	20-day trend
Yesterday more than +0.5% above trend	50%	54%
Yesterday near trend *(+0.5% to -0.5%)*	61%	*44%
Yesterday more than -0.5% below trend	36%	46%

Looking ahead: odds of rise in future

	Next 3 days	Next 5 days
Today rose over +0.25%	67%	67%
Today small swing *(+0.25% to -0.25%)*	61%	57%
Today fell below -0.25%	64%	64%

NOVEMBER 25 ODDS OF A PRICE RISE: 43%

Odds of different size price shift

	1935 to present
Large rise *(above +0.25%)*	30%
Small swing *(+0.25% to -0.25%)*	30%
Large fall *(below -0.25%)*	40%

Odds of rise based on yesterday

	1935 to present
Large rise yesterday *(above +0.25%)*	70%
Small swing yesterday *(+0.25% to -0.25%)*	33%
Large fall yesterday *(below -0.25%)*	38%

DIAGNOSTICS

Odds of price rise based on direction of 5-day and 20-day trend yesterday

	5-day trend	20-day trend
Yesterday rose more than +0.1%	47%	39%
Little change *(+0.1% to -0.1%)*	*38%	42%
Yesterday fell more than -0.1%	40%	50%

Odds of rise based upon distance between trend and yesterday s closing price

	5-day trend	20-day trend
Yesterday more than +0.5% above trend	54%	48%
Yesterday near trend *(+0.5% to -0.5%)*	47%	*17%
Yesterday more than -0.5% below trend	32%	43%

Looking ahead: odds of rise in future

	Next 3 days	Next 5 days
Today rose over +0.25%	50%	57%
Today small swing *(+0.25% to -0.25%)*	50%	43%
Today fell below -0.25%	58%	58%

* *Per cent based on fewer than 10 observations*

NOVEMBER 26 ODDS OF A PRICE RISE: 61%

Odds of different size price shift

	1935 to present
Large rise *(above +0.25%)*	41%
Small swing *(+0.25% to -0.25%)*	30%
Large fall (*below -0.25%)*	28%

Odds of rise based on yesterday

	1935 to present
Large rise yesterday *(above +0.25%)*	69%
Small swing yesterday *(+0.25% to -0.25%)*	50%
Large fall yesterday (*below -0.25%)*	62%

DIAGNOSTICS

Odds of price rise based on direction of 5-day and 20-day trend yesterday

	5-day trend	20-day trend
Yesterday rose more than +0.1%	54%	56%
Little change *(+0.1% to -0.1%)*	67%	59%
Yesterday fell more than -0.1%	62%	73%

Odds of rise based upon distance between trend and yesterday s closing price

	5-day trend	20-day trend
Yesterday more than +0.5% above trend	*44%	52%
Yesterday near trend *(+0.5% to -0.5%)*	75%	*67%
Yesterday more than -0.5% below trend	53%	71%

Looking ahead: odds of rise in future

	Next 3 days	Next 5 days
Today rose over +0.25%	63%	47%
Today small swing *(+0.25% to -0.25%)*	57%	50%
Today fell below -0.25%	69%	62%

NOVEMBER 27 ODDS OF A PRICE RISE: 63%

Odds of different size price shift

	1935 to present
Large rise *(above +0.25%)*	43%
Small swing *(+0.25% to -0.25%)*	33%
Large fall (*below -0.25%)*	24%

Odds of rise based on yesterday

	1935 to present
Large rise yesterday *(above +0.25%)*	82%
Small swing yesterday *(+0.25% to -0.25%)*	67%
Large fall yesterday (*below -0.25%)*	25%

DIAGNOSTICS

Odds of price rise based on direction of 5-day and 20-day trend yesterday

	5-day trend	20-day trend
Yesterday rose more than +0.1%	67%	80%
Little change *(+0.1% to -0.1%)*	70%	56%
Yesterday fell more than -0.1%	56%	40%

Odds of rise based upon distance between trend and yesterday s closing price

	5-day trend	20-day trend
Yesterday more than +0.5% above trend	77%	71%
Yesterday near trend *(+0.5% to -0.5%)*	58%	*38%
Yesterday more than -0.5% below trend	57%	64%

Looking ahead: odds of rise in future

	Next 3 days	Next 5 days
Today rose over +0.25%	55%	50%
Today small swing *(+0.25% to -0.25%)*	53%	53%
Today fell below -0.25%	36%	27%

* *Per cent based on fewer than 10 observations*

NOVEMBER 28 ODDS OF A PRICE RISE: 56%

Odds of different size price shift

	1935 to present
Large rise *(above +0.25%)*	42%
Small swing *(+0.25% to -0.25%)*	27%
Large fall (*below -0.25%)*	31%

Odds of rise based on yesterday

	1935 to present
Large rise yesterday *(above +0.25%)*	68%
Small swing yesterday *(+0.25% to -0.25%)*	53%
Large fall yesterday (*below -0.25%)*	36%

DIAGNOSTICS

Odds of price rise based on direction of 5-day and 20-day trend yesterday

	5-day trend	20-day trend
Yesterday rose more than +0.1%	71%	67%
Little change *(+0.1% to -0.1%)*	*14%	53%
Yesterday fell more than -0.1%	57%	40%

Odds of rise based upon distance between trend and yesterday s closing price

	5-day trend	20-day trend
Yesterday more than +0.5% above trend	67%	59%
Yesterday near trend *(+0.5% to -0.5%)*	50%	*71%
Yesterday more than -0.5% below trend	50%	44%

Looking ahead: odds of rise in future

	Next 3 days	Next 5 days
Today rose over +0.25%	47%	42%
Today small swing *(+0.25% to -0.25%)*	67%	67%
Today fell below -0.25%	43%	36%

NOVEMBER 29 ODDS OF A PRICE RISE: 49%

Odds of different size price shift

	1935 to present
Large rise *(above +0.25%)*	36%
Small swing *(+0.25% to -0.25%)*	38%
Large fall (*below -0.25%)*	27%

Odds of rise based on yesterday

	1935 to present
Large rise yesterday *(above +0.25%)*	56%
Small swing yesterday *(+0.25% to -0.25%)*	46%
Large fall yesterday (*below -0.25%)*	43%

DIAGNOSTICS

Odds of price rise based on direction of 5-day and 20-day trend yesterday

	5-day trend	20-day trend
Yesterday rose more than +0.1%	44%	53%
Little change *(+0.1% to -0.1%)*	54%	42%
Yesterday fell more than -0.1%	50%	55%

Odds of rise based upon distance between trend and yesterday s closing price

	5-day trend	20-day trend
Yesterday more than +0.5% above trend	64%	48%
Yesterday near trend *(+0.5% to -0.5%)*	36%	50%
Yesterday more than -0.5% below trend	*56%	50%

Looking ahead: odds of rise in future

	Next 3 days	Next 5 days
Today rose over +0.25%	56%	50%
Today small swing *(+0.25% to -0.25%)*	41%	53%
Today fell below -0.25%	42%	42%

* *Per cent based on fewer than 10 observations*

NOVEMBER 30 ODDS OF A PRICE RISE: 47%

Odds of different size price shift

	1935 to present
Large rise *(above +0.25%)*	38%
Small swing *(+0.25% to -0.25%)*	31%
Large fall (*below -0.25%)*	31%

Odds of rise based on yesterday

	1935 to present
Large rise yesterday *(above +0.25%)*	69%
Small swing yesterday *(+0.25% to -0.25%)*	33%
Large fall yesterday (*below -0.25%)*	36%

DIAGNOSTICS

Odds of price rise based on direction of 5-day and 20-day trend yesterday

	5-day trend	20-day trend
Yesterday rose more than +0.1%	53%	57%
Little change *(+0.1% to -0.1%)*	54%	42%
Yesterday fell more than -0.1%	31%	42%

Odds of rise based upon distance between trend and yesterday s closing price

	5-day trend	20-day trend
Yesterday more than +0.5% above trend	53%	72%
Yesterday near trend *(+0.5% to -0.5%)*	42%	25%
Yesterday more than -0.5% below trend	*44%	33%

Looking ahead: odds of rise in future

	Next 3 days	Next 5 days
Today rose over +0.25%	53%	53%
Today small swing *(+0.25% to -0.25%)*	50%	43%
Today fell below -0.25%	50%	50%

DECEMBER

PROFIT ODDS SUMMARY FOR THE MONTH

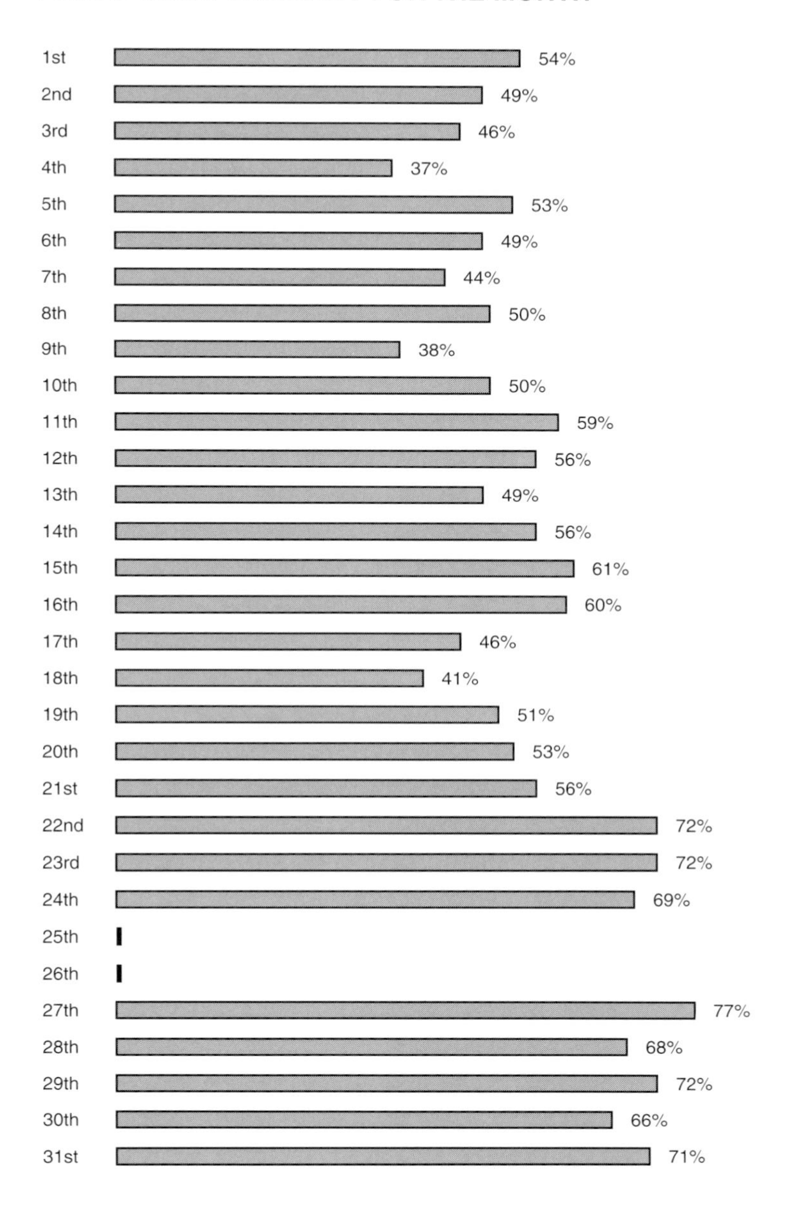

DECEMBER 1 ODDS OF A PRICE RISE: 54%

Odds of different size price shift

	1935 to present
Large rise *(above +0.25%)*	39%
Small swing *(+0.25% to -0.25%)*	33%
Large fall *(below -0.25%)*	28%

Odds of rise based on yesterday

	1935 to present
Large rise yesterday *(above +0.25%)*	53%
Small swing yesterday *(+0.25% to -0.25%)*	65%
Large fall yesterday *(below -0.25%)*	42%

DIAGNOSTICS

Odds of price rise based on direction of 5-day and 20-day trend yesterday

	5-day trend	20-day trend
Yesterday rose more than +0.1%	63%	61%
Little change *(+0.1% to -0.1%)*	55%	60%
Yesterday fell more than -0.1%	44%	*25%

Odds of rise based upon distance between trend and yesterday s closing price

	5-day trend	20-day trend
Yesterday more than +0.5% above trend	57%	65%
Yesterday near trend *(+0.5% to -0.5%)*	57%	60%
Yesterday more than -0.5% below trend	45%	38%

Looking ahead: odds of rise in future

	Next 3 days	Next 5 days
Today rose over +0.25%	56%	50%
Today small swing *(+0.25% to -0.25%)*	33%	20%
Today fell below -0.25%	62%	77%

* *Per cent based on fewer than 10 observations*

DECEMBER 2 ODDS OF A PRICE RISE: 49%

Odds of different size price shift

	1935 to present
Large rise *(above +0.25%)*	28%
Small swing *(+0.25% to -0.25%)*	36%
Large fall (*below -0.25%)*	36%

Odds of rise based on yesterday

	1935 to present
Large rise yesterday *(above +0.25%)*	61%
Small swing yesterday *(+0.25% to -0.25%)*	27%
Large fall yesterday (*below -0.25%)*	57%

DIAGNOSTICS

Odds of price rise based on direction of 5-day and 20-day trend yesterday

	5-day trend	20-day trend
Yesterday rose more than +0.1%	58%	53%
Little change *(+0.1% to -0.1%)*	43%	42%
Yesterday fell more than -0.1%	43%	55%

Odds of rise based upon distance between trend and yesterday s closing price

	5-day trend	20-day trend
Yesterday more than +0.5% above trend	59%	55%
Yesterday near trend *(+0.5% to -0.5%)*	41%	*43%
Yesterday more than -0.5% below trend	*50%	44%

Looking ahead: odds of rise in future

	Next 3 days	Next 5 days
Today rose over +0.25%	62%	62%
Today small swing *(+0.25% to -0.25%)*	41%	47%
Today fell below -0.25%	35%	18%

DECEMBER 3 ODDS OF A PRICE RISE: 46%

Odds of different size price shift

	1935 to present
Large rise *(above +0.25%)*	28%
Small swing *(+0.25% to -0.25%)*	35%
Large fall (*below -0.25%)*	37%

Odds of rise based on yesterday

	1935 to present
Large rise yesterday *(above +0.25%)*	57%
Small swing yesterday *(+0.25% to -0.25%)*	40%
Large fall yesterday (*below -0.25%)*	41%

DIAGNOSTICS

Odds of price rise based on direction of 5-day and 20-day trend yesterday

	5-day trend	20-day trend
Yesterday rose more than +0.1%	32%	38%
Little change *(+0.1% to -0.1%)*	50%	44%
Yesterday fell more than -0.1%	59%	57%

Odds of rise based upon distance between trend and yesterday s closing price

	5-day trend	20-day trend
Yesterday more than +0.5% above trend	55%	45%
Yesterday near trend *(+0.5% to -0.5%)*	41%	*13%
Yesterday more than -0.5% below trend	46%	61%

Looking ahead: odds of rise in future

	Next 3 days	Next 5 days
Today rose over +0.25%	54%	69%
Today small swing *(+0.25% to -0.25%)*	44%	50%
Today fell below -0.25%	35%	41%

* *Per cent based on fewer than 10 observations*

DECEMBER 4 ODDS OF A PRICE RISE: 37%

Odds of different size price shift

	1935 to present
Large rise *(above +0.25%)*	26%
Small swing *(+0.25% to -0.25%)*	30%
Large fall (*below -0.25%)*	43%

Odds of rise based on yesterday

	1935 to present
Large rise yesterday *(above +0.25%)*	50%
Small swing yesterday *(+0.25% to -0.25%)*	29%
Large fall yesterday (*below -0.25%)*	33%

DIAGNOSTICS

Odds of price rise based on direction of 5-day and 20-day trend yesterday

	5-day trend	20-day trend
Yesterday rose more than +0.1%	50%	24%
Little change *(+0.1% to -0.1%)*	25%	47%
Yesterday fell more than -0.1%	31%	42%

Odds of rise based upon distance between trend and yesterday s closing price

	5-day trend	20-day trend
Yesterday more than +0.5% above trend	*56%	35%
Yesterday near trend *(+0.5% to -0.5%)*	27%	*44%
Yesterday more than -0.5% below trend	40%	35%

Looking ahead: odds of rise in future

	Next 3 days	Next 5 days
Today rose over +0.25%	58%	67%
Today small swing *(+0.25% to -0.25%)*	50%	50%
Today fell below -0.25%	45%	40%

DECEMBER 5 ODDS OF A PRICE RISE: 53%

Odds of different size price shift

	1935 to present
Large rise *(above +0.25%)*	31%
Small swing *(+0.25% to -0.25%)*	36%
Large fall (*below -0.25%)*	33%

Odds of rise based on yesterday

	1935 to present
Large rise yesterday *(above +0.25%)*	80%
Small swing yesterday *(+0.25% to -0.25%)*	50%
Large fall yesterday (*below -0.25%)*	43%

DIAGNOSTICS

Odds of price rise based on direction of 5-day and 20-day trend yesterday

	5-day trend	20-day trend
Yesterday rose more than +0.1%	50%	50%
Little change *(+0.1% to -0.1%)*	70%	77%
Yesterday fell more than -0.1%	47%	33%

Odds of rise based upon distance between trend and yesterday s closing price

	5-day trend	20-day trend
Yesterday more than +0.5% above trend	62%	58%
Yesterday near trend *(+0.5% to -0.5%)*	53%	*67%
Yesterday more than -0.5% below trend	47%	41%

Looking ahead: odds of rise in future

	Next 3 days	Next 5 days
Today rose over +0.25%	50%	50%
Today small swing *(+0.25% to -0.25%)*	56%	69%
Today fell below -0.25%	13%	40%

* *Per cent based on fewer than 10 observations*

DECEMBER 6 ODDS OF A PRICE RISE: 49%

Odds of different size price shift

	1935 to present
Large rise *(above +0.25%)*	24%
Small swing *(+0.25% to -0.25%)*	40%
Large fall (*below -0.25%)*	36%

Odds of rise based on yesterday

	1935 to present
Large rise yesterday *(above +0.25%)*	69%
Small swing yesterday *(+0.25% to -0.25%)*	44%
Large fall yesterday (*below -0.25%)*	36%

DIAGNOSTICS

Odds of price rise based on direction of 5-day and 20-day trend yesterday

	5-day trend	20-day trend
Yesterday rose more than +0.1%	47%	50%
Little change *(+0.1% to -0.1%)*	*63%	47%
Yesterday fell more than -0.1%	44%	50%

Odds of rise based upon distance between trend and yesterday s closing price

	5-day trend	20-day trend
Yesterday more than +0.5% above trend	69%	50%
Yesterday near trend *(+0.5% to -0.5%)*	37%	*75%
Yesterday more than -0.5% below trend	46%	35%

Looking ahead: odds of rise in future

	Next 3 days	Next 5 days
Today rose over +0.25%	45%	55%
Today small swing *(+0.25% to -0.25%)*	67%	61%
Today fell below -0.25%	50%	63%

DECEMBER 7 ODDS OF A PRICE RISE: 44%

Odds of different size price shift

	1935 to present
Large rise *(above +0.25%)*	31%
Small swing *(+0.25% to -0.25%)*	53%
Large fall (*below -0.25%)*	16%

Odds of rise based on yesterday

	1935 to present
Large rise yesterday *(above +0.25%)*	46%
Small swing yesterday *(+0.25% to -0.25%)*	35%
Large fall yesterday (*below -0.25%)*	53%

DIAGNOSTICS

Odds of price rise based on direction of 5-day and 20-day trend yesterday

	5-day trend	20-day trend
Yesterday rose more than +0.1%	64%	50%
Little change *(+0.1% to -0.1%)*	33%	38%
Yesterday fell more than -0.1%	38%	43%

Odds of rise based upon distance between trend and yesterday s closing price

	5-day trend	20-day trend
Yesterday more than +0.5% above trend	60%	55%
Yesterday near trend *(+0.5% to -0.5%)*	42%	*17%
Yesterday more than -0.5% below trend	36%	41%

Looking ahead: odds of rise in future

	Next 3 days	Next 5 days
Today rose over +0.25%	64%	50%
Today small swing *(+0.25% to -0.25%)*	58%	63%
Today fell below -0.25%	*29%	*57%

* *Per cent based on fewer than 10 observations*

DECEMBER 8 ODDS OF A PRICE RISE: 50%

Odds of different size price shift

	1935 to present
Large rise *(above +0.25%)*	35%
Small swing *(+0.25% to -0.25%)*	30%
Large fall (*below -0.25%*)	35%

Odds of rise based on yesterday

	1935 to present
Large rise yesterday *(above +0.25%)*	79%
Small swing yesterday *(+0.25% to -0.25%)*	48%
Large fall yesterday (*below -0.25%*)	*11%

DIAGNOSTICS

Odds of price rise based on direction of 5-day and 20-day trend yesterday

	5-day trend	20-day trend
Yesterday rose more than +0.1%	57%	55%
Little change *(+0.1% to -0.1%)*	47%	53%
Yesterday fell more than -0.1%	47%	*33%

Odds of rise based upon distance between trend and yesterday s closing price

	5-day trend	20-day trend
Yesterday more than +0.5% above trend	73%	53%
Yesterday near trend *(+0.5% to -0.5%)*	46%	*56%
Yesterday more than -0.5% below trend	36%	44%

Looking ahead: odds of rise in future

	Next 3 days	Next 5 days
Today rose over +0.25%	56%	50%
Today small swing *(+0.25% to -0.25%)*	79%	64%
Today fell below -0.25%	38%	56%

DECEMBER 9 ODDS OF A PRICE RISE: 38%

Odds of different size price shift

	1935 to present
Large rise *(above +0.25%)*	28%
Small swing *(+0.25% to -0.25%)*	26%
Large fall *(below -0.25%)*	47%

Odds of rise based on yesterday

	1935 to present
Large rise yesterday *(above +0.25%)*	44%
Small swing yesterday *(+0.25% to -0.25%)*	57%
Large fall yesterday *(below -0.25%)*	18%

DIAGNOSTICS

Odds of price rise based on direction of 5-day and 20-day trend yesterday

	5-day trend	20-day trend
Yesterday rose more than +0.1%	53%	52%
Little change *(+0.1% to -0.1%)*	50%	33%
Yesterday fell more than -0.1%	20%	18%

Odds of rise based upon distance between trend and yesterday s closing price

	5-day trend	20-day trend
Yesterday more than +0.5% above trend	50%	50%
Yesterday near trend *(+0.5% to -0.5%)*	43%	*38%
Yesterday more than -0.5% below trend	21%	26%

Looking ahead: odds of rise in future

	Next 3 days	Next 5 days
Today rose over +0.25%	54%	69%
Today small swing *(+0.25% to -0.25%)*	50%	75%
Today fell below -0.25%	59%	59%

* *Per cent based on fewer than 10 observations*

DECEMBER 10 ODDS OF A PRICE RISE: 50%

Odds of different size price shift

	1935 to present
Large rise *(above +0.25%)*	35%
Small swing *(+0.25% to -0.25%)*	41%
Large fall (*below -0.25%)*	24%

Odds of rise based on yesterday

	1935 to present
Large rise yesterday *(above +0.25%)*	44%
Small swing yesterda y*(+0.25% to -0.25%)*	50%
Large fall yesterday (*below -0.25%)*	56%

DIAGNOSTICS

Odds of price rise based on direction of 5-day and 20-day trend yesterday

	5-day trend	20-day trend
Yesterday rose more than +0.1%	53%	47%
Little change *(+0.1% to -0.1%)*	*56%	56%
Yesterday fell more than -0.1%	45%	46%

Odds of rise based upon distance between trend and yesterday s closing price

	5-day trend	20-day trend
Yesterday more than +0.5% above trend	33%	59%
Yesterday near trend *(+0.5% to -0.5%)*	56%	36%
Yesterday more than -0.5% below trend	56%	50%

Looking ahead: odds of rise in future

	Next 3 days	Next 5 days
Today rose over +0.25%	81%	88%
Today small swing *(+0.25% to -0.25%)*	42%	47%
Today fell below -0.25%	55%	64%

DECEMBER 11 ODDS OF A PRICE RISE: 59%

Odds of different size price shift

	1935 to present
Large rise *(above +0.25%)*	46%
Small swing *(+0.25% to -0.25%)*	15%
Large fall (*below -0.25%)*	39%

Odds of rise based on yesterday

	1935 to present
Large rise yesterday *(above +0.25%)*	71%
Small swing yesterday *(+0.25% to -0.25%)*	61%
Large fall yesterday (*below -0.25%)*	43%

DIAGNOSTICS

Odds of price rise based on direction of 5-day and 20-day trend yesterday

	5-day trend	20-day trend
Yesterday rose more than +0.1%	59%	64%
Little change *(+0.1% to -0.1%)*	*100%	65%
Yesterday fell more than -0.1%	45%	42%

Odds of rise based upon distance between trend and yesterday s closing price

	5-day trend	20-day trend
Yesterday more than +0.5% above trend	77%	69%
Yesterday near trend *(+0.5% to -0.5%)*	55%	70%
Yesterday more than -0.5% below trend	45%	45%

Looking ahead: odds of rise in future

	Next 3 days	Next 5 days
Today rose over +0.25%	81%	62%
Today small swing *(+0.25% to -0.25%)*	*29%	*29%
Today fell below -0.25%	83%	61%

* *Per cent based on fewer than 10 observations*

DECEMBER 12 ODDS OF A PRICE RISE: 56%

Odds of different size price shift

	1935 to present
Large rise *(above +0.25%)*	40%
Small swing *(+0.25% to -0.25%)*	38%
Large fall (*below -0.25%)*	22%

Odds of rise based on yesterday

	1935 to present
Large rise yesterday *(above +0.25%)*	56%
Small swing yesterday *(+0.25% to -0.25%)*	*13%
Large fall yesterday (*below -0.25%)*	71%

DIAGNOSTICS

Odds of price rise based on direction of 5-day and 20-day trend yesterday

	5-day trend	20-day trend
Yesterday rose more than +0.1%	39%	50%
Little change *(+0.1% to -0.1%)*	*33%	50%
Yesterday fell more than -0.1%	76%	67%

Odds of rise based upon distance between trend and yesterday s closing price

	5-day trend	20-day trend
Yesterday more than +0.5% above trend	50%	45%
Yesterday near trend *(+0.5% to -0.5%)*	39%	*40%
Yesterday more than -0.5% below trend	76%	70%

Looking ahead: odds of rise in future

	Next 3 days	Next 5 days
Today rose over +0.25%	72%	50%
Today small swing *(+0.25% to -0.25%)*	47%	47%
Today fell below -0.25%	20%	40%

DECEMBER 13 ODDS OF A PRICE RISE: 49%

Odds of different size price shift

	1935 to present
Large rise *(above +0.25%)*	36%
Small swing *(+0.25% to -0.25%)*	31%
Large fall *(below -0.25%)*	33%

Odds of rise based on yesterday

	1935 to present
Large rise yesterday *(above +0.25%)*	74%
Small swing yesterday *(+0.25% to -0.25%)*	28%
Large fall yesterday *(below -0.25%)*	*38%

DIAGNOSTICS

Odds of price rise based on direction of 5-day and 20-day trend yesterday

	5-day trend	20-day trend
Yesterday rose more than +0.1%	47%	63%
Little change *(+0.1% to -0.1%)*	38%	27%
Yesterday fell more than -0.1%	60%	57%

Odds of rise based upon distance between trend and yesterday s closing price

	5-day trend	20-day trend
Yesterday more than +0.5% above trend	50%	42%
Yesterday near trend *(+0.5% to -0.5%)*	43%	*50%
Yesterday more than -0.5% below trend	58%	55%

Looking ahead: odds of rise in future

	Next 3 days	Next 5 days
Today rose over +0.25%	56%	50%
Today small swing *(+0.25% to -0.25%)*	36%	71%
Today fell below -0.25%	53%	67%

* *Per cent based on fewer than 10 observations*

DECEMBER 14 ODDS OF A PRICE RISE: 56%

Odds of different size price shift

	1935 to present
Large rise *(above +0.25%)*	40%
Small swing *(+0.25% to -0.25%)*	36%
Large fall (*below -0.25%)*	24%

Odds of rise based on yesterday

	1935 to present
Large rise yesterday *(above +0.25%)*	65%
Small swing yesterday *(+0.25% to -0.25%)*	58%
Large fall yesterday (*below -0.25%)*	38%

DIAGNOSTICS

Odds of price rise based on direction of 5-day and 20-day trend yesterday

	5-day trend	20-day trend
Yesterday rose more than +0.1%	72%	60%
Little change *(+0.1% to -0.1%)*	50%	53%
Yesterday fell more than -0.1%	40%	54%

Odds of rise based upon distance between trend and yesterday s closing price

	5-day trend	20-day trend
Yesterday more than +0.5% above trend	85%	61%
Yesterday near trend *(+0.5% to -0.5%)*	45%	70%
Yesterday more than -0.5% below trend	40%	41%

Looking ahead: odds of rise in future

	Next 3 days	Next 5 days
Today rose over +0.25%	56%	61%
Today small swing *(+0.25% to -0.25%)*	69%	63%
Today fell below -0.25%	45%	45%

DECEMBER 15 ODDS OF A PRICE RISE: 61%

Odds of different size price shift

	1935 to present
Large rise *(above +0.25%)*	37%
Small swing *(+0.25% to -0.25%)*	39%
Large fall (*below -0.25%)*	24%

Odds of rise based on yesterday

	1935 to present
Large rise yesterday *(above +0.25%)*	47%
Small swing yesterday *(+0.25% to -0.25%)*	78%
Large fall yesterday (*below -0.25%)*	55%

DIAGNOSTICS

Odds of price rise based on direction of 5-day and 20-day trend yesterday

	5-day trend	20-day trend
Yesterday rose more than +0.1%	55%	60%
Little change *(+0.1% to -0.1%)*	*38%	63%
Yesterday fell more than -0.1%	81%	58%

Odds of rise based upon distance between trend and yesterday s closing price

	5-day trend	20-day trend
Yesterday more than +0.5% above trend	69%	64%
Yesterday near trend *(+0.5% to -0.5%)*	43%	45%
Yesterday more than -0.5% below trend	*89%	69%

Looking ahead: odds of rise in future

	Next 3 days	Next 5 days
Today rose over +0.25%	71%	71%
Today small swing *(+0.25% to -0.25%)*	56%	72%
Today fell below -0.25%	55%	73%

* *Per cent based on fewer than 10 observations*

DECEMBER 16 ODDS OF A PRICE RISE: 60%

Odds of different size price shift

	1935 to present
Large rise *(above +0.25%)*	49%
Small swing *(+0.25% to -0.25%)*	28%
Large fall (*below -0.25%)*	23%

Odds of rise based on yesterday

	1935 to present
Large rise yesterday *(above +0.25%)*	75%
Small swing yesterday *(+0.25% to -0.25%)*	42%
Large fall yesterday (*below -0.25%)*	67%

DIAGNOSTICS

Odds of price rise based on direction of 5-day and 20-day trend yesterday

	5-day trend	20-day trend
Yesterday rose more than +0.1%	65%	54%
Little change *(+0.1% to -0.1%)*	63%	57%
Yesterday fell more than -0.1%	50%	69%

Odds of rise based upon distance between trend and yesterday s closing price

	5-day trend	20-day trend
Yesterday more than +0.5% above trend	73%	62%
Yesterday near trend *(+0.5% to -0.5%)*	52%	55%
Yesterday more than -0.5% below trend	*56%	60%

Looking ahead: odds of rise in future

	Next 3 days	Next 5 days
Today rose over +0.25%	74%	70%
Today small swing *(+0.25% to -0.25%)*	46%	92%
Today fell below -0.25%	36%	73%

DECEMBER 17 ODDS OF A PRICE RISE: 46%

Odds of different size price shift

	1935 to present
Large rise *(above +0.25%)*	39%
Small swing *(+0.25% to -0.25%)*	37%
Large fall (*below -0.25%)*	24%

Odds of rise based on yesterday

	1935 to present
Large rise yesterday *(above +0.25%)*	68%
Small swing yesterday *(+0.25% to -0.25%)*	31%
Large fall yesterday (*below -0.25%)*	18%

DIAGNOSTICS

Odds of price rise based on direction of 5-day and 20-day trend yesterday

	5-day trend	20-day trend
Yesterday rose more than +0.1%	52%	46%
Little change *(+0.1% to -0.1%)*	43%	48%
Yesterday fell more than -0.1%	36%	42%

Odds of rise based upon distance between trend and yesterday s closing price

	5-day trend	20-day trend
Yesterday more than +0.5% above trend	60%	43%
Yesterday near trend *(+0.5% to -0.5%)*	30%	60%
Yesterday more than -0.5% below trend	*50%	40%

Looking ahead: odds of rise in future

	Next 3 days	Next 5 days
Today rose over +0.25%	61%	56%
Today small swing *(+0.25% to -0.25%)*	71%	82%
Today fell below -0.25%	55%	55%

* *Per cent based on fewer than 10 observations*

DECEMBER 18 ODDS OF A PRICE RISE: 41%

Odds of different size price shift

	1935 to present
Large rise *(above +0.25%)*	28%
Small swing *(+0.25% to -0.25%)*	37%
Large fall (*below -0.25%)*	35%

Odds of rise based on yesterday

	1935 to present
Large rise yesterday *(above +0.25%)*	60%
Small swing yesterday *(+0.25% to -0.25%)*	25%
Large fall yesterday (*below -0.25%)*	40%

DIAGNOSTICS

Odds of price rise based on direction of 5-day and 20-day trend yesterday

	5-day trend	20-day trend
Yesterday rose more than +0.1%	46%	46%
Little change *(+0.1% to -0.1%)*	9%	45%
Yesterday fell more than -0.1%	64%	31%

Odds of rise based upon distance between trend and yesterday s closing price

	5-day trend	20-day trend
Yesterday more than +0.5% above trend	63%	43%
Yesterday near trend *(+0.5% to -0.5%)*	30%	43%
Yesterday more than -0.5% below trend	*29%	36%

Looking ahead: odds of rise in future

	Next 3 days	Next 5 days
Today rose over +0.25%	77%	85%
Today small swing *(+0.25% to -0.25%)*	59%	76%
Today fell below -0.25%	56%	56%

DECEMBER 19 ODDS OF A PRICE RISE: 51%

Odds of different size price shift

	1935 to present
Large rise *(above +0.25%)*	33%
Small swing *(+0.25% to -0.25%)*	40%
Large fall (*below -0.25%)*	27%

Odds of rise based on yesterday

	1935 to present
Large rise yesterday *(above +0.25%)*	62%
Small swing yesterday *(+0.25% to -0.25%)*	50%
Large fall yesterday (*below -0.25%)*	44%

DIAGNOSTICS

Odds of price rise based on direction of 5-day and 20-day trend yesterday

	5-day trend	20-day trend
Yesterday rose more than +0.1%	50%	57%
Little change *(+0.1% to -0.1%)*	70%	47%
Yesterday fell more than -0.1%	38%	50%

Odds of rise based upon distance between trend and yesterday s closing price

	5-day trend	20-day trend
Yesterday more than +0.5% above trend	54%	40%
Yesterday near trend *(+0.5% to -0.5%)*	55%	71%
Yesterday more than -0.5% below trend	40%	38%

Looking ahead: odds of rise in future

	Next 3 days	Next 5 days
Today rose over +0.25%	67%	87%
Today small swing *(+0.25% to -0.25%)*	83%	83%
Today fell below -0.25%	67%	75%

* *Per cent based on fewer than 10 observations*

DECEMBER 20 ODDS OF A PRICE RISE: 53%

Odds of different size price shift

	1935 to present
Large rise *(above +0.25%)*	44%
Small swing *(+0.25% to -0.25%)*	33%
Large fall (*below -0.25%)*	22%

Odds of rise based on yesterday

	1935 to present
Large rise yesterday *(above +0.25%)*	47%
Small swing yesterday *(+0.25% to -0.25%)*	65%
Large fall yesterday (*below -0.25%)*	45%

DIAGNOSTICS

Odds of price rise based on direction of 5-day and 20-day trend yesterday

	5-day trend	20-day trend
Yesterday rose more than +0.1%	47%	47%
Little change *(+0.1% to -0.1%)*	57%	73%
Yesterday fell more than -0.1%	58%	40%

Odds of rise based upon distance between trend and yesterday s closing price

	5-day trend	20-day trend
Yesterday more than +0.5% above trend	42%	50%
Yesterday near trend *(+0.5% to -0.5%)*	64%	69%
Yesterday more than -0.5% below trend	45%	42%

Looking ahead: odds of rise in future

	Next 3 days	Next 5 days
Today rose over +0.25%	85%	85%
Today small swing *(+0.25% to -0.25%)*	80%	87%
Today fell below -0.25%	90%	80%

DECEMBER 21 ODDS OF A PRICE RISE: 56%

Odds of different size price shift

	1935 to present
Large rise *(above +0.25%)*	38%
Small swing *(+0.25% to -0.25%)*	44%
Large fall *(below -0.25%)*	18%

Odds of rise based on yesterday

	1935 to present
Large rise yesterday *(above +0.25%)*	60%
Small swing yesterday *(+0.25% to -0.25%)*	50%
Large fall yesterday *(below -0.25%)*	*56%

DIAGNOSTICS

Odds of price rise based on direction of 5-day and 20-day trend yesterday

	5-day trend	20-day trend
Yesterday rose more than +0.1%	52%	44%
Little change *(+0.1% to -0.1%)*	*63%	63%
Yesterday fell more than -0.1%	57%	64%

Odds of rise based upon distance between trend and yesterday s closing price

	5-day trend	20-day trend
Yesterday more than +0.5% above trend	63%	52%
Yesterday near trend *(+0.5% to -0.5%)*	50%	53%
Yesterday more than -0.5% below trend	*57%	*67%

Looking ahead: odds of rise in future

	Next 3 days	Next 5 days
Today rose over +0.25%	94%	94%
Today small swing *(+0.25% to -0.25%)*	75%	75%
Today fell below -0.25%	*75%	*75%

* *Per cent based on fewer than 10 observations*

DECEMBER 22 ODDS OF A PRICE RISE: 72%

Odds of different size price shift

	1935 to present
Large rise *(above +0.25%)*	46%
Small swing *(+0.25% to -0.25%)*	43%
Large fall *(below -0.25%)*	11%

Odds of rise based on yesterday

	1935 to present
Large rise yesterday *(above +0.25%)*	76%
Small swing yesterday *(+0.25% to -0.25%)*	71%
Large fall yesterday *(below -0.25%)*	*63%

DIAGNOSTICS

Odds of price rise based on direction of 5-day and 20-day trend yesterday

	5-day trend	20-day trend
Yesterday rose more than +0.1%	57%	81%
Little change *(+0.1% to -0.1%)*	85%	73%
Yesterday fell more than -0.1%	83%	*50%

Odds of rise based upon distance between trend and yesterday s closing price

	5-day trend	20-day trend
Yesterday more than +0.5% above trend	85%	80%
Yesterday near trend *(+0.5% to -0.5%)*	64%	64%
Yesterday more than -0.5% below trend	*80%	60%

Looking ahead: odds of rise in future

	Next 3 days	Next 5 days
Today rose over +0.25%	81%	95%
Today small swing *(+0.25% to -0.25%)*	85%	85%
Today fell below -0.25%	*100%	*100%

DECEMBER 23 ODDS OF A PRICE RISE: 72%

Odds of different size price shift

	1935 to present
Large rise *(above +0.25%)*	40%
Small swing *(+0.25% to -0.25%)*	49%
Large fall (*below -0.25%)*	11%

Odds of rise based on yesterday

	1935 to present
Large rise yesterday *(above +0.25%)*	68%
Small swing yesterday *(+0.25% to -0.25%)*	79%
Large fall yesterday (*below -0.25%)*	*67%

DIAGNOSTICS

Odds of price rise based on direction of 5-day and 20-day trend yesterday

	5-day trend	20-day trend
Yesterday rose more than +0.1%	69%	83%
Little change *(+0.1% to -0.1%)*	81%	68%
Yesterday fell more than -0.1%	*60%	60%

Odds of rise based upon distance between trend and yesterday s closing price

	5-day trend	20-day trend
Yesterday more than +0.5% above trend	76%	79%
Yesterday near trend *(+0.5% to -0.5%)*	72%	*63%
Yesterday more than -0.5% below trend	*60%	60%

Looking ahead: odds of rise in future

	Next 3 days	Next 5 days
Today rose over +0.25%	79%	89%
Today small swing *(+0.25% to -0.25%)*	87%	87%
Today fell below -0.25%	*100%	*80%

* *Per cent based on fewer than 10 observations*

DECEMBER 24 ODDS OF A PRICE RISE: 69%

Odds of different size price shift

	1935 to present
Large rise *(above +0.25%)*	26%
Small swing *(+0.25% to -0.25%)*	60%
Large fall (*below -0.25%)*	14%

Odds of rise based on yesterday

	1935 to present
Large rise yesterday *(above +0.25%)*	80%
Small swing yesterday *(+0.25% to -0.25%)*	50%
Large fall yesterday (*below -0.25%)*	*83%

DIAGNOSTICS

Odds of price rise based on direction of 5-day and 20-day trend yesterday

	5-day trend	20-day trend
Yesterday rose more than +0.1%	74%	76%
Little change *(+0.1% to -0.1%)*	75%	60%
Yesterday fell more than -0.1%	*43%	70%

Odds of rise based upon distance between trend and yesterday s closing price

	5-day trend	20-day trend
Yesterday more than +0.5% above trend	87%	78%
Yesterday near trend *(+0.5% to -0.5%)*	62%	*44%
Yesterday more than -0.5% below trend	*50%	70%

Looking ahead: odds of rise in future

	Next 3 days	Next 5 days
Today rose over +0.25%	73%	91%
Today small swing *(+0.25% to -0.25%)*	88%	76%
Today fell below -0.25%	*83%	*67%

DECEMBER 27 ODDS OF A PRICE RISE: 77%

Odds of different size price shift

	1935 to present
Large rise *(above +0.25%)*	46%
Small swing *(+0.25% to -0.25%)*	46%
Large fall (*below -0.25%)*	8%

Odds of rise based on yesterday

	1935 to present
Large rise yesterday *(above +0.25%)*	*88%
Small swing yesterday *(+0.25% to -0.25%)*	73%
Large fall yesterday (*below -0.25%)*	*67%

DIAGNOSTICS

Odds of price rise based on direction of 5-day and 20-day trend yesterday

	5-day trend	20-day trend
Yesterday rose more than +0.1%	80%	*75%
Little change *(+0.1% to -0.1%)*	80%	64%
Yesterday fell more than -0.1%	*67%	*100%

Odds of rise based upon distance between trend and yesterday s closing price

	5-day trend	20-day trend
Yesterday more than +0.5% above trend	*75%	90%
Yesterday near trend *(+0.5% to -0.5%)*	80%	*57%
Yesterday more than -0.5% below trend	*67%	*78%

Looking ahead: odds of rise in future

	Next 3 days	Next 5 days
Today rose over +0.25%	83%	83%
Today small swing *(+0.25% to -0.25%)*	67%	92%
Today fell below -0.25%	*50%	*0%

* *Per cent based on fewer than 10 observations*

DECEMBER 28 ODDS OF A PRICE RISE: 68%

Odds of different size price shift

	1935 to present
Large rise *(above +0.25%)*	39%
Small swing *(+0.25% to -0.25%)*	45%
Large fall (*below -0.25%)*	16%

Odds of rise based on yesterday

	1935 to present
Large rise yesterday *(above +0.25%)*	71%
Small swing yesterday *(+0.25% to -0.25%)*	68%
Large fall yesterday (*below -0.25%)*	*50%

DIAGNOSTICS

Odds of price rise based on direction of 5-day and 20-day trend yesterday

	5-day trend	20-day trend
Yesterday rose more than +0.1%	73%	92%
Little change *(+0.1% to -0.1%)*	64%	53%
Yesterday fell more than -0.1%	*60%	*67%

Odds of rise based upon distance between trend and yesterday s closing price

	5-day trend	20-day trend
Yesterday more than +0.5% above trend	80%	81%
Yesterday near trend *(+0.5% to -0.5%)*	62%	*43%
Yesterday more than -0.5% below trend	*50%	60%

Looking ahead: odds of rise in future

	Next 3 days	Next 5 days
Today rose over +0.25%	47%	67%
Today small swing *(+0.25% to -0.25%)*	82%	88%
Today fell below -0.25%	*67%	*67%

DECEMBER 29 ODDS OF A PRICE RISE: 72%

Odds of different size price shift

	1935 to present
Large rise *(above +0.25%)*	54%
Small swing *(+0.25% to -0.25%)*	33%
Large fall (*below -0.25%)*	13%

Odds of rise based on yesterday

	1935 to present
Large rise yesterday *(above +0.25%)*	75%
Small swing yesterday *(+0.25% to -0.25%)*	70%
Large fall yesterday (*below -0.25%)*	*71%

DIAGNOSTICS

Odds of price rise based on direction of 5-day and 20-day trend yesterday

	5-day trend	20-day trend
Yesterday rose more than +0.1%	72%	90%
Little change *(+0.1% to -0.1%)*	62%	53%
Yesterday fell more than -0.1%	*100%	*71%

Odds of rise based upon distance between trend and yesterday s closing price

	5-day trend	20-day trend
Yesterday more than +0.5% above trend	74%	72%
Yesterday near trend *(+0.5% to -0.5%)*	71%	*75%
Yesterday more than -0.5% below trend	*67%	*67%

Looking ahead: odds of rise in future

	Next 3 days	Next 5 days
Today rose over +0.25%	76%	60%
Today small swing *(+0.25% to -0.25%)*	80%	87%
Today fell below -0.25%	*67%	*83%

* *Per cent based on fewer than 10 observations*

DECEMBER 30 ODDS OF A PRICE RISE: 66%

Odds of different size price shift

	1935 to present
Large rise *(above +0.25%)*	40%
Small swing *(+0.25% to -0.25%)*	47%
Large fall (*below -0.25%)*	13%

Odds of rise based on yesterday

	1935 to present
Large rise yesterday *(above +0.25%)*	71%
Small swing yesterday *(+0.25% to -0.25%)*	53%
Large fall yesterday (*below -0.25%)*	*100%

DIAGNOSTICS

Odds of price rise based on direction of 5-day and 20-day trend yesterday

	5-day trend	20-day trend
Yesterday rose more than +0.1%	61%	71%
Little change *(+0.1% to -0.1%)*	75%	44%
Yesterday fell more than -0.1%	*100%	*100%

Odds of rise based upon distance between trend and yesterday s closing price

	5-day trend	20-day trend
Yesterday more than +0.5% above trend	65%	64%
Yesterday near trend *(+0.5% to -0.5%)*	63%	*67%
Yesterday more than -0.5% below trend	*100%	*80%

Looking ahead: odds of rise in future

	Next 3 days	Next 5 days
Today rose over +0.25%	74%	68%
Today small swing *(+0.25% to -0.25%)*	73%	68%
Today fell below -0.25%	*83%	*100%

DECEMBER 31 ODDS OF A PRICE RISE: 71%

Odds of different size price shift

	1935 to present
Large rise *(above +0.25%)*	44%
Small swing *(+0.25% to -0.25%)*	44%
Large fall (*below -0.25%)*	11%

Odds of rise based on yesterday

	1935 to present
Large rise yesterday *(above +0.25%)*	76%
Small swing yesterday *(+0.25% to -0.25%)*	68%
Large fall yesterday (*below -0.25%)*	*60%

DIAGNOSTICS

Odds of price rise based on direction of 5-day and 20-day trend yesterday

	5-day trend	20-day trend
Yesterday rose more than +0.1%	77%	81%
Little change *(+0.1% to -0.1%)*	*75%	65%
Yesterday fell more than -0.1%	*33%	*57%

Odds of rise based upon distance between trend and yesterday s closing price

	5-day trend	20-day trend
Yesterday more than +0.5% above trend	83%	79%
Yesterday near trend *(+0.5% to -0.5%)*	62%	*33%
Yesterday more than -0.5% below trend	*0%	*67%

Looking ahead: odds of rise in future

	Next 3 days	Next 5 days
Today rose over +0.25%	65%	50%
Today small swing *(+0.25% to -0.25%)*	70%	75%
Today fell below -0.25%	*20%	*40%

* *Per cent based on fewer than 10 observations*